WATER MADE CLEAR

Communicating with the
Spirit World

Barbara Bridgford

First published in Great Britain by
Pen Press Publishers Ltd
39-41, North Road
Islington
London N7 9DP

ISBN 1-904018-25-4

Printed and bound in the UK

A catalogue record of this book is available
from the British Library

Dedication

I dedicate this book with love to my mother.

With special thanks and love to my children; Penny,
Vicki, Steph and Rod for their enduring patience and
understanding with a mother who communicates in
'Two Worlds'.

I wish to acknowledge the help and encouragement given to me by my dear friends; Michael Smith, Stephen Gill, Roger Steel, Joan Newton, Elsie Stobbart, Detective Inspector Gert Khan, Barbara Gray, Trisha George and all circle members. And to all those I have mentioned in this book, a big thank you.
Without them it would not have been possible.

My love to Brian Knibb for encouraging me to send my manuscript for publication.

Contents

Introduction

I was born during the Second World War in 1944, and in those days the subject of spiritualism was never discussed. As a child I often saw things others couldn't and learnt, eventually, to keep it to myself, quietly accepting the fact that I possessed an amazing gift, extraordinary powers that could bring joy and comfort to thousands of people. My gift led me to visit many countries, and on occasion, to help the police solve serious crimes, including murders.

This book is about my experiences. A connection between mind, body and spirit has enabled me to live my life as an almost transformed human being. It has been a long journey, gradually revelational and at times amazing. I hope it will prove invaluable not only to those who wish to become mediums, but also to those who aspire to cultivate the higher senses that lie latent in the vast majority of people.

What is possible is the ability to discover what exists after we die; if we believe this, then we can prepare for it. It all happened slowly for me, but people can only progress when they are ready, and according to what they're equipped for.

I am a convinced spiritualist because life after death has been proved to me, beyond a shadow of doubt. The years I have been working with spirits I have experienced extraordinary psychic phenomena that can have only one explanation: that intelligent individuals do exist after the death process. The dead communicate with me regularly, they are as real to me as the living. I feel their love, affection, support and inspiration. They have guided me through good times and bad, always by my side.

It takes all kinds to make a world. My world, like that of most mediums and healers, has been filled with sceptics, gullible people and those who live by intuition and direct contact with spirits. I have tried in this book to cover the questions asked by all who seek explanations and enlightenment, giving easily-understood answers to often-raised questions about reincarnation, mediumship and healing, and observations that are both simple and thought-provoking.

I have shared some of my extraordinary experiences covering 50 years of contact and communication with spirit beings. Some are hair-raising, some reassuring and inspiring; most importantly, all are true. Nothing is dogmatic or forced, but is left for the reader to decide for him- or herself. This book aims to enlighten, not to convert.

Everyone is capable of developing supernormal faculties and powers, and I have tried to instruct, in the best way, those who desire to do so. I have devoted 35 years to my work as a medium. Furthermore, during these years I have conducted weekly classes for the cultivation of mediumship and healing. Many students have passed successfully through my hands.

What makes my work particularly attractive and worthwhile is that I am able to share many experiences of an unusual nature with those seeking enlightenment, together with knowledge and explanations. If this book takes its readers down the path to understanding, it will have achieved its purpose. But as a reader you must be prepared to follow the path to its end before making your final judgement.

Foreword

When I was asked to write a short Foreword for this book, I decided that perhaps the best way would be to tell you readers about just a couple of the many moments I have experienced with Barbara over about five years.

We are friends now, Barbara and I, and meeting her changed my thinking entirely. From trying to tackle life by reasoning, intellectualising and only concentrating on the material side of life, I now find I can focus more on the spiritual aspect. And very rewarding it has turned out to be for my inner peace and hope.

Someone suggested I make an appointment to see Barbara after I found myself facing a death in the family about 20 years after I had last faced one. This time it was my father and again it had left me feeling bewildered, angry and frightened at what I saw as the pointlessness of human and all life. To live and then not to live – how absurd, I thought. To live and gain earthly knowledge, learn about love, have fun with friends, and then *kaput!* What a waste of time, my naive mind reasoned.

So, exhausted and tearful, I made the appointment. Barbara was a perfect stranger of my own age and when I arrived she sat me down to give me a reading. She proceeded to tell me all about my husband's business difficulties, the fact that my horse had eye cancer, and various other problems I was experiencing at the time. It was all true: we were going through everything except murder, all at once.

I listened, stunned, as she started to talk about my deceased parents being 'here, with us now', and how they were telling Barbara about these dramas. There was, they said, nothing in my husband's or my life that they did not know about. They described themselves to her: the way they had died, what they had looked like, and the fact that I was brought up far to the south of England. They even described the cottage we had all lived in, and our family traditions.

In an emotional haze, I realized that she had put into my lap that box of buried treasure one dreams of finding as a child when playing pirates. But how could this woman possibly know all this? I reasoned. Was she reading my mind, or was I carrying this information around my body somewhere and she was simply reading it?

No. Barbara explained that she was looking at my parents with her 'inner eye', and that she was simply repeating what they told her to pass on.

As I sat there suffering from information overload, and emotionally choked, as if to cap the experience and leave me in no doubt as to what I was hearing, she told me one last thing.

'When you were very small,' she said, 'you had a close friend called Gillian.'

'That's right,' I agreed.

'Well, your mum is saying Gillian is over there with them now: she died eighteen months ago, and she's well and happy.'

Gillian would have been in her fifties now, the same age as me. We were at primary school together half a century ago, but had lost touch as we got on with our own lives. I only ever had one friend called Gillian.

This was a marvellous opportunity for me to check out what Barbara had said, and a few weeks later found me ringing Gillian's elderly father in the south-east of England. I explained who I was to him, that we had met long ago, and that I would love to speak to Gillian, whereupon he gently told me that eighteen months ago she had died of breast cancer. I told him to sit down, because I wanted to explain to him that I knew this already, but could I explain to him how I knew the fact? I told him that my parents were both not with me, and that a perfect stranger, a medium, had told me about Gillian's death, and that I wanted to check that this sad fact was true. I also wanted to explain to him that she had said she was now well and happy.

He was quiet for a moment, and then told me that he was pleased and grateful that I had phoned him. He was in fact nursing his frail, very elderly wife who was dying, and soon he would be on his own.

I like to think that when his wife finally meets up with her daughter again, he will take comfort in the fact that he is not alone really, he is just biding his time until thay are all together once more. Could it be that Gillian had come to Barbara, hoping that I would comfort her father? I like to think so.

Barbara explained to me that she had been born able to see and play with her dead pets, which got up and walked away through the wall. They had felt like any cat or dog would, and she got used to seeing people and energy colours as she had grown up, and hearing voices also came to be normal for her.

She has an air of softness and kindness about her, and one cannot help but like her and feel comforted by the words she passes on. The best of these types of people who can raise their consciousness levels to the higher realities, and help mankind on the way to inner peace and knowledge, are always quiet and compassionate, gentle and thoughtful, and need to be treated by others close to them with great love and care. For they need to keep their lives harmonious and as happy as possible to keep their degree of sensitive connection to other spheres open. Connections such as these cannot flow through a disturbed and turbulent mind. It takes a peaceful, positive inner mind, born of conviction of experience and knowledge, to pass on such beautiful, precious words of hope and love. They are like tender flowers in a hothouse that need to be nurtured.

Mankind, right down throughout the ages, has always had this other worldly connection to the hierarchical spheres. It is as if it is there for the times when a person is brought to his knees by life's circumstances, and prompted to visit the type of person with their other worldly channels open, whereby they can receive comfort and strength to go on with life, and spiritual guidance.

Once a week, Barbara and I sit in her little prayer-meditation group with a few others. Like people all over the world, we sit in closeness of spirit, sending out to the world our prayers of peace and love. Remembering that part of the Bible where Jesus said. 'Where two or more meet in my name, I shall be there'. And aiming our open hearts to the creator, we ask that he send his Holy Ghost to be amongst us, to fill us with the highest knowledge: Our spiritual inheritance.

Rita Clifford - Wilkinson

BOOK ONE

CHAPTER ONE

Early Psychic Experiences

I must have been a strange child, perhaps even then drawing spirit towards me, for my favourite game was telling ghost stories to my playmates, sitting round the back of my friend's house next door, on the step. In the early 50's there was no television so children had to entertain themselves; boys played football in the street and girls skipped with skipping ropes. It was a real fun time for us all, we even had football and skipping teams with very strict rules. However, as a form of entertainment, story-telling seemed to win every time.

Many times Mum told me off for being late for tea. She would call my name but the kids would say, 'Just another five minutes, Barbara!' I couldn't resist it, for I enjoyed the stories I told just as much as they did, and couldn't stop until I had them spellbound.

It all started with two or three children and then they asked their friends along. Finally, my audience grew to around 20 or more local children and became a regular thing. I even got into trouble with their parents, who said I was frightening their little ones to death and they couldn't sleep at night; if I didn't stop they would tell my mum to give me a good hiding. I didn't stop and it was well worth the trouble I got myself into. I derived a great deal of pleasure seeing the children's faces as I told my stories.

I didn't know it then but as a child, my spiritual path and schooling must have already been 'written'. I hadn't been long in this world before I started to see Spirit, though I was much too young to understand what was happening to me. Like most very young children I accepted everything my parents said without question, doing what was expected

1

of me each day, not giving any thought to the unseen world.

I remember my first experience of the unknown world very clearly as if it was yesterday. I was about five or six and wasn't in the least bit afraid. I was playing with my dolls in the bedroom, quite engrossed in my own little world of make-believe, when suddenly my kitten, which had recently died, appeared to me. I remember the happiness I felt as I bent down to stroke her saying, 'Hello Tibby, where have you been, are you better now?' She responded by arching her back and rubbing herself against my legs. It was as though she had never gone away. Suddenly she ran out of my bedroom, across the landing and disappeared through the wall. I called her but she was gone. Like all young children, I never really understood what death was all about, or gave it much thought. All I knew was that my lovely kitten was no longer there to play with me and cried because I missed her. I must have thought something was wrong when she disappeared through the wall, although I should think children of that young age do not think that deeply.

I ran downstairs saying, 'Mum, Mum, I've seen Tibby.'

All she could say was 'How lovely, sweetheart', but I thought it was absolutely wonderful.

For many years during my infancy, I saw pets I had loved that had passed on to the spirit world. Most of them had died from distemper; I don't think in those days the vets had a cure for that disease, and many times my heart was broken when I lost an animal. I would sit up all night looking after them, cradling them in my arms, hoping they would get well. Finally they left me and passed on to the next world, a new vibration. I think the worst times were when I had to take them to the vet to be put to sleep. How my heart ached when I had to leave them to die. Eventually I realised they would come back to me to say hello, which is not the same as having them in this world but better than nothing. I did become accustomed to the idea and looked forward to seeing them again; they never let me down.

A few months later Mum took me to a strange place where we sang hymns and said prayers, though it wasn't like an ordinary church. After the singing had finished those who stayed behind placed chairs in a row in the middle of the room, and one by one people sat down. Some men and women were dressed in white coats and they put their hands on the people sitting on the chairs. I was fascinated by it all and watched with interest. But soon, as most children do after quite a long time sitting still and having to be quiet, I became a little fidgety.

Then it was my turn. Mum picked me up and carried me to one of those important chairs and sat me on her knee. A nice lady in a white coat said to me, 'It's all right, sweetheart, we're not going to hurt you.' She then proceeded to touch my head; I knew she was nice because she smiled all the time. A man also wearing a white coat stood behind me and he too put his hands on my head. I wasn't sure about him; I couldn't see what he was doing and I always liked to know what was going on. A few minutes later I started to feel a funny sensation of warmth and then cold as they both touched me. I started to cry quietly, the tears pouring down my face. I couldn't understand why this was happening as I wasn't in the least bit sad; on the contrary, I felt very happy. I know now that the powerful healing energy from the spirit doctors made me react that way. Afterwards, we had tea and biscuits and then went home. It was very late and the stars were shining. I felt very excited at being up so late.

That same week a strange and frightening thing happened to me. I had been in bed for what seemed like hours but couldn't get to sleep. It was a very warm evening and I had been tossing and turning, trying to find a cool spot. I couldn't settle and was fed up. I eventually got comfortable, lying on my front, and grew drowsy and relaxed with not a care in the world.

Suddenly, I froze to the bed, terrified as invisible hands

3

picked me up and gently turned me over onto my back. The strong, firm hands seemed to come through the bed and grasp my waist. Immediately I was on my back a warm sensation flowed through my body, taking away all fear. The top of my head was like ice and for some reason I just accepted what was happening to me. Strange as it may seem, I gave in to the wonderful feeling as I sank deeper and deeper into a lovely dream-like state. It was as though I had been hypnotised; I was warm, relaxed and comfortable.

It was still very dark outside as I came back to reality, remembering what had happened to me. Then terror struck, my heart started pounding in my chest as I looked around my bedroom for signs of a visitor. My entire body broke out in a cold sweat. I stared into the darkness trying to see if anyone was there. I couldn't see anyone, but I was too scared to get out of bed in case someone was hiding underneath it. The more I thought about where the hands had come from, the more I was convinced the stranger must still be there, waiting to pounce on me. I finally plucked up courage to lean over and look underneath my bed. What a relief to find I was on my own!

My feet hardly touched the floor as I ran into my parents' bedroom, shouting hysterically, 'Mum, Mum, someone has just picked me up and turned me over!'

Startled by my sudden outburst, Mum jumped up and said, 'You're all right, calm down, you must have been dreaming.'

By this time I was sobbing uncontrollably. 'No, Mum!' I exclaimed, trying to speak through all the tears, 'I was still awake.'

I described to her what had happened to me. It was real and I wasn't going to be put off; I knew I hadn't been dreaming. She listened to what I had to say very patiently, repeating that I must have been dreaming. Finally, to satisfy me, she took me into every room in the house saying, 'Look, you see there's nobody here and look, all the doors

4

and windows are locked.'

After trying to console me for a long time, my mother persuaded me to return to bed, promising to leave the light on. Reluctantly I went back to bed where I stayed undisturbed but awake until it was time to get up.

This was my first experience of being touched by spirit, an experience I will never forget. I had suffered from very bad headaches for years. I remember sometimes turning upside down on the settee, crying with pain. Mum had taken me to the doctor several times but the pain didn't go away. After that night when I was turned in my bed, my headaches suddenly disappeared and I never had another one until I was much older and a mother myself. It was years later, when I reminded my mother about my so-called 'nightmare', that she explained I had been taken to a spiritualist church for healing. That night must have been a healing act by spirit doctors.

I think this must have been the start of my spiritual development as a clairvoyant.

After that experience, nothing much happened to me in the psychic sense for a few years, apart from seeing deceased pets, until one night when I was in my early teens.

It must have been the middle of the night when something woke me. I jumped up and peered around the dark room, trying to focus on a shuffling noise coming from the direction of my window. Straining my eyes, I saw to my horror an apparition of an old lady standing in front of me. I could 'feel' the awful way that she had died. I was terrified, I couldn't breathe, and I was choking. The air in the room was heavy, thick and oppressive. I shook the bedclothes, hoping she would go away, hearing my own screams. Sweat ran down both sides of my face and my heart felt as though it was going to jump out of my chest. I don't know what I would have done if the apparition had spoken to me, I think my heart would have stopped. Her contorted face was vaguely familiar to me.

My mother came dashing into my bedroom, wondering

what on earth was going on. I garbled something about how a ghost that looked like the sick lady we had been to visit the day before had woken me up and was standing in front of me. Mum tried to comfort me, saying I had just had a bad dream. She explained how far away this lady lived, and that a sick old lady couldn't and wouldn't come into our house in the middle of the night. The very idea was ridiculous.

But then it wasn't so ridiculous after all. Two days later a visitor came to our house and Mum sent me out to play while they talked. Reluctantly I dragged myself out into the kitchen, sulking. It was very naughty of me but I decided I would stay there and try to listen through the door. I felt very uneasy and knew something was wrong. Even at that early age, I heeded my 'gut' feelings that told me when there was a problem. I recalled seeing this man the previous week when we had visited the sick old lady I had seen in my bedroom. I decided I definitely wasn't going to play outside, I was too interested in why this man had come to see my mother.

Their voices were very low, almost whispers. I found it very difficult to hear, but I strained my ears and heard the words: 'I thought I would call myself to tell you my mother passed away the night before last in the early hours. It wasn't very nice, she choked to death.'

'I'm so sorry to hear that. But she's at peace now, it's a welcome release after all the pain she suffered.'

'Yes, you're right, it's a comfort for me to know that. Thank you for all you did for her, she did appreciate your visits even though she didn't tell you herself.'

I gasped, putting my hand over my mouth. A chill ran down my spine and at the same time I felt the hair at the back of my neck stand on end. Now I was scared; I knew then that I really had seen a ghost. But what better place had she gone to, what was Mum talking about? The lady was dead, wasn't she?

I had no idea why this dead old lady had visited me.

Perhaps it was easier for her to show herself to me, so that I could let my mother know she had died. Or did a higher intelligence want me to know that, after the death process, life does indeed continue? Both explanations are acceptable to me. No-one can ever tell me I didn't see her, or that life doesn't continue on another plane of existence.

I eventually stopped telling Mum about my strange experiences. It seemed pointless. In those days mediumship and spiritualism were never talked about, they were very hush-hush subjects.

As a child I had a lot of strange and frightening things to put up with. For example, on several occasions when I was sitting at the table having tea with my mother, father and Colin, Dad would suddenly start speaking very aggressively in a foreign language. This was a very frightening experience and my mum got very cross with him, saying, 'You should be in control, fancy behaving like that in front of the children.' I never understood what she was talking about, I just accepted it all as part of my everyday life.

During my teenage years, when I became old enough to understand and realise what had happened to me as a child, my mother finally told me that she too could see dead people, and that she was a clairvoyant. She went on to explain about spiritualism, telling me my maternal grandmother had worked as a medium and healer serving spiritualist churches up and down the country, and that she was well known and respected by the name of 'Sandy'. Both my grandmother and my father were members of the SNU (Spiritualist National Union), and the NFSH (National Federation of Spiritual Healers) I must have been very naive and not as sharp as I thought I was.

Until it has happened to you, you don't realise how many other people are experiencing the same sort of things, as I later found out.

During my young adult years I saw more and more spirit beings who had died, which really frightened me; in those days I didn't know any better. I know now that they never come to upset or to scare you, that they come because they love you and want to help. Spirit people I hardly knew came to visit me, almost total strangers. Other times I saw aunts and uncles who had died, leaving me with a wonderful feeling of peace and love as they looked at me and smiled. Sometimes they would speak to me and help me with a particular problem. It was only when they disappeared, faded away, that I realised that I had seen a dead person.

Only in later years, after reading as many spiritualist books as I could lay my hands on and visiting spiritualist churches, did I understand a little more of the spiritualist movement, what had happened at our tea table, and what my mother had meant by my father being 'in control'. He had allowed a spirit person to take over his body when they wanted and without preparation. This is what development is all about, and those with a psychic gift should develop it. In time you learn to work with spirit using your talents correctly, and always in control. Usually, only good loving spirit guides, relatives and friends come to us. Obviously my father hadn't had the correct amount of training or development. With proper tuition this would never have happened and the spirit entity would have been sent away until an acceptable time could be found.

My mother brought Colin and me up; Dad was never at home, was always working away. For years they kept separating and reuniting, until finally Mum realised it would never work out and divorced him. She stopped going to spiritualist churches because divorce in those days was frowned upon.

When I reached the age of 16, I asked Mum if she would take me to a church service, but she wasn't very happy about it. She felt she had been away too long. I explained to her how I felt, how I was drawn to the spiritualist movement like a magnet and couldn't pull myself away.

Reluctantly she agreed. I was thrilled to bits, and we

8

arranged a day and time to go.

We finally arrived at the church in Leeds after struggling for hours through several inches of snow. The roads were impassable and the driver of the bus had to turn around and go back. We decided to get off and trundle the remaining distance on foot, arriving terribly cold and wet. Eager to see what spiritualism was all about I couldn't wait to sit down in the warm welcoming church. The platform speaker, Mrs Allan, gave a talk on the basics of spiritualism, looking at me all the way throughout her demonstration, as if she knew why I had come.

It was loud and clear that the message was directed at me from spirit friends. God indeed does work in a mysterious way: from that day on spiritualism became my life.

I decided I wanted to go to development circles and become a first-class medium. Nothing less was good enough for me, I had to be one of the best. I returned to the same church once a week for my development, sat with lots of other people of like mind and tried to develop my mediumistic gifts. I was surprised to find in just a couple of weeks that I was giving accurate messages to the other circle members; I felt on top of the world. All I wanted was to go on the platform and be a star, giving clairvoyance – typical of a young teenager. However, that wasn't to be for quite some time, as unseen forces had different ideas.

You can only develop your psychic gifts successfully after a great deal of dedication and effort in a development circle. If it's worth having, it's worth working for and cannot be rushed. I always wanted things done yesterday, and it took me a long time to learn patience. I got fed up when spirit constantly reminded me of this. Do strive to gain as much knowledge as possible, and be patient. In time you will be able to give your best and become a good medium and instrument for spirit use. If only I had known then what an exciting spiritual life lay ahead of me.

CHAPTER TWO

Gifts Come In Strange Ways

At the age of 18 I left home and married Michael Smith. I was very grown up for my years and couldn't wait to have my own home, family and a dog curled up asleep in front of the fire.

Eleven months after we were married I gave birth to my first beautiful daughter on 1 May 1963, a tiny little thing with dark brown hair and dark blue/black eyes which later turned brown. We christened her Penelope Michel Lesley, three names to compensate for the common surname. I was on top of the world. I had a nice comfortable home, a husband I loved, a baby and a Boxer dog: what more could I possibly want?

However, in those days we had very little money as Michael was on a training course and only received a weekly wage of £6, so it was hard for us both, trying to manage the little money we had to pay our bills.

One day Penelope, or Penny as we came to know her, had fallen asleep and I intended to make the most of it. She was one of those children who hardly ever slept and I was exhausted. I decided to relax and watch television with a welcome cup of tea. Every channel was showing horse racing. Disappointed at not being able to watch the usual afternoon film, I left it on anyway and curled up on the sofa.

The horses were parading up and down in the paddock, getting ready for the next race. Picking up the newspaper, I thought I might try and guess the winner of the next race, just for fun. It was all new to me. It had never crossed my mind to watch racing, let alone bet on a horse, but I became quite interested after watching one or two races.

About a week later, I watched the horse-racing again. It was time for the first race and the horses were lined up for the start. Then they were off. I placed the newspaper on the table and looked at all the horses', jockeys' and trainers' names. It was all double Dutch to me, I couldn't understand any of it and I decided to give it up as a bad job. I walked into the kitchen to make a cup of tea, when suddenly I heard somebody say quite clearly the name of a horse. I looked around the living room to see who had spoken; no one was there. I then proceeded to investigate the rest of the house, looking in every room to see where the voice had come from.

Over the years I had become used to 'spooky' happenings, so when I couldn't find anyone I put it down to spirit or imagination. I thought it couldn't hurt to take a look in the newspaper to see if this horse did exist, and I couldn't believe my eyes: the horse was listed in the very next race! I was so excited – obviously someone was trying to tell me something. I wondered what I should do about it. If I placed a bet and the horse won, it would be wonderful as I would be able to pay the outstanding electricity bill.

There was a betting shop around the corner only two streets away. Opening my purse, I discovered I had only a shilling left; it wasn't much but it would be enough. But even if I wanted to put a bet on a horse I didn't know how to do it, or even dare to go into one of those awful places alone. Time was running out and the next race was about to start.

I took a deep breath, picked Penny up and set off to the betting shop, shaking as I opened the door. The room was filled with thick cigarette smoke and there wasn't another woman in sight. As I walked into the room everything seemed to come to a standstill and there was deathly silence. I was aware of the radio blaring out the starting price of each horse as I pushed my way through sweating queues of men towards the counter. All the men in the room stopped and stared at me, taking time out from placing their bets to make rude suggestions.

'Yes love,' said the man behind the counter, smiling.

'I want to make a bet,' I said, wanting desperately to

flee from this awful scene.

'You're supposed to write out your own bet. Here, love, let me help you,' said a voice from the back of the room. 'I'll do it for you. Now, what race meeting, which horse and how much? Do you want it placed on the nose or each way?'

I thought to myself, Oh God, what am I going to do? I didn't know. 'What do you mean?' I said. 'All I know is the name of the horse and I have a shilling to make a bet with.'

'Tell me the name of the horse and I'll look and see if I can find which course it's running at,' said the man behind the counter, and I handed him the piece of paper with the horse's name on it.

'Oh, here it is, Kempton Park, 2.30. They're under starter orders so we'd better be quick. How much?'

'Err, one shilling on the nose,' I said, not knowing what the 'on the nose' meant.

Then, grabbing the piece of paper he had given me, I rushed out of the shop and into the street. I took a deep breath as I looked down at Penny's little face; thank goodness she was asleep. Furtively I glanced up and down the road to see if anyone had seen me. My mother-in-law's shop was only one street away and I was worried that she might see me, so I ran home and closed the door behind me.

I must be crazy, I thought as I sat down to watch the race. I just hoped it was going to be worth all the embarrassment. To my disappointment my horse wasn't even mentioned once. I thought, that's that, never again. Then I realised the man had said Kempton Park; I was watching the wrong race. I didn't know what to do; I couldn't go back to the betting office to see if my horse had won. I went to make a cup of tea and decided I would wait to see the winners in the next day's newspaper.

Suddenly I heard: 'Here are the results of the 2.30 at Kempton Park.' I rushed back into the living room as the man announced that my horse had come in first at 5-1. I jumped up and down with joy, then reality dawned on me. I would have to go and collect my winnings, and I shuddered at the thought.

The next day I tried to figure out how I could get someone else to pick them up for me. I didn't know anyone and anyway, I didn't want it known what I had done. So I would have to do it myself. I had bills to pay and 5-1 winnings would give me five shillings plus my own shilling back. Not a fortune, but not to be sneezed at.

Most days for the next 12 to 18 months I gambled, winning on every bet I placed. I didn't hear any more voices; I just knew instinctively which horse would win by looking at the paper. I only ever had enough money to place a small bet, winning just enough to pay my bills.

I could go on telling stories about my gambling days but I must come to the point I want to make. While I was struggling to pay bills, I won every race I put money on. I know it's hard to believe, but that's how it was: winning just enough to keep my head above water, never having a penny left over. When my husband started earning a proper wage and I could pay my bills, my lucky streak disappeared as quickly as it came. I honestly believe this was due to spirit intervention on my behalf.

I had been seeing spirit relatives of people I came into contact with, and always passed this information on to them, though more in a casual way than as a practising medium. I have been asked many times over the years the same questions: What is clairvoyance? What is it like to see 'ghosts'? Do you see them like solid people? Doesn't it scare you at all?

Like other clairvoyants I have the advantage of seeing spirit guides and the spirit bodies of those who have died. This can be extremely valuable in proving the existence of life after death, as I can describe those who have died. It is so rewarding to bring comfort to the bereaved. Most people have a natural desire to contact their loved ones, to find out if they are happy and well in their new environment.

The death of a loved one can be extremely traumatic for those left behind, especially if they have no belief in life after death to hang on to. This is why mediums are so sought after, to prove to the bereaved that life does in fact continue after the death process. I thank God that I am fortunate to have this faith and gift; they have carried me through many a traumatic time.

Penny was almost two years old when my second daughter was born at home on the 10 March 1965. Unlike Penny, she had white hair and light blue eyes. We named her Victoria Alison. By this time we were in a position to buy our own home, and needed the space. Not long after we moved to our new house my mother came to stay with us. She was suffering from chronic asthma and bronchitis and was in a terrible state. I honestly thought it was her time to leave this world as she was fighting for every breath she took. I prayed constantly for healing to reach her and make her well again. My prayers for healing were answered and several weeks later she had recovered from her illness. I cannot thank my spirit healers enough for all the hard work and healing power they transmitted to Mum.

I wasn't what you would call a practising spiritualist as such. I believed in life after death and I could communicate with dead people but I didn't particularly give it much thought. I wasn't looking in any way to use my gifts; I had enough to do looking after my two children. Looking back now, I think spirit had different ideas for me.

I remember one particular occasion, it was Christmas night and the children were in bed fast asleep, exhausted and full to bursting after their exciting day of opening presents and eating lots of goodies. My mother, my husband and I were appreciating the meaning of Christmas, singing carols and hymns thanking God for a wonderful day. The atmosphere in the room was lovely; we were relaxed and very happy. Without any warning the whole room lit up with a wonderful brilliant white light, and as I looked into the light I could see numerous beautiful spirit lanterns. The colours were beyond description, nothing like the ordinary colours we have here on this earth plane. These had been placed around the room for extra decoration amongst our Christmas trimmings. What a beautiful sight!

I was admiring these when I suddenly became aware of a spirit visitor. He was an elderly oriental gentleman, and by the way he was dressed he must have been very important. He wore the most splendid gold brocade mandarin coat with a matching hat, plain black trousers and gold brocade slippers. His beautiful clothing was exquisitely embroidered and his long black hair was neatly plaited down his back. His moustache was very long and drooped down at each side of his mouth to past the bottom of his chin. The radiance of the light that surrounded him was awe-inspiring. It blinded me as I tried hard to take it all in and to capture all the details of this wonderful spirit person, wondering if I were dreaming. Not only had he showed himself to me, he went on to explain that he was one of my spirit helpers, a Mandarin and sage. He told us that it had been hundreds of years since he was last on the earth plane. As I gazed into his wise old face I could see a knowing twinkle in his eyes. He then faded away, leaving me with a wonderful feeling of wellbeing as a powerful love poured through me, almost reducing me to tears of joy. I sat in silence trying to understand what had happened to me. What a wonderful Christmas present spirit had given me. I will never forget and know that spirit is around me all the time.

I had started giving clairvoyance to the public on a part-time basis, and had been doing it for about five years, without ever really trying to develop my psychic gift. I had very little time left to devote to psychic work as my children were still so young. However, spirit always let me know they were working with me.

To my surprise, I was soon to experience spirit taking over my body for the first time. One night as I lay in bed, awake and relaxed following meditation, without warning I felt a tremendous power flow through me and my whole being started to change. The love I felt was so powerful, I had no reason to be afraid, so I allowed spirit to continue

15

with whatever they had planned for me. (By this time I had learnt to trust spirit implicitly; knowing that no harm would ever come to me.)

To describe what happened to me is very difficult. I felt I had become another human being. Even with my beliefs, I was a little apprehensive, as this strange feeling was something new; I had never experienced anything like it before. I remember feeling very confused as I changed into my Aunt Eunice. It's hard to imagine, and I know it sounds ridiculous, but I knew what was happening to me was real, though I kept thinking how stupid it all was. It was also very uncanny, not feeling in the least bit afraid when I became another person. I felt like my Aunt Eunice, I *was* her, but as far as I was aware she was still alive.

It was very unnerving for me, knowing she was still in this world. How could this happen to me? Yet the feeling was so wonderful, I found I didn't want to be myself again, I thoroughly enjoyed this powerful feeling of love that spirit was transmitting. I was so convinced I was Eunice I wanted to get up and look in the mirror, believing I would see her reflection staring back at me. She didn't speak a word or show herself to me but how could she. I was Eunice.

I was only 23 at the time and still in my infancy as a medium, never dreaming something like this would happen. I couldn't quite grasp the reason behind it but I knew all would be revealed eventually.

I was very close to Eunice, we were like sisters. She was only in her forties, one of my younger aunts, and we got along wonderfully. But she had been suffering from bone cancer for quite a long time and was in a tremendous amount of pain. The good thing was that she believed in spiritualism and was very psychic. I don't know if she was afraid of her ability to see dead people, but she never actively worked in any way for spirit.

That night it took me a long time to finally drift off to sleep, as I didn't want to miss anything or let go of the experience, of the spiritual love that was directed at me. I found it very hard having to wait until morning before I could give a detailed description of the night's extraordinary psychic phenomenon.

A few days later we were watching television when the phone rang; it was my Aunt Margaret. She began asking me why we hadn't gone to Eunice's funeral that day, saying she thought we were awful. I was speechless and very upset to hear the news. I told her that no-one in the family had informed us of her passing.

We now know why Eunice had visited to me, and I will never forget. She was letting me know that she had finally received her promotion, a release from the awful pain she had suffered in this life. It was good to know this.

I did see Eunice again clairvoyantly on several occasions over the next few years. When she was in the physical body she used to sing folk songs. She had a lovely voice, even performing on television sometimes. On future occasions when Eunice made her spirit presence known to me, I found myself singing her songs. There was never any doubt it was her because I could suddenly sing with a much sweeter voice.

Following that episode I gradually increased my involvement with the spiritualist movement and gave sittings regularly. I used clairvoyance most of the time, my seeing faculty. I find the majority of people like to come to see me so that I can bring their family and friends closer to them. It is positive proof of an afterlife when I can describe their loved ones and give detailed descriptions of how they looked when they were alive. I tell them things about themselves that only spirit friends or relatives could possibly know, such as nicknames, what they bought the day before, who came to visit them last week, if they had a birthday party and so on.

Most people would expect mediums and clairvoyants to be able to see all their family and friends who have passed to the spirit world. However, this is not always the case. I have seen some of my aunts and uncles but not all

17

of them. I haven't seen my grandmother either. I would have thought that because of her mediumistic ability she would have found it easier to contact me. I have felt her presence on occasions but I have never seen her clairvoyantly. Nor has my grandfather appeared to me; he died when I was very small and thought I was the 'bees-knees'. Yet again, I have only felt his presence and one would imagine with the love link between us that I would have seen him. For whatever reason, it must not be possible.

We cannot 'call up' anyone we wish to communicate with, and we cannot make things happen. Spirit people come because they want to visit us. Perhaps those we haven't seen have gone on to a higher plane of existence and don't particularly wish to come back to this heavy dark world of ours. Maybe they have been reborn onto the earth plane again – what we call reincarnation. All this is explained in more detail in Book Two.

CHAPTER THREE

Earthbound

In 1971, my husband and I decided to emigrate to South Africa. It was a sudden and impulsive decision on my part and Michael was only too eager to go along with it. He had always wanted to travel but until then I had always been the 'home bird'.

By this time I had four children. My third daughter was the spitting image of Penny, and we named her Stephanie Claire. My youngest child was a son at last, whom we named Roderick Jason. He looked like Victoria, with fair hair and complexion. He was still only a baby of 11 months when we left.

Off we went to live at a place called Randburg, situated on the outskirts of Johannesburg towards the bush land. I knew when I left I would be able to continue with my mediumistic work. It doesn't matter where you live, life after death still exists and so does spiritualism. I would find my own little niche and when the time was right I knew the spirit world would work with me and pass on knowledge wherever it was needed.

It's strange how news travels fast about a medium moving into the area. At times over the years I have found it difficult to hide away, even for a short while to unpack and settle into my new home. South Africa was no exception, even though it was 6000 miles away from home.

My first sitting in a strange country proved to be less than satisfactory. A gentleman came to see me accompanied by his two friends. I made them comfortable before I started the sitting; my spirit guides were waiting, ready to help. I proceeded to pass on to the sitter all the information given to me by spirit. Unfortunately, everything I told this man was met with a negative response and after a while I gave up. I knew I was correct, as the information from spirit came loud and clear to me, and there was no mistake.

Eventually, to my relief, he and his two companions left, leaving me confused, upset and a little embarrassed.

Several weeks later I gave an 'evening of clairvoyance', inviting a group of approximately 20 people. The evening went very well and everyone seemed to be happy with the information they had received. I noticed amongst the group of people the man I had seen earlier for a sitting. When everyone had left he stayed behind and asked if he could have a word with me. I was still somewhat embarrassed but said yes anyway. He went on to tell me the sitting I had given him several weeks earlier was indeed correct. I was angry and pointed out to him that he should have said so at the time, as it wasn't fair to the spirit communicators or to myself. He explained it was because his friends were there. I asked why he had brought them with him if he wanted the sitting to be private. I recalled the information I gave to him and there was nothing for him to be ashamed of. I explained that, in any case, spirit always 'wrap' personal information up so only the recipient can understand the message. He apologised and eventually left. I must admit I did feel much better knowing he had finally confirmed the accuracy of the information he had been given.

When I was settled and got used to my new environment I decided to form a 'Development Circle', helping those who wanted to become a medium or healer.

A young man, an unbeliever, decided one evening, following long discussions with me about spiritualism, to come to a meeting at my home. The messages he received from spirit must have astounded him, because from that day on I couldn't keep him away. I finally agreed that he could join my development circle. He must have been keen, as it was a considerable distance for him to travel to my home. To my surprise his development as a healer came on in leaps and bounds; it took only a few months of attending my development circle before he was almost able to practice his healing gift and clairvoyance without supervision. It is very rewarding seeing someone change

20

so drastically.

Sadly, after ten years my marriage came to an end and the children and I returned to England in June 1972. I was sorry I couldn't stay and watch all the circle members blossom and grow mediumistically. It was very hard for me starting again without a home and four children to look after, but where there's a will there's a way. We stayed with my mother while we waited for a nice council house to become available; it took about six months. I had ample savings to furnish it and to buy a small car.

I had been living on my own with the children for about six months and was very content. One night the children were in bed and I was relaxing in my nightclothes watching television, following the usual hectic day entertaining four young children. The ten o'clock news was about to begin when I heard a loud banging at the front door. I wasn't expecting anyone at that late hour; reluctantly I went to the door and peered through the glass panel to see who was there. It could have been an emergency of some kind. I could see the visitor was a woman, but I couldn't make out who she was through the thick glass. Feeling safe, I opened the door. I couldn't believe my eyes; standing in front of me was my cousin Roberta, holding her two-year-old son. I hadn't seen her in ten years, in fact I had not given her much thought during that time. I had no idea that she knew where I was living.

'Good heavens, what on earth are you doing here at this time of night, Roberta? I asked.

'Hi, Barbara can we come in? I need your help,' she said, looking very upset.

'Of course you can, what's wrong?' Closing the door behind her, I thought: Oh no, not at this time of night. But she was family, after all.

'My house is haunted and I'm frightened!' she blurted out. 'I didn't know where else to go. I thought you might be able to help me. You don't mind, do you?'

I ushered her inside. What do you mean, haunted?'

21

'A ghost, what do you think? Will you help me, Barbara, you know about spooks and things, don't you, you mess about with them?'

Smiling at her interpretation of what I did, I said, 'You'd better start at the beginning, and tell me all about it. Let's put the little one to bed first, he can go in with Rod, they're about the same age. I heard you had a little boy shortly after Roderick was born. Sorry, what's his name?'

His name was Lee. While Roberta settled Lee down for the night I made us both a sandwich and a cup of tea, knowing it was going to be a long hard night. Settling down, I asked, 'Have you been playing with a ouija board?'

'No, I don't think so.' She hesitated, then: 'What's a ouija board?'

I explained that it was a board with the alphabet printed on it, with a separate pointer for discarnate beings to move and spell out words, messages.

'Oh! No, just pieces of paper with the alphabet on and a glass,' She replied, unconcerned.

'The glass and alphabet are the same as the ouija board. Didn't you realise how dangerous it can be?' I growled at her.

'Well, no,' she said, rather sheepishly.

'Oh, Roberta, what have you done? Never mind, what's happening to you is probably something and nothing, easily explained. Start at the beginning and tell me everything. And I mean everything.'

I wasn't sure I believed she had a ghost, it seemed a little far-fetched. Perhaps she was over-reacting. It took most of the night for her to tell me what had been happening. Things had been thrown around the house, she explained, and objects moved around the bedrooms. The baby's toys had been moved when she wasn't there and the lights would go on and off on their own.

Crying, she said. 'I cut out some cardboard crucifixes and pinned them on all the doors around the house. I even placed a Bible next to me on the bedside table. What am I

22

going to do? Please help me, Barbara.' Putting my arm around her, I promised to do all I could.

She went on, 'The doors open and close by themselves. I thought the crosses on the doors would have stopped this from happening, and the Bible, but it was thrown across the bedroom. It must be very evil to do that to a holy book.'

I said I would go with her the following morning to her house and have a look for myself, I would try and 'pick up' any presence. If necessary we would try and get the church involved. I still wasn't convinced; she could have been exaggerating a little.

I was soon to find out for myself.

The next day after breakfast we dressed the children, and then set off for Dewsbury where she lived. The journey would take us about three-quarters of an hour. Roberta lived with her son in a two-bedroom council house on an estate in West Yorkshire. Roberta and I had spent a lot of time together when we were children and in those days I was quite fond of her. We had grown apart when we both married. Her house had been my Aunt Eunice's home before she died and Roberta, her daughter, carried on living there after her mother's passing.

When we arrived, Roberta was a little apprehensive about going inside but I persuaded her to show me around, saying, 'Come on then, don't be afraid I'm here with you.' This was a stupid statement, as I had no idea what we were up against. Who was I to think I had some special power over the invisible forces, good or evil, that might be in the house?

As soon as we set foot in the entrance hall I could feel the presence of something evil. It was daylight, but I could feel heaviness, darkness through the house. I said something ridiculous like, 'Come out, come out wherever you are', as I had done when playing hide-and-seek as a child. What a shock I would have got if someone invisible had said 'Boo!' to me.

23

'Don't, Barbara, please. It's not funny,' pleaded Roberta.

'I know, I'm sorry, I just thought I would try and lighten the situation.'

I couldn't believe the next stupid thing I said out loud: 'Have no fear, Barbara is here.' I didn't have any experience of exorcisms and I thank God nothing happened. As we left the house I said to Roberta, 'I think you should ring the local priest and see if he'll help.'

We arrived back at my house safe and sound, though feeling a little stressed. I made a cup of tea while Roberta looked through the telephone directory for the number of her local church. After tea she took a deep breath, picked up the phone and said, 'Well, here goes then. What if he doesn't believe me?'

'We'll face that situation if it arises.'

After talking to the priest she told me: 'He said he would have to get permission from the church to carry out an exorcism, but he'll meet me at the house tomorrow morning and see for himself. I don't think he believed me. Will you come along with me and talk to him?'

I agreed, and we went the following day to see him. Roberta and I had been waiting inside the house for about ten minutes and during that time I was aware once again of a terrible heavy, dark feeling around and eyes watching us. A cold shudder ran through me from the top of my head to my toes and I could feel the hair at the back of my neck stand on end. I tried hard not to show my fear to Roberta; I had no idea what was going to happen.

The priest arrived 15 minutes late. 'So, what's all this nonsense about? You say the house is haunted. What makes you think such a thing?' he demanded. I decided at once I didn't like this arrogant and condescending man at all. Roberta told him the whole story; admittedly she did sound rather like a little girl making up a fairy tale. I interrupted and confirmed what she had said. He looked at both of us, smiling in disbelief. I was so angry, I wanted to wipe the smirk of his face – not very Christian of me, I know, but I did hope something paranormal would happen and he would get the fright of his life.

'Show me where this haunting is supposed to have happened,' he said sarcastically.

'Both bedrooms, and downstairs,' Roberta mumbled nervously.

He climbed the stairs two at a time as though he was the king of the castle, unafraid, like a father showing his child it was only a bad dream after all. Then, turning to Roberta, he said, 'I think there could be something here. I do feel an atmosphere, perhaps a presence, but I'll have to ask permission to perform an exorcism. Give me your telephone number and I'll be in touch with you soon.'

A long week later, the priest rang Roberta at my home to say he had received permission to carry out the exorcism. They made arrangements to meet the following day, and Roberta asked me if I would come along, which I readily agreed to.

I prayed very hard that night, as I always do. I asked God to protect us all, keeping us safe from evil forces and asking for the light of love to fill Roberta's home again.

Morning came; there was silence, apart from the usual playful noises of the children. Roberta and I were deep in thought, thinking about the afternoon's ordeal ahead of us. Time dragged as we waited for 2.15 to arrive to set off on our journey to Dewsbury. This time I decided we were going to wait for the priest outside in the car so we could all go in together.

He arrived, thank goodness, on time. My heart was thumping as we went inside. I began saying the Lord's Prayer to myself over and over. Poor Roberta looked scared to death, pale and drawn. The atmosphere indoors was oppressive and cold, and for the first time I felt very frightened. It seemed to take forever for the priest to prepare all his regalia. While he was praying, he went through the house throwing holy water into all the corners of the rooms, blessing the house. When you're scared, time

25

stands still.

Finally we stood on the landing at the top of the stairs. The priest said to us, 'Let us put our hands together in prayer.'

We stood with our hands clasped together and eyes closed while he said a prayer. The next thing I knew the priest was running down the stairs and out of the front door. Fear struck me as my mind ran riot and I remember thinking: Oh my God, it's all up to me now, what am I going to do? Roberta by now was beginning to panic. Putting on a brave face, I started to say out loud the Lord's Prayer with my hands clasped tightly together. Suddenly I could see a man's face clairvoyantly which knocked me off my guard a little; I wasn't expecting this to happen. He had short light brown curly hair, his face was round and full and his eyes glared and seemed to go right through me. His evil face was grinning as saliva dripped from the side of his mouth. I remember thinking: As long as I can see him, we're all right and please God, don't let him touch me, I will die of fright.

Clairaudiantly I heard a voice tell me how this man wanted Roberta to take her own life. It wasn't his voice, perhaps it was a guardian angel. My heart beat so fast I thought it would jump out of my chest. I tried to swallow but I couldn't, my throat was too dry and I could hardly breathe. I was beginning to feel sick as the evil power tried to pull my hands apart as I stood praying. The power was so strong it took all my strength to keep my hands clasped together. I fought hard to sustain the power of light, knowing my faith in God was too strong for any evil to enter my being or harm us in any way. I insisted, in the name of our Lord Jesus Christ, that the evil spirit go away and leave us in peace, telling him to look towards the light for help and to be gone from this place for good. We stayed like that for a while, then suddenly I took Roberta's hand and we ran just as the priest had done. We got into the car and drove off at great speed.

'Barbara I can't go back there again!' Roberta's voice was pleading and very shaky.

'You don't have to, love, not until it's safe for you,' I reassured her, wondering what I was going to do next. I thought the priest was awful leaving us like that. His faith couldn't have been very strong. I was really worried about Roberta's future, wondering where she was going to stay. She could stay with me temporarily, but on a permanent basis it would not work out for either of us. All I could do now was pray for guidance and hope spirit friends would help us.

Roberta and her son stayed with me for several weeks until it was safe for her to return home. We plucked up courage to visit the house twice a week to see if there had been any more unusual occurrences and we placed the Bible back on the bedside table, hoping it would remain there. The atmosphere in the house seemed to be quite normal but we couldn't take any chances; we had to be absolutely sure. It took time for the house to become 'quiet'. Eventually Roberta moved back, knowing she could come back to me if anything happened again. I don't know what I did on that horrendous day but whatever it was, it must have worked. Roberta remained in that house for several years. My prayers must have been answered.

Looking back, I must have been crazy: a novice thinking she could put the world to rights. I should never have attempted anything remotely like that, as I did not know the first thing about performing an exorcism. I didn't know it then but this was the beginning of my spiritual journey.

I had been on my own for 17 months when I met and married a lovely man by the name of Keith. I had packed so much into my life and I was still only 29 years old. Keith had three children, two daughters and a son, the later who lived with us, making five children in all to look after. My husband was a chartered accountant with his own business. This demanded a great deal of my time, entertaining business colleagues and travelling all over the

27

world, meeting chartered accountants of different nationalities. This again put a strain on my mediumistic work but somehow I managed to fit it all in.

After the wedding we all moved to my husband's house just outside Ilkley. It wasn't long after we moved that I realised there was something bothering the children, then aged between four and 13. I was having difficulty getting them to go upstairs alone, as they said they were frightened. At the time I thought it was the change of house and having a new dad that caused this unsettled feeling. Every time they went upstairs, I had to stand at the bottom watching them. Having five children constantly going up and downstairs made life very difficult for me. About halfway up the stairs the children would suddenly run at full speed to the top, across the landing and into their rooms, banging their doors behind them. I must admit, when I reached the top of the stairs I always felt uneasy, as though I was being watched. It was becoming more and more difficult to persuade the children to go to bed at night, so I had to find out what was going on.

Whoever the unseen visitor was, they hadn't shown themselves to me. I wondered why I couldn't 'pick up' this spirit visitor. That night I decided to 'tune in' to the next world during meditation, ask who it was upsetting my children and would they show themselves to me. Soon after I started my meditation I could feel the presence of a spirit person, but to my disappointment nothing happened that night. I wasn't unduly worried, as I could feel nothing evil, only a strange presence, and I knew the children were safe.

About a week later, as I was about to climb the stairs, I saw a lady dressed in white. As she floated down the stairs, I automatically stepped to one side but I could feel the hair at the back of my neck stand on end. It was a real ghostly apparition like one would see in a film. She seemed to pass through me, leaving a chill that froze me to the spot. I was used to seeing spirit people but under different circumstances, and I was never left feeling uncomfortable.

As I looked at her I noticed her lovely long auburn hair and slender shapely body. She was probably in her 20s and looked terribly distressed. I remember asking her mentally to talk to me, tell me what her problems were, what was disturbing her. I promised I would try to help, but without warning she disappeared. All that evening, however much I tried, I couldn't get her out of my mind, though I didn't think it wise to tell anyone just yet.

I went to bed before my husband and propped myself up, ready to start my meditation. I had just closed my eyes, trying to link with our visitor, when I felt her in the room. She didn't walk; she glided through the bedroom door and across the room towards me, coming to a halt at the foot of the bed right in front of me. I must have looked ridiculous with my mouth wide open in surprise.

I said to her, 'You're very welcome, who are you? Are you the lady I saw earlier?' That was rather stupid of me, as I already knew it was she who had passed me on the stairs earlier.

'Yes, it was me,' she said.

'How can I help you, why are you here?'

'I feel very alone, I have to tell you what I did, then I can leave this place, move on. I have waited a long time for someone to talk to,' she said.

'Go on, love, tell me what you want me to know.' By this time I felt so sorry for her, she was obviously very distressed and wanted my help.

'I lived here with my husband and children but I became so depressed, I took my own life.'

She was sobbing, and my heart ached for her. 'Tell me all about it you will feel better, don't be afraid. How did you take your life?'

'I made sure everyone was out. I was so depressed I couldn't think clearly, I was desperate. I no longer wanted to go on living, all I could think about was ending my life. It seemed easy at the time, and it never crossed my mind that I would cause my family so much pain. I went into the

29

kitchen and turned on the gas oven, then placed my head so that I could breathe in the fumes.' As she was telling me this, tears poured down her face.

Tears were also falling down my face as she told me the story. I knew she had to open her heart to me before she could move on.

'The next thing I knew I was here. I feel so terribly lost. Will you help me and tell my family how very sorry I am and ask them to forgive me?'

'Yes, of course I will, but who are you and where does your family live?'

To my astonishment, she said. 'Next door to you.' Before I could ask her name or which house next door, she was gone.

What a difficult situation to find myself in! I didn't know my neighbours on my left. The people on my right I knew quite well but never discussed spiritualism with them. I wasn't sure how they would take this news, if in fact it was for them.

It was a small village where I lived and everyone knew everyone else's business. My husband was a member of the local Methodist church and people were beginning to wonder why I never went to church with him. I refrained from going because it had nothing to offer me; I was a spiritualist and had different ideas.

What should I do? I didn't want to cause any embarrassment to my family, but I had promised this young woman I would talk to her family. I wasn't prepared to let her down, she needed my help.

It was several weeks later when I found the right time to approach my next door neighbour, who had invited me round for coffee. All I had to do was direct the conversation onto the subject of spiritualism. The time had come. I tried to talk generally about life after death. I wasn't sure if she was at all interested in my conversation but her expression was strange. She was a regular churchgoer and I wasn't sure if she would show me the door or not. Her face didn't give much away and I wondered when would be the right time to broach the subject of my spirit visitor. I swallowed, asked her if she knew anything about the previous occupants of my house, then blurted out: 'Did you know that the house was haunted?' Knowing what the spirit woman had told me, it was rather insensitive on my part. With a little more thought I could have chosen a better approach.

She looked shocked at my sudden statement. I asked her if she was all right, as she looked rather pale. After a very long silence, I said. 'Is there anything you would like to tell me or think I should know?'

'My son and daughter in-law lived in your house. Tell me about the ghost,' she said very abruptly, staring right through me.

I gave her the full story about the lovely auburn-haired woman I had seen and spoken with, passing on the message from this spirit person word for word. My neighbour's face began to soften and with tears in her eyes, she said, 'Thank you, you are right, my daughter-in-law did take her own life by inhaling gas fumes. She was very depressed at the time. My son has been going through hell ever since this happened.'

Just to make sure, she asked me to describe this apparition again. I finished my cup of coffee and left feeling much better. A weight had been lifted from my shoulders. From that day on we never had any further eerie experiences, and my children started to go to bed without any problems. I never saw the spirit visitor again; she must have gone on to her place of rest.

CHAPTER FOUR

New Beginnings

A short while later we moved to Ilkley where I stayed for the next 13 years. The new house was very large and beautiful. We needed lots of room to accommodate all the family, and I was able to have my own sanctuary to continue the work spirit wanted me to do.

One hot summer's day, I had cleaned the house from top to bottom and was feeling very tired. I loved the house, but there were such a lot of rooms to clean. I had been suffering from terrible headaches for several weeks, which I had put down to over-work. My children were like most other kids and at times took some coping with. I decided to phone my doctor for some medication, and he told me I could pick up a prescription later that morning. However, it was around lunchtime before I felt well enough to drive there. My head was still pounding, I had to get the tablets and sooner rather than later, so I set off in the car to the surgery, which was only a few minutes away in the next village.

I had just turned left onto the main road when the sun blinded me through the windscreen. I had to screw up my eyes in order to see the oncoming traffic. My headache was so bad and the last thing I needed was to have difficulty driving.

Presently I heard an enormous bang, and when I turned the second bend I saw immediately what it was: a car had smashed into the wall along the side of the road. I looked around but I couldn't see any other vehicle involved in the accident. I wasn't at all surprised that this could have happened, the sun was so strong and this particular sharp bend was well known as a black spot for accidents. I drove past slowly, looking to see if I could help in any way, and was relieved to see the five occupants of the car get out. They looked very shaken but seemed uninjured. I leaned out of my car and shouted, 'Is everyone OK, is there anything I can do?' I was hoping I wouldn't have to stop; thank goodness there was no response. I could see they were all right and other drivers were stopping. They would be looked after.

As I drove down the road I remember thinking what an awful wreck the car was in, and how lucky they were to come out of it unscathed.

It took me about ten minutes in all to get my prescription, and I was back on the road home again. As I approached the scene of the accident, I was beginning to feel a little ashamed of myself for not stopping earlier. By this time I could see police cars and ambulances. The policemen were slowing down the traffic, and as I slowly passed the smashed vehicle, I could see to my horror five bodies lying at the side of the road. I took a second look in amazement. By the way they were dressed, I could see they were the same five people I had spoken to earlier. My heart sank, for I knew then that the five people I had seen must have been the dead occupants of the car. They hadn't realised they had been killed in the accident, and were getting out of the car as though nothing had happened.

I was stunned and couldn't think straight. I questioned myself as I drove the rest of the way home. Should I have stopped on the way to the surgery and offered some help? I turned into the drive, home at last. The first thing I did was to put the kettle on and make myself a strong cup of tea. I couldn't believe what I had just seen, and I was in a state of shock myself.

Later that day on the six o'clock news there was a story about the accident, in which all five occupants of the vehicle had died instantly. I felt relieved that they had not suffered, and realised then that I could not have done anything for them if I had stopped.

The experience made me think, and confirmed to me that spirit people do exist, although spirit had proved this to me many times over the years. However, having said that, I am one of the most sceptical people you can imagine. I always tell my sitters, 'Accept only what has been proved beyond doubt to you. Never be a sponge, absorbing all the information given to you as gospel. There are mediums who are not what they seem, and will tell you anything to get a fee.'

We all have our off-days; some are harder than others for whatever reason. We are, after all, human and we make mistakes. However, there is no excuse for lying or cheating; the only rule for a good medium is honesty at all times. In some cases, a medium has to be very careful what she/he says to someone who comes for a sitting, even though the information is given with the best possible intentions. Quite a lot of the time, they really do not want to hear what you have to say, just what they want you to tell them.

There are good evidential sittings as well as poor ones. For whatever reason it happens on occasions.

I remember one time, it must be 20 years ago, when a couple booked an appointment to see me for clairvoyance. I was still living in Ilkley, West Yorkshire, and they were travelling all the way from the Isle of White. It was a long way to come to spend an hour or so with a medium that they had never met. They were about two hours late for their appointment, during which time their spirit relatives and I patiently waited for them. I became increasingly tired and irritable after a hard day's work. I didn't want to let the sitters down, so I remained 'tuned in' to spirit even though it was for a considerable length of time. The appointment was for eight o'clock in the evening, and by ten o'clock I had given up all hope of it materialising at all. I made myself a cup of tea and joined my husband in the lounge. I had just put my feet up when the doorbell rang. It was the couple from the Isle of White, apologising for their late arrival, but asking if they could still come in and have their sitting. Under normal circumstances I would probably have said no. It was very late and I was exhausted. It was only because of the distance they had travelled that I agreed, knowing spirit relatives were still waiting to say hello.

As I opened the door to my sanctuary, I could feel the peace and tranquillity that spirit had brought with them. I showed the couple in, and they sat down.

But what an awful experience! I've never felt so embarrassed in all my life. The sitting took about two minutes from start to finish. I did give them clairvoyance; I described the spirit relatives giving names and how they had passed into the spirit world. Suddenly there was, dare I say it, a 'deathly' silence. No matter what I did and how hard I tried, the sitting was over. My biggest mistake was apologising to the couple; I had proved the existence of life after the so-called death process. No matter how short and sweet it was, I had done all that spirit asked of me. But I can still see their faces to this very day as they sat there, waiting for more. I finally said, 'I'm sorry, I can't pass on any more information because I'm not receiving anything else. I appreciate you have come a long way, but that's all spirit are prepared to offer this evening.'

After I had said goodbye and closed the door behind them, I stood with my back against the front door, fighting away the tears. It was such a long way to come; my reputation was at stake and I felt so terribly embarrassed. That night I went to bed vowing that this was the last sitting and the end of my mediumistic work. I felt totally inadequate, and I no longer wanted to practise my mediumship.

As I always do each night when I go to bed, I began to meditate, sending out healing prayers. I had so many people on my absent healing list, I was up until the early hours of the morning. I also received many phone calls during the night from those in need of my help. How can you refuse to help those who desperately need you? Naturally, these middle-of-the-night calls didn't go down very well with my husband; he had to get up for work in the morning. But spiritualism is my life, so the arguments were all worthwhile. I finally went to sleep thinking: Well, this is it, no more,

35

the end.

I can only say that unseen forces had different ideas regarding my future work.

When morning came the telephone never stopped ringing with people asking for sittings or thanking me for their postal readings, telling me how wonderful and accurate they were and what a wonderful medium I was. The postman delivered a mountain of letters, people asking for appointments for clairvoyance and healing, including requests for postal readings. I remember standing in the hall laughing at the thought that it was near impossible for me to give up this wonderful gift bestowed on me. The previous night was forgotten. For whatever reason, the sitters were given only what they needed to know. I have learnt not to question myself or spirit any more; the only time I would do it would be to improve my standard of mediumship.

I had to make good use of my time between clairvoyance and healing as I had so many patients who were sick, and I hardly had time to give sittings. For the time being I could only take emergencies for clairvoyance; my healing work had to come first. I opened a healing clinic where anyone could pop in free of charge; those who wanted could leave a donation on a plate.

Unanswered letters started to pile up, and I had such a backlog of people waiting for sittings I didn't know where to start. Mediumship is not like most jobs when you can delegate the work to someone else in the building if you are overworked. It got to a point when I couldn't see everyone; I had no alternative but to advise them to see another medium. However, there were very few good mediums I knew in Yorkshire to recommend.

I became quite ill through over-work. I found it very difficult to turn people away when they needed help, but you have to say no occasionally, for your own sake and others'. If you don't, everybody suffers. I had to learn the hard way, and eventually everything worked out well.

There are countless examples I could give of good evidential sittings over the years, but I have chosen only a few of the very interesting ones to mention here.

When a sitter arrives, one never knows what information one is going to receive, from whom or even for whom. All you have is a name to write in your diary. On one occasion, a lady called Doris came to see me from the outskirts of Bradford. After welcoming her with a cup of tea, I started the sitting. It was hard work; she couldn't place any of the information I gave to her from spirit. I was embarrassed, and asked spirit to try to sort out this mess. At the end of the sitting, spirit gave me the name of Marjorie who was still living. It was only then that she replied, 'Oh that's a friend of mine, she's been staying with me recently, and I've just put her on a train for home. All I can think of is this information must be for her, would that be possible?' I agreed it was.

She finally left, leaving me feeling rather inadequate. I think I felt worse than Doris did; she seemed to be quite happy. I knew that the information I had given was correct, but that didn't help me on the day to prove survival. I had to put it out of my mind, and get on with trying to prove survival to my next sitter.

Later that day, 11 July, the phone rang. 'This is Doris, I came to see you earlier today for a sitting. As soon as I arrived home I rang Marjorie in Liverpool, and told her about our meeting. She was amazed at what I told her and agreed the sitting was meant for her. She said she's going to write to you this week.'

I did receive a letter from Marjorie about two days later. This is what she had to say:

Dear Mrs Bridgford,

My friend Doris saw you by appointment this afternoon for clairvoyance. I have spoken on the phone to her this evening and feel I must write to you. I am Marjorie who stayed with Doris over the weekend; I will mention the things Doris can remember you saying to her, which I think apply to me. You told her that you could see me changing trains at Manchester, carrying a bulging bag, also a bag with pottery at the bottom, which you said had broken. I can confirm I did change trains at Manchester from Bradford and was carrying the luggage you described. The pottery was broken and of sentimental value, belonging to Doris. I brought it back with me to see if my brother could salvage something for her. You also said that I had just purchased new curtains. I bought and hung a pair last week. You mentioned my aunt, an old lady with a stick with hip trouble, who had reached the age of 96. You were also correct when you said she passed into the spirit world in 1970. The old gentleman and the soldier you mentioned being my father or brother, I can also accept. Joan passed with breast cancer, a special friend who died six days before my Aunt. Rachel is also a name I can accept, my aunt's sister; she passed seven years ago as you stated. Yes, I do have leg and chest trouble.

I feel that all the information you gave Doris was for me, directed from the spirit world to my friend to pass on to me. I would like to convey my thanks to you and would very much like some more information, if it were possible to make an appointment to see you.

My sincere thanks,
Marjorie

God does indeed move in a mysterious way. It is obvious that when Doris came to see me, spirit had decided her friend needed help more than she did. Therefore, the information was passed on through Doris. Sometimes there are messages from our spirit friends which are not verified until much later. This can be embarrassing during the sitting because of the negative response. However, I have learnt over the years never to doubt spirit communications. More often than not, the receiver of the messages will let you know when it has been proved to them at a later date. It is also very rewarding, for one cannot under these circumstance ever be accused of having read the sitter's mind.

Some things may seem very unlikely, but are true. A good example of this was when Ann came to see me one June. At the end of the sitting, having told her of all the spirit family and friends who were around her, with descriptions and names, I went on to say. 'I am being told by spirit that you will give birth to a lovely baby girl on 7 January next year. You mustn't worry, all will be well with the birth.'

'I don't think so,' Ann replied. 'I'm not pregnant, and anyway, I'm not sure if I'm ready for children yet. It certainly isn't on my mind to start a family. I'm sorry, but you're definitely mistaken.'

'Spirit are very adamant about this, perhaps you should check with the doctor. They're telling me that you conceived at the beginning of April.' The look of disbelief on her face said, 'Stupid woman.'

How can you insist that a person is pregnant? They obviously know their own bodies better than anyone else. Ann finally left, and I must admit I was glad to see her go. I thought I had really put my big foot in it again, although I knew that spirit were correct. If mistakes are made, it is usually through the medium's misinterpretation of a message, and I knew I hadn't got it wrong. I tried to put it out of my mind but I hoped one day she would come back to me and tell me what had happened.

It was August, a lovely summer's day. I had planned to take the day off from my psychic work and relax in the garden, something I very rarely had the opportunity to do.

I had no appointments that day, and I was looking forward to a little peace and quiet. Then the phone began to ring. I was tempted to leave it but I had to answer, in case it was urgent.

'Hello. Barbara Bridgford,' I said.

'Mrs Bridgford, this is Ann. Do you remember you gave me a sitting a few months ago? You told me I was expecting a baby in January?'

'Yes, I do recall the sitting, Ann, how are you, love?'

'I'm very well, thank you. Except, I am pregnant like you said. I thought it only right that I should let you know you were correct. However, you did tell me the baby would be born on 7 January next year. I'm sorry, but you're wrong with the dates, according to the doctor. He says it is due at the end of January, beginning of February.'

'Well, thank you for letting me know, I was sure I wasn't wrong. How do you feel about it?'

'Quite honestly, I don't know how it happened, we were definitely not planning a family just yet. I'm not sure how I feel, I suppose I'll get used to the idea eventually.'

I thanked her again for letting me know, and asked her to keep in touch and let me know when the baby was born, which she agreed to.

'Yes certainly I will, I'm sure you'll be curious to see if the baby turns out to be a little girl, won't you?'

'I'm sure if spirit says it will be, then yes I believe you will have a little girl.'

That was the end of the conversation. I was pleased to hear that I had not given her incorrect information.

I thought about Ann several times during the next few months, wondering how she was getting on, especially on 7 January. I could remember the date I had given, because the baby was due two days before my birthday on the ninth.

About five or six months later I received another phone call from Ann. 'You were right, I gave birth to a little girl on 7 January. I will never doubt what you and spirit say again, and as soon as I feel better can I come and see you again?'

40

'Yes, I'd like that very much. Will you bring the baby with you?'

Spirit always know what is going on, even before we do. It is always wonderful to receive letters or telephone calls confirming that the messages received from our friends in spirit are correct after all.

I saw a lot of Ann and her husband over the next few years, and we became friends, as I have done with many of my sitters. She was very apprehensive about becoming a mother during her first pregnancy, but she must have soon realised the joys children can bring, because eventually she had another baby, a little boy.

A similar experience happened another time. I gave a friend a message while we were having coffee together. 'Congratulations, Elsie, spirit tell me your daughter is expecting another addition to the family,' I blurted out.

'Oh, I hope not for her sake, she has enough children. I've just had a letter from her and there was no mention of her being pregnant again. Are you sure? Could it be someone else in the family?' she said, sounding rather concerned.

'Quite sure, Elsie. Write back to her and ask, or wait for her next letter to arrive. I'm sure she'll tell you then.' Later Elsie left looking rather worried. I was beginning to wonder if I should have waited for her daughter to tell her the news, although at that time I didn't know that Elsie wasn't already aware of this.

Elsie wrote to her daughter, who was then living in Zimbabwe, telling her what I had said. Her daughter responded very quickly, saying she was definitely not pregnant, and to 'tell Barbara Bridgford she's wrong'. She did not believe in such things as spiritualism, and did not want anything to do with it.

Naturally, Elsie showed me the part of the letter that involved me. 'You must be wrong, Barbara. I know spirit have never given me anything that has been incorrect, but I think on this occasion it must be a mistake. When all's said and done, my daughter must know whether she's

41

pregnant or not.'

'I don't think I've made a mistake, Elsie,' I said, remembering the experience I'd had with Ann. 'Let's wait and see, shall we?' No more was said on this subject, and I put it to the back of my mind. I knew that if I had been correct, I would eventually find out through Elsie, as we were very close friends and met regularly.

Eventually Elsie's daughter wrote to her to say she was pregnant, and the dates she gave her mother coincided with the time the message was given. I also had a further problem regarding Elsie's daughter and the pregnancy; this followed further information received from my spirit guides. I knew I could tell Elsie, but also knew that we could not tell her daughter what I had gleaned from spirit friends.

I told Elsie spirit was concerned that her daughter should never have tried for another child. She would have problems holding on to the baby, problems with her womb. Spirit also told us that the baby was in a breach position and the doctors would have difficulty turning it. Elsie agreed with me that we should not worry her daughter with this information, although she wouldn't have believed me anyway, and would never have wanted anything to do with any psychic information. We did nothing until she confirmed it in a letter: 'Mum, I'm having awful problems carrying this baby. The doctor says I may have to have my womb stitched to stop me from losing it.'

Later on in the pregnancy, she wrote again. 'The baby is in the breach position, and the doctors can't turn it.'

When I received this information, Elsie had asked me to give her daughter absent healing. With spirit help, she never had to have her womb secured and spirit doctors turned the baby.

A letter received later from Elsie's daughter contained some good news. 'The doctor said it was a miracle, the baby turned at the last minute. They don't know how it could have happened.'

She had a normal delivery after all.

CHAPTER FIVE

Strange But True

When my son Roderick was 14, I was asked by his school to give a talk on spiritualism to his classmates. I went to Ilkley Grammar School and talked to these teenagers, expecting the children to ask silly questions about ghosts. I was astounded at the intelligent questions they did ask, and their interest. Following my talk, I received a letter from the English teacher thanking me for an interesting afternoon, enclosing letters from every pupil in the class asking further questions, wanting to see me at home. *Psychic Newspaper* printed an article about my visit to the school, quoting the questions asked by the youngsters and my replies, with the heading 'Grammar School class has lesson about spiritualism'.

I started the discussion with the words, 'There's nothing more sure than the fact that in time we will all die. My job,' I said, 'is to prove there is a life after death.'

I explained that the physical body is like a caterpillar, restricted in movement and focused only on its primary needs for survival. When its life-span as a caterpillar ends, it evolves into a beautiful butterfly (spirit), with the ability to explore the world around it and to feel the infinite wonders which freedom brings.

'There is nothing to worry about,' I assured them. 'Death is just a stepping stone to a better place.' I told them I had been developing for 25 years and still didn't know it all! Everyone has some psychic gift, because we are a spirit in a physical body, and everyone can use their own spirit body to see other spirit people.

I explained that I could bring the two worlds together for a short period of time through my mediumship. 'You must know from your science lessons that everything vibrates,' I told the children. 'We vibrate at a much lower level than the spirit world, so I have to try and raise my

43

level of vibrations, and spirit entities lower theirs to enable us to communicate with each other. Before a sitting, I tune into the spirit world, it's like a radio set when you turn the knobs gently, although there is nothing I can do if spirit entities do not wish to come.'

One child asked, 'Can anyone become a medium or healer?'

'To a point,' I replied. 'Every healer is a medium but not every medium is a healer. Everyone is a spirit body clothed by a physical body. Development means that you become more aware of your own spirit body.' It was refreshing to see these youngsters with a thirst for spiritual knowledge, wanting to find out more and more.

In the New Testament you will find the words 'In my Father's house there are many mansions', but there is nothing that describes what the mansions or planes of existence are like, how they are made or who dwells in them. When you are thinking of going on holiday or going to visit a strange place, you gather as much information as possible. You read brochures, go to tourist information and travel agents, and ask people who have already been there for their views. Having collected all your information, you decide whether or not you would like to go to that particular place. When you have made your choice, you then make all the necessary preparations for your journey.

Where do you find out about life after death? You have very few options: the church, which tells you very little; mediums; the Bible; or other books. Mediums usually write these books, or those who have gained some knowledge of life after the death process.

There are no hard and fast rules about where to pass on knowledge from spirit friends. Over the years, when I have visited my local pub and it became known that I was a medium, my evenings out for a quiet relaxing drink always turned into a gathering of people asking questions about spiritualism. Their thirst for knowledge was amazing.

It is hard to understand that in the world beyond this

one, people do live in houses, although they are not made of bricks and mortar, they are constructed by thought, in a world where thought is substantial, tangible and perceivable, just as bricks and mortar are in the physical world. This also applies to clothing, which is not always like earthly fashion. It usually consists of robes which differ to show an individual's spiritual growth and attainment.

In the winter of 1975 my mother-in-law Evelyn went to see her doctor as she had problems swallowing her food. The doctor referred her to a specialist for tests and she was admitted to hospital. Although the tests showed there was nothing to worry about, she was losing weight rapidly and looked as though she was at death's door. We were very concerned but had to go by what the doctors had said. All we could do was visit her and cheer her up, hoping that whatever was wrong with her would be discovered and treated.

On 10 March 1976 it was my daughter Victoria's 11th birthday. There was extra work to be done, birthday cakes to bake etc. Amongst Vicki's presents was one from Evelyn. I was very tired, and my usual practice after a heavy day was to lie flat on the lounge carpet to relax and unwind. I needed five minutes' quiet before I started the birthday tea, though it was just for the immediate family. The children were upstairs doing their homework, Keith wasn't back from work yet and the house was peaceful.

I was very relaxed with nothing in particular on my mind, in a meditative state. Within seconds I found myself suddenly travelling down a dark tunnel. I could see a light at the end, and it felt good. I experienced a floating sensation as though I had no legs, and I was at peace with the world. I remember looking to my left and I saw Evelyn holding my hand; she also floated down the tunnel with me. I assured her there was nothing to worry about, and told her to look towards the light. At the end of the tunnel, this beautiful light seemed to beckon us, calling us forward. I could hear beautiful music playing. We both felt wonderful, on top of the world, smiling at each other as we continued. As we reached the end, we could see several people with their arms outstretched, welcoming us. Suddenly I felt a little panic inside me, as I was told I would have to turn back and leave Evelyn with her family and friends. I wanted to stay and see what was ahead, it looked so beautiful and inviting, but I wasn't allowed. Then, without warning, I suddenly came back to reality, finding myself back on the lounge carpet. I jumped up onto my feet, confused and disorientated for a few moments, and then the sad reality dawned on me: my mother-in-law had just died and I had taken her on to the next level of existence.

I immediately phoned the hospital, asked for the ward sister, and enquired about Evelyn Bridgford, explaining who I was. The nursing sister told me she had died peacefully two minutes earlier. I was in a state of shock, but knew she had gone to a better place. What a day for this to happen! How would I tell my husband that his mother had gone, and the children, especially Vicki the birthday girl? If only we had been told to prepare ourselves for this. Yet I was happy knowing I had taken her to the 'departure lounge', so to speak, for her exciting journey forward, her well deserved promotion. It was an experience I will never forget.

My husband arrived home half an hour later and I broke the news to him and the children. It was a sad time and I wanted to explain to them what had happened, that I had taken her to a beautiful place, that there was no need to be sad as she was very happy. I did eventually tell Keith about the wonderful journey his mother and I had made, and I told the children later when they were old enough to understand.

When people pass from this life, they face new experiences gradually, getting used to their new life and clothing created from their own thoughts. Everything in the next world, such as communication, homes etc, is brought into being through thought. During our earth life, we know very little of our true nature, our real selves, our spirit body. This is because we are prisoners within our own physical bodies, unable to express ourselves wholly.

In the early stages of the next life, we learn how to recognise ourselves, to dismiss all illusions of what we were so that we can see more clearly and fully parts of ourselves we have not seen before – our true selves which we were not able to express whilst in the physical body on the earth plane.

Once we have done this, we are in a better position to understand our new surroundings and the differences our new world offers. We learn how to change things just by thought, such as our clothing and the scenery around us. It eventually dawns on us that we do not need to have these old visions because we do not require them any longer.

I wonder what Evelyn found and what she would say about her new home.

When spirit relatives come back through a medium and describe their environment, which they have made purely by thought, it will vary considerably from person to person because everyone 'sees' things differently. We are allocated to the place we have grown to spiritually, a plane of existence that suits us and which has some bearing of how we will see things.

My youngest daughter Stephanie, who was ten when Evelyn died, saw her about a year later during the early hours of the morning. She woke up to see her step-grandmother standing at the end of her bed, smiling at her. I asked Stephanie if Evelyn had said anything to her, but she said not. She said she hadn't been frightened, because she had felt so much love from Evelyn's presence.

I have not seen Evelyn since that day, but if I had I would have asked her what it was like for her after I left her, and what she had experienced immediately after her passing.

Harold, Evelyn's husband, joined her some years later

when he died of cancer. He believed in spiritualism, so I had been able to talk to him about Evelyn's transition and the wonderful spiritual experience I'd had. He did marry again and was very happy with his second wife, which leads me to a question I have been asked several times by people who have lost their partners and loved ones: 'What would my late husband or wife think if I remarried?' In the spirit world there is no jealousy. Time and time again the message is very clear: if a person's new partner is good and kind and they love each another, their previous partner will rejoice in the knowledge that they are happy on the earth plane. The attraction is love, an indescribable love that we have not yet experienced, but which we will experience when we join our loved ones who are waiting for us.

There are several planes of existence, and on the lowest level you will find people who still want to eat and drink, or even smoke. They have the illusion of still wanting the same things they wanted when living on the earth plane, as familiarity brings them comfort. But such things are not necessary. On the first level one can create beautiful landscapes and dwellings, all of a permanent nature, because this is the level where the mental process operates. One day they will progress to a higher level and leave all the unimportant things behind them.

Each level of existence is more refined than the preceding one. Progressing through these different levels could be compared with passing exams to reach a higher grade at school, learning as you travel. You pass through different layers of consciousness, attaining true harmony with your own spiritual environment, then moving on again when the time is right. Layers of consciousness of existence overlap and blend into the next ones, which are all part of the same universe. This makes the passage from one sphere to another within easy reach. You can only move on by awakening, becoming aware, reaching a state of consciousness shared by others of like mind, where you can expand and grow.

When we die, we find ourselves on a level of existence suitable to our personal growth at that particular moment. For example, if a person on the earth plane learns very little during their earth life, their spiritual growth and progression will have been slow, therefore they will find themselves on an appropriate plane.

On the other hand, someone who has grown considerably and learned what they came here to learn will find him- or herself on a completely different plane of existence, one that their growth has determined. If both these people found themselves on the same plane, they would find it difficult to communicate, to understand one another and would feel uncomfortable. Therefore, we come to the material world to better ourselves, to learn lessons from our experience of life. Our sorrows, pain, difficult and happy times, our mistakes and how we treat our fellow man are all lessons to be learned. This is our spiritual growth dictating where we are allocated when the so-called death process takes place.

Unlike in our world, there are no language problems on these other planes. Nationality no longer exists, and thought, telepathy and feelings are the only languages, the only means of communication. Lying, cheating, pretending to have secrets, are impossible for every individual is seen and known for what they are mentally and spiritually. Our spirit body is like a fingerprint: no-one is the same. We cannot say, 'I didn't mean to do that', because our body will show the truth.

Only those of the same spiritual quality can dwell on the same plane in this new life, therefore we cannot climb the ladder and try to exist on a higher level if this is not our proper place. We can only dwell on the one our spiritual status resonates with.

However, a person of a higher level may occupy a lower one for a specific purpose, such as to help or teach a particular spirit person. We might ask, 'What happens when I die if my husband or wife is on a different level? We won't be together.' The answer is that if you love one another, the person on the higher plane will come down to be with the one on the lower, helping them to progress.

It has been proved to me and to many other mediums that there is no age in the world of spirit, that is, in the physical sense; only a growth towards spiritual maturity. There are no old, frail or imperfect bodies in the next world, those old bodies were shed during the death process, and the real you transcends, moves on, is reborn. This must not be looked upon as some sort of miracle; it is simply a change of consciousness when your feelings adapt to your own self. Some people prefer to remain in their youth, forgetting the miseries of old age; for others, maturity suits them more as it is a time which brought them the most happiness. Children grow older as they evolve, while old people grow younger in spirit. However, spirit friends and relatives always come back as we know and remember them.

There is no need for money in the spirit world, there is only wealth and poverty of spirit. Spirit life is one of continual progression towards perfection. There is no heaven and hell as we know them; these are places we make for ourselves. If we have been evil or selfish, we will go to a level that suits us, and on that level we will not find the beauty that we would find on a higher level. This is the hell we make for ourselves. Heaven, of course, is the opposite. The higher the level, the more beautiful it becomes, and it too is what we have made for ourselves by our actions, words and thoughts.

There are laws of cause and effect, which are perfect in their operation. No-one sits in judgement; we judge ourselves. We look at ourselves and what we were responsible for, what we moulded in our earthly lives and how we have become what we are. We then have to accept ourselves. There is no hiding the true self, it is there for all to see and with this self-judgement, we will gradually see the need to change.

50

We will take stock and realise that material possessions on the earth plane are of no use. We must look towards spiritual possessions, the spiritual growth we have brought with us. Our character, memories, the power to think and feel, these are the only possessions that will uphold us in our new environment. Days of reckoning lie ahead for good as well as bad. Coming to terms with ourselves, knowing ourselves as never before, can be a very painful process.

The day of judgement is not as we pictured it on the earth plane. It certainly isn't a punishment, simply an opportunity to learn and grow. A kind, compassionate and understanding teacher is allocated to us to enable us to have deeper insights. This knowledgeable spirit being shows us pictures of our past lives, so that we can see what we were really like, not what we thought we were like. The teacher shows us where we went wrong, and how to feel the thoughts and feelings of pain and pleasure which our actions caused in the lives of others, so that we can feel them within ourselves.

Self-judgement may only take place when we are ready to face up to new growth by looking at our bad and good qualities. This can consist of healing the wounds we have created, which the soul must find, allowing us to re-grow in a positive way. This will require hard work and understanding when the defects are discovered and revealed in the spirit body. As I said earlier, no two bodies are the same. We are spiritually 'naked' in our new home; all those around us can see who and what we really are. However, once this is evident and we learn to live with ourselves, we will grow more rapidly and move on to a different area of consciousness. When time has elapsed, we will have fully worked out what has been holding us back on other levels. Only when we are ready, and feel we want to atone and make amends for all the wrong actions in our lives, are we able to move to another level, another promotion.

If we believe in this process, we should never feel the need for revenge against those who have hurt us in the past. When we read or hear about murderers and criminals who are given shorter sentences than they deserve, remember that all of us will be punished for our actions in the end. We will receive our just deserts from the heaven or hell we have chosen for ourselves. What a shock this will be for all those evil people who believe once they are dead, that is it – to find themselves in a place and situation where there is nowhere to hide, no-one to cheat and lie to, and no-one they can harm. They will find they are amongst people of the same level of consciousness as themselves, with no escape. Only when they have spent considerable time looking at who they really are, seeing the harm and pain they have caused others whilst on the earth plane; only when they have atoned for their wrongdoings will they be able to move on.

If there is any delay in remorse, those who are in the same sorry condition continue to be grouped together and help one another, each within the same confinement, a prison without bars. They can remain thus for long periods of time, refusing the help of others who are reaching out to them in love. All the spirit helpers who come down to this level of existence experience considerable distress as they seek to lift other souls from this bad state of existence. By trying to reach these people, they have to lower their own consciousness to a level that is understandable to those they wish to help and hope to rescue. Eventually the obstacles are overcome, but in some cases it can take many earth years.

We do not die and rot in the grave; this only happens to our material body. But although we go on to a better place, this does not mean we change and become nicer people. If people were selfish and unkind while in the material body, they will remain that way in the spirit world, until the time is right for them to want to change.

There is no sitting around doing nothing in the spirit world, as there is much to learn. There are halls of learning and libraries. When a practising doctor on the earth plane dies, he or she may still wish to practise medicine. But this time they have at their fingertips all the wonders of the power of spirit, and are not restricted by 'matter'. They use their hands and the power that is accessible to them in the spirit world, which can penetrate all earthly matter through the spiritual healer.

There are people who are constantly working to make it easier to communicate with us. There are childless women who spend time looking after spirit children, artists who like to paint and people who want to learn to sing or play a musical instrument. Being released from their physical body enables them to learn to do all the things they wanted to do whilst on the earth plane. There is so much to look forward to, so much to learn and so many spirit helpers who want to come forward and prove to us that life does indeed continue.

During one of my development circles in Guiseley, West Yorkshire, and after roughly two years sitting with the same circle members, I decided to try for physical phenomena. We started with a trumpet, which had luminous paint around the largest part of the rim so that it could be seen clearly in the darkened room. This was placed in the centre of the room with a circle drawn around it so that we could see afterwards if spirit friends had moved the trumpet. We sat patiently for some weeks before we saw the slightest movement, but in time it did move.

I must also point out that under no circumstances must anyone in the circle interfere with the physical phenomena taking place, such as a hand or foot in the path of the moving object. This can cause severe injury to the medium, as the psychic rod carrying the object may snap and its elements return with force back to the medium.

We didn't have a great deal of success with physical phenomena until my son-in-law Stephen joined the circle. He was neither a believer or a disbeliever, he had an open mind. He always asked questions about spiritualism with growing interest. One day he asked if he could visit the circle. I agreed and the following week he came to see what spiritualism was all about. I thought he would have changed his mind by the time the circle members had gathered, but to my surprise he was already waiting for me to take him.

After his first visit he continued coming to the circle for quite some time. He must have been the person spirit were looking for to enable physical phenomena to take place. One has to have the correct balance of sitters in the circle for this particular phenomenon. From that day on we had some wonderful experiences of transfigurations.

It is very important in any circle, whether sitting for physical phenomena or not, to meet at the same time on the same day each week. It is the same with meditation; spirit like punctuality and they are always ready and waiting at any given time. Discipline in any psychic work is very important. I have always sat for development and meditation at the same time each day. On very rare occasions I have been late for my appointment with spirit. Each time this has happened, as I have entered the room I have felt the presence of spirit waiting for me. I have always apologised for my delay; after all it is no different from arranging to meet with someone in this world. Good manners are a must; spirit never let us down and are always waiting to help us.

We always met on Friday evenings at eight o'clock. On this occasion, I picked Stephen up at 7.30 and we set off to Elsie's house. The usual crowd were waiting for us to arrive – the 'circle of light' (this is the name spirit gave the circle) Elsie's job, apart from sitting in the circle, was to transcribe and make sure the tape recorder worked properly. The room we used was kept free from cigarette smoke etc. We had bought a red light bulb for this meeting, to help spirit operators produce physical phenomena. I didn't know what was happening during the time I was in trance, and looked forward to listening to the tapes afterwards. I am glad we recorded everything, as I can now look back and listen to the wonderful messages from spirit. The only problem is that I cannot see what happens during the transfiguration process. For a long time I had to rely on the members of the circle to inform me of the evening's events. I have missed such a lot, it's never the same when relayed to you second hand.

This particular evening Elsie had moved us out of the living room to the dining room, and we tried for physical phenomena using the small red light. I wasn't sure that anything would happen because of the change of rooms, but we all sat in our usual order, making a circle of chairs. We always said several prayers, and we asked spirit to help us succeed in our request for physical phenomena, not knowing what form of phenomena, if any, would materialise.

Before we started I asked Stephen if he would be all right, explaining what we were trying to accomplish. He was a little nervous, never having sat in a circle before; we were throwing him in at the deep end.

During our meditation I could feel the tremendous power from spirit fill the room. It seemed to pulsate with love and I knew everything would be all right. The meeting went well, with spirit talking to the members of the circle as usual, giving messages and bringing knowledge about spiritual matters. I came out of trance briefly, thinking the meeting had come to an end. It was strange; I couldn't 'come back' fully. I felt as though I was floating, and I wasn't sure if I liked it. It had never happened before. I closed my eyes, trying to recover, and within a few minutes I could feel my cheeks starting to move, a rippling sensation. My jaw felt as though it was growing and jutting outwards, and I could hear circle members whispering, 'Look, look!'

My feelings about this were mixed, to say the least, I didn't particularly like the idea of still being awake while this was going on. Before I knew it, I had been taken fully back into a deep trance state and don't remember any more.

55

It was only when I woke up that I discovered what had taken place, and the faces of the circle members were a picture I'll never forget.

We were not expecting anything to happen, we just hoped something would. Usually spirit told us in advance what to expect and what we should do, but on this particular evening we were told nothing.

I was eager to listen to the tape. We all sat down with tea and biscuits, and the smokers lit their cigarettes. Naturally I couldn't see what had happened, but I got a good idea from what was said. It was wonderful.

The tape began with Elsie saying, 'She's gone off now, look, her face is changing. I think it's a woman.'

'I think I know that face,' said Stephen.

'Are you sure it's a woman? The face looks very old, it could be a man,' said another member of the circle.

'I do know that face, look, it's still changing. It's getting much clearer now,' said Stephen, trying to clear a frog in his throat.

'Oh, look, now it's really changed!' someone else said in amazement.

'I wonder if it's my mum,' said Elsie.

'Cor, I don't believe it, that's my gran!' said Stephen.

'Are you sure? How wonderful,' said Elsie, sounding very pleased. She said to the spirit person, 'God Bless you, thank you for coming.'

All the time I could hear everyone saying how wonderful the face was, and thanking spirit for coming. Stephen kept saying, 'It is my grandmother, I'd know that face anywhere. Cor, fantastic! I can't take it all in. Wait till I tell Penny, she's not going to believe this. It's great. I definitely believe in spirit now.'

I looked at Stephen's smiling face and I said, 'Was it really your grandmother, Stephen? You're not mistaken?'

'Positive, Mother.'

It was worth all the time and effort I had given to spirit in my years as a medium. Stephen's face looked a picture, and I can still see it to this day. He had a look of, shock, wonderment and amazement, in fact all the circle members had the same expression on their faces.

It's wonderful how spirits are able to clothe themselves temporarily in a form so exact it resembles the body and the flesh of a physical person.

Stephen came to the circle for several months, enjoying the experiences which spirit brought us. However, my daughter Penny was a little afraid of my work and found the idea of her husband taking part in the circle unacceptable, so Stephen eventually left. One thing is for sure: he will always carry with him the experiences and knowledge he gained whilst in the circle, so it was all worthwhile.

I never liked the idea of a stranger coming to the circle, I think due to one terrible evening when my dog Sam jumped onto my knee while I was still in trance. I suppose the thought of being touched unexpectedly by someone frightened me a little.

However, a few years later I was persuaded to allow a neighbour of a friend of mine to visit. This woman had been feeling very depressed since the passing of her son a few years earlier.

Before we started I instructed our visitor not to touch me without first asking permission from spirit. We all sat in our usual places, with our visitor a little way outside of the circle. We first sang hymns and said prayers, followed by meditation. Before I went into trance for physical phenomena, I always felt my wonderful spirit operators touch me and reassure me that all would be well. I was relaxed and felt on top of the world, and very quickly I was taken into trance as spirit operators began their wonderful work of transfiguring.

A young man showed himself to the circle by transfiguring my face as before. I became very young-looking and was identified as this woman's son. She was thrilled by the experience, and was able to communicate with her son. Although he was unable to speak to her, he did nod in answer to her questions and spirit allowed her to give him a big hug. She thanked me profusely, and asked if she could come again.

Her depression soon left her, and she had a reason for living, knowing she would meet her son again in the next life. I was told she now visits local spiritualist churches regularly, and I have seen her on a few occasions since that night.

CHAPTER SIX

Unexpected

It was cold and raining, my first appointment for the day was due to arrive. I was 'tuning in' to spirit friends when I was aware of a spirit gentleman in the room waiting patiently for the visitor, telling me he was her husband. The doorbell rang. I opened the door and saw a tall, blonde woman standing in the porch. She was very attractive, with her hair tied back neatly at the nape of her neck. She was dressed very smartly and looked in her mid-30s. I showed her into the dining room, my little sanctuary. Everyone entering this room would make a point of telling me they could feel a wonderful peace and tranquillity. Even so, I was very uncomfortable with this spirit visitor, though I couldn't explain why. All I knew was that he didn't bring with him the usual nice feelings from spirit.

I made my sitter comfortable and offered her a cup of tea. After some general chit-chat about the weather, I began the sitting. The next hour or so proved very interesting. During the conversation with the woman I discovered why I felt as I did about her husband. I found myself treading very carefully, as something was not quite right.

My opening words were, 'I have your husband here, he's been waiting for you.' I then went on to describe him in detail.

'Yes, that's exactly how he looked,' she said, not sounding over-excited at the prospect of communicating with him. Usually a sitter wants to communicate with a close relative, and I presumed she must have been divorced and no longer had any feeling for her ex-husband. I felt dreadful and couldn't understand why I felt so nervous and a little afraid. I was receiving terrible evil thoughts and information from this man. I asked him to repeat what he had said, wondering if I had misheard. How could I pass on this message to her? I couldn't suddenly say 'Your husband was a very evil man', so I found myself saying, 'Your husband wasn't a very nice man, was he?'

She could have given me a real telling-off, perhaps even slapped my face. Thank goodness she responded favourably. 'Yes, you're right, but that's putting it mildly.' She looked upset and frightened.

I wasn't sure if she wanted me to continue, so I said, 'If you prefer I could move on to another link, another family member. You look so upset.'

'No, no, please continue. Tell me everything he's saying.'

I felt much better then and found I could continue with the sitting and relay all the information as I received it, withholding nothing. I endured about half an hour of horrendous detail regarding his acts of rape and cruelty. I felt sick at the information given to me. It turned out that he was a notorious rapist.

The woman was pleased with some of the information her husband had given her, most of which was not public knowledge. The sitting also helped to clear up one or two ideas she'd had regarding the cause of his death in prison.

After the sitting we talked for quite a while. She was depressed and needed solace. We discussed spiritualism in general and she asked lots of questions. It was a real pleasure talking to her. I explained that if I could be of help to her she could call me any time. She thanked me, saying she would come to see me again. We became friends and I saw quite a lot of her during the next few months. Due to her husband's crimes, she and her sons had a terrible life. My heart went out to her and her family. In a small way I helped her, though I wish I could have taken away more of her pain. Eventually we lost contact when she had to move away because of the unpleasantness she and her children had to endure when people found out who they were.

Strange information can come out of the blue when you least expect it. I was in my sanctuary at home giving healing to a patient when I heard clairaudiently the name Peter Sutcliffe. I was told that he was 'the Yorkshire Ripper', the serial killer. I then saw his face clairvoyantly: what an awful fright when I realised who it was – the man who had been butchering young women in the red light area of Leeds. I often give clairvoyance following healing but this information was for my eyes and ears only. It was difficult but I had to ignore this intrusion from spirit and continue with my healing. I was pleased when I had finished and could relax.

I tried for days not to think about the information I had received, putting it to the back of my mind. However, soon it all started again. I was pestered night and day by spirit repeating the information over and over. This was something I could do without, but I wasn't sure how to handle it. If I went to the police, what would they think? Another one of those crazy psychic people to add to their long list?

I eventually told my children, who were then old enough to understand. They were adamant that I should risk embarrassment and reminded me that it was my duty to pass on all knowledge from spirit. I reluctantly dialled the number of our local police station, explaining who I was and giving them the name of the killer along with other information I had received from spirit. The police officer who came to see me was most polite and listened to what I had to say but I was not sure if he believed me or not. But as far as I was concerned, I had done all that was asked of me by spirit for the time being. As soon as I had given the information to the police I was no longer pestered by spirit and could get on with my daily life.

Months later, when I was meditating in my bedroom, to my distress more information about Sutcliffe came through as clear as a bell. It came from the next victim's relatives, who were already in the world of spirit. Obviously they wanted to prevent the murder of their loved one. It was around October when this information was given to me. I could see clairvoyantly the killer's next victim and where the murder would take place. It was dark and I was shown a bend in the road. As I turned to the left I could see a church. Since the road was very clear, it remained imprinted on my mind. I recall thinking to myself that I knew this place that spirit were showing me; it was somewhere I had visited on the outskirts of Leeds. I had been brought up in this area and knew it well but I couldn't say exactly where the road was. I know now. It was ten minutes away from where I had lived as a child. Spirit told me she would be murdered around Christmas time, which was only a couple of months away. I remember my feelings of apprehension, yet I really didn't want to get involved and tried to dismiss it. Spirit desperately wanted me to do something to prevent this murder and kept pestering me, going to such lengths as interrupting my healing and clairvoyant appointments. I decided it was pointless to contact the police again, as there had been so many psychics taking up their time. I hoped I had made the right decision for the young girl's sake.

The weeks up to the festive season were a nightmare for me but Christmas went by with no news of any more murders. I was relieved I had not made a fool of myself by going to the police with such a bizarre story; this time I must have been wrong.

The months went by without the killer striking again until around Christmas the following year. I was sitting watching television when there was a news flash: another young woman had been viciously attacked and murdered on such-and-such a street near a church. This was exactly the same place spirit had told me. My heart sank and I started to cry. I wondered if there was anything I could have done to prevent this poor girl from dying. My family assured me that I had done my best but it didn't help me at all. I wondered what the spirit relatives of the young girl thought of my poor efforts to save her life. They had warned me of the dreadful murder that was about to happen to their lovely girl and I had let them down.

A few weeks later the same young girl who was so

brutally murdered visited me from the spirit world during one of my weekly circle meetings. She assured me she was all right and thanked me for my assistance, but despite what everyone told me, I still think about it. I wonder if I could have changed the outcome, or was it meant to be? Could I have left my body as I have done on many occasions, astral travelled to where she was going to be murdered and prevented this dreadful murder?

One day I was going through my absent healing list in bed. I had so many patients it took me hours to complete the healing prayers for each one, as I never wanted to group them all together when asking spirit for help; I found it better to spend more time on the serious cases.

During one healing intercession with a patient, to my surprise I found myself visiting her home. I vividly remember being with my healing doctors. Suddenly I found myself standing in my patient's bedroom, seeing the colour of her carpets and curtains, what furniture she had in the room and so on. She was very ill at the time and I stood at the bottom of her bed looking at her.

I recall helping the spirit doctor to heal this lady as if I had been a doctor's assistant for years. I recognised him instantly and we had a non-verbal conversation through thought: I could read his mind and he mine. When it came to speaking to my patient I used the normal way of talking. Surprisingly, she could hear me. I asked her to turn over for me. She smiled at me and turned over, thanking me for coming. We gave healing to her using the spirit power available to us. What amazed me was that I seemed to know what I was doing. Perhaps I had been doing this for years, never remembering any of it in my waking moments.

It is only when you wake up or return to your physical body that you start to analyse the events that have taken place. It all seems so natural.

Later, I received a letter from my patient, thanking me for the wonderful healing. She said, 'Would you believe it,

I actually saw you at the bottom of my bed. You were with Dr Panner, and you spoke to me.' I wrote back, telling her I knew about this and went on to describe her bedroom for evidential purposes. (Most of my astral travelling has been done during absent healing sessions and when I wrote to my patients I always described their bedrooms, to prove later that I was correct.)

How can anyone fear death when the next life is so beautiful? People who have told their story about out-of-body experiences have always said they no longer fear death, in fact they look forward to it and welcome it. Most of these people have also said it has changed their lives drastically, as they have a different outlook on the meaning of life.

One particular evening I had been thinking about my spirit control Grey Buffalo as I climbed into bed, wondering if I could will myself out of my body and talk to him. There were so many things I wanted to know. I had never attempted to visit my spirit guides and helpers before, and I was wondering if this would be possible. The only way was to find out and try to reach them.

I settled down in bed. It was very early but I didn't know how long it would take me. Relaxing, I went through my usual meditation, followed by willing my spirit body out of my physical body, mentally watching myself being thrown out by the reverse of a whirlpool. I was being pulled up towards a light above me, trying so hard to reach the top with my mind fixed on Grey Buffalo.

Suddenly I found myself on the top of a mountain ridge. I knew I was in North America; I don't know how, but this is usual for most mediums. It's as though we have been told by someone mentally. The sky was very black and the stars were twinkling brightly above me. As I looked down and across the great vast space below me, I could just make out what looked like hundreds of buffalo grazing peacefully. I felt as though I had come home and was at peace with the world. To my left I could see small camp fires everywhere and hear lots of laughter, as though a party was in progress.

As I walked towards the fires I could see a village of North American Indian tepees, typical of those seen in cowboy and Indian films. I wasn't in the least bit afraid it all seemed so natural and safe. As I approached, I could see the Indians waving to me and mentally asking me to join them. I was very excited and naturally I wanted to be part of this wonderful experience.

Braves and squaws were dancing around the large crackling fires, all wearing splendid robes and having a good time. Some were sitting round in a circle, watching and eating as the children ran about chasing one another. They invited me to sit down with them and share their food, which I did.

I looked around, hoping to see Grey Buffalo, praying I would find him and be able to communicate with him. Within a matter of seconds, as though my thoughts had been heard, I saw an Indian man walking through the crowd of dancers towards me. He looked so tall and handsome, but not as I remembered him. My heart sank as it crossed my mind that this must be someone else. He was wearing long brown pants and on his head was the most magnificent chieftain headdress. The beautiful coloured feathers reached all the way down to his bare feet. His naked muscular chest was adorned with numerous necklaces made of beads and what looked like pieces of fur.

I remember feeling very disappointed as he sat down beside me on my left. I remembered Grey Buffalo with only two white feathers placed towards the back of his hair. I turned to him and smiled, only then realising that this was indeed Grey Buffalo. My heart started to pound as he smiled back at me with a wonderful loving look on his face. I felt as though I would melt away on the spot.

By this time I was beginning to feel a little intoxicated with the smell from the firewood, a lovely sweet smell that reminded me of vanilla. I was so comfortable and relaxed, enjoying every minute when suddenly I had this awful feeling of having to go back. Panic gripped me as I fought hard to stay where I was and heard Grey Buffalo say to me, 'You have to leave now.'

'But I don't want to go yet,' I said.

'You must,' he replied gently.

I felt myself being pulled backwards at speed and reached out for a hand to stop me. The next thing I knew I was back in the bedroom. Keith had come to bed early, which had disturbed me. I was so angry and upset, I snapped at him, 'You've interrupted my meditation.' He apologised, but that wasn't enough. All I wanted was to go back to this lovely place again. I have tried many times since then and experienced so much more. I have often wondered if I visited the place where Grey Buffalo and I once lived when on the earth plane. Or was I visiting a spirit place that had been created by thought? One thing is for sure, I visit Grey Buffalo through meditation and sheer will power most days.

I will never forget a time when I left my physical body and found myself standing on a small country path, at the very end of which was a farm gate. Beyond this, green fields rose to form a small hill obscuring my view. On my left and down along the rest of the path was a beautiful hedge of wild pink roses. Their delicate perfume was absolutely glorious. To my right was another hedge of wild white flowers; this also went the whole length of the path. Both these hedges were about eight feet tall, not allowing me a glimpse of what was on the other side. As I was looking down at my feet I noticed the soil on the path was red and had little tufts of grass growing from it. Then I noticed, to my delight, beautiful white doves emerging from within the white hedgerow as if to say hello. I put out my hands and one by one the doves rested on them. I could see their tiny hearts beating in their tiny breasts as I stroked them gently, sending my loving thoughts to them. The sky was blue, peaceful and very relaxing. It was warm, the sun was shining and I felt at home.

Soon I was aware of a person standing next to me. All

I can say is that he looked as we imagine Jesus Christ the Nazarene to look. His smile was indescribable, with a love that poured through me. He placed his arm around my shoulder as we walked together down this path. I could feel myself absorbing his love as it enveloped and embraced me. I cannot remember any words being spoken, mentally or otherwise, until we reached the farm gate. Preparing to open the gate and step through with him, I was told I was not allowed to just yet. I felt very disappointed at having to remain behind and at that moment I found myself back in my physical body. I wanted so desperately to go back and did try, though without success.

Since that night I have attempted many times to visit this wonderful place. I can journey there but I stand alone. All I want to do is to look into this man's eyes. Someone told me if you gaze into the eyes of the Nazarene you will be truly blessed. I will never give up and one day I hope I will feel his love again and receive a blessing from him, whoever he is.

It is good to be able to travel at will on this plane of existence, especially when someone is ill. There have been times when the process of leaving my body has been so rapid that it has been like a thought. It's like anything you do: practice makes perfect. It has been a long, long time since I last went travelling. I just haven't given it much thought until now.

It will probably be very difficult to start again after all this time, but I may give it a try again soon. There are so many places in the spirit world one can visit at will, all by the power of thought. However, I believe that when you are in need of a particular experience that's where you will be taken. When I need strength, one of my favourite places to visit is a place where there is a large old oak tree. I lean against this trusty tree and draw strength from it. Sometimes I put my arms around it and feel its power flowing through me. If I am ever feeling down, this is where I am taken.

The oak tree is situated on top of a grassy hill. This beautiful place is warm and peaceful and it makes me feel good. I am alone and the only sounds I can hear are birds singing. I cannot see them but I can hear their wonderful happy songs. At the bottom of the hill there is a small brook. Lilies float gently on the crystal clear water. I can paddle in the warm water and this relaxes me as I am drawn to peer into the centre of the flowers. If I look deep into them I can see pictures of other spiritual places. If I want, I can go there. When I return to my physical body I feel strong and rejuvenated as though I have been away for a long holiday.

These experiences I have talked about are astral travelling, not pictures given to me through meditation. Once I am out of my body I can always see myself in bed before I set off on my travels. On my return I step back into my physical body either by sitting up or lying down, depending on the way I left it.

During meditation one can experience similar pictures. They also seem real, but this is not astral travelling.

'Out-of-body' experiences are quite different. They do not happen voluntarily, usually occurring when a person is going through a traumatic time such as an operation, near-death experiences or when they have actually died for a short period of time. Suddenly they find themselves hovering somewhere above the bed near the ceiling and watch everything that is happening to them. Once the operation has finished, or the patient has been revived, they find they are back in their physical body once again.

Reincarnation is a subject that is talked about often and at great length. Some spiritualists believe in rebirth but there are a considerable number who do not. I am one of the few who definitely believe in this. How can I think differently when I know of several lives I have already experienced on this earth plane? I believe that we come here to learn and that it takes many incarnations to obtain a pure and rich spirit. With the help and guidance of the Great Spirit we can climb the ladder to perfection.

This is what one of my spirit guides had to say about reincarnation: 'If it were possible to learn all things that are expected of us, to attain perfection in one life on the material plane, it would make our understanding much easier. Life goes on for all eternity in your world and mine, to enable us to learn in the knowledge that we will eventually succeed in the truest form.

'To bring about a blending with the Great Spirit, to obtain the perfect Soul, the perfect spirit that we are or, if not now, will be – all this takes time and time spent in a material body in each incarnation is but a short period of learning in the schools of practical development.

'Theory can come in time with the wisdom of age and cannot be rushed. This is why we come here time and time again into the heavy world of matter, reliving our imperfections to the fullness of our growth so we can come into our own through the rebirth of our spirit body, embracing the faults and failings of our human nature.

'Greatness only comes with practice of the unfolding of the soul in search of knowledge and perfection, given to us through our development of learning the lessons in our limited way, each time we set out on our new path and new life in the knowledge that time on your earth plane is short. Otherwise we would reluctantly hold back from the torment of the dark world in which we are expected to grow.

'Deliverance from your world is our reward, to be earned in all that is good and kind. Pretending to live the path we chose is unacceptable. Serving the Great Spirit by loving each other is the only means to obtain promotion. Only when the spirit is ready can perfection come and growth take place.

'Every action, every thought is registered in the spirit world. There is no hiding from what we truly are. How many more lives we have to endure is entirely up to us, and only our actions and thoughts can bring about a new beginning in the wonderful world of spirit, our home.'

Each time I have been shown a past life it has been through meditation. I know it is real and not a dream because spirit has told me before I have been taken through the visual experience.

I was so excited when spirit said to me, 'I am now going to show you a time when you were on the earth plane many years ago. Just relax and continue with your meditation.' This was difficult for me as my mind was now focused on new, exciting things. Eventually I managed to relax and give myself to spirit.

I was taken to Egypt, where I found myself in what looked like a pyramid. I must have been in my mid-20s and was very attractive with a well-shaped figure and long, straight dark hair. I knew it was me; I wasn't an observer, I was living this experience. My clothes were long to my ankles, a white gown with a narrow gold belt pulled tight at the waist. I noticed my feet were bare except for a thick ankle band made of solid gold. I had matching jewellery around my neck and hair.

The pyramid was warm and comfortable, although all I could see were stone floors, walls and seating. A small fire was burning in front of me, giving out a nice familiar smell of aniseed. A handsome young man was in the room with me, dressed in a much shorter white robe, the material not as splendid as mine. Around his waist he wore a brown belt and he had brown sandals on his feet. His hair was black and cut short. He seemed to be an aide of some kind and was busy preparing a bowl of water to wash my feet. I sat down while he gently lifted my foot and bathed it. All the time he kept his head lowered, never looking into my eyes once. When he had dried my foot, he proceeded to lift the other, unclasping the ankle bracelet and washing that foot also. I knew this man very well, intimately. His hands occasionally stroked my leg lovingly and I stroked his head in approval.

I could hear noises outside and I felt very uneasy. There seemed to be a lot of tension in the room, a fear of death. The muffled noise outside grew louder and closer until I could hear shouting and jeering. I knew they were coming for me; I had committed a crime and was going to be severely punished. My heart was pounding and I felt faint. The young man put his arms around me, trying to comfort and protect me, but it was too late. I didn't experience my death but I knew this was the end.

I came back from my meditation knowing that I had just been killed, yet I was not afraid. I thought about my experience for some time, totally convinced of my past life. Several years later I met the same young man in this life, my soul mate.

Our spirit body is a seed of growth. If it's looked after it will blossom out and mature just as a plant will. If we take a cutting from an old dying plant and place it in the ground it will grow and live again as we do.

Regression is practised more and more, taking people back in time to past lives through hypnosis. So much information has been given by people being regressed and investigations into records have proved that these people have indeed existed in the past. In some cases the regressed person has shown that they have lived several times on this earth plane, going back in time hundreds of years.

I find this subject fascinating and I would like one day to be regressed and prove all that I have told you. It would be wonderful to be able to record my past lives on tape. If I am fortunate, perhaps dates, time and names will all be given during hypnosis or even something real, tangible that one could investigate.

I have found that most people continue to come back to this life in the same gender and with the same sexual tendencies. Only on very rare occasions are they the opposite sex. I don't know why this is, but I must have been told it by someone in spirit. I am sure some people would disagree with this theory, but I believe it is true. Only once to my knowledge have I ever come back as a male.

During another insight into a past life, I found myself in a market square outside a castle wall. There were wooden stalls full of all kinds of fruit, vegetables, curios, trinkets etc. The square was bustling with traders buying and selling their wares, and animals were being sold and slaughtered. It all seemed quite natural but looking back now it had a sickening effect on me.

I was in my mid-30s, tall, buxom, with long, thick auburn curls cascading down to my waist. I was wearing an off-the-shoulder cream blouse and a long brown flared skirt. Lively music was playing and on my feet were soft brown sandals. I was happy, swinging my skirt and dancing in the centre of the crowd, who were clapping their hands and stamping their feet. My lover was in the crowd. He smiled at me and I returned the smile with a deep feeling of love for him.

I could hear a loud noise in the distance that sounded like thunder. I felt a fear inside of me. Everyone in the square was trying to quickly collect their possessions and some were leaving everything and running away. I recognised the noise as it came closer; it was the sound of horses galloping. The square was suddenly overrun with horses ridden by the King's army. The soldiers were laughing as they sliced into men, women and children with their swords. The screaming crowd were running in all directions trying to escape the cruel soldiers and their horses' hooves as they were cut down one by one, just for the fun of it. I felt a burning sensation as the blade sliced down my right side, splitting me wide open. I fell to the ground. As I looked up, my sweetheart gently picked me up and carried me away.

Several times during meditation and also during my sleep state, I saw the following past life in every detail, which never changed. My clothes were very modern, so I presume it was the last reincarnation before this one. If I had come back to this earth plane almost immediately after my most recent passing, this would mean I had last died around 1943.

It was summertime and I was standing at the bottom of a cliff. Looking up I could clearly see a shop. It looked as though it had been built within the rock face, though it hadn't been. There was a path and steps leading up to the shop with a road at the back for vehicles. It was quite a climb to reach the shop. I was aware that it was also my home and I had got used to the climb. The view was wonderful, one could see all the way out to sea. Directly below I could see fishing boats moored by a short pier.

I was about 14 years old, dressed in school uniform: navy skirt, tie and white shirt. My straight dark brown hair was cut short and swept back at the sides, my build was a little chubby. The sea was behind me as I climbed up the path. As I entered the open door I noticed tassels of shells hanging down in the open space of the outside door, which I had to part to enter the shop. 'I'm home, Mum,' I called as I walked through the shop to the back where we lived. I could see various gifts for holidaymakers to buy. At this point the dream or meditation ended. I wasn't to know at that time that the story would continue later.

Several years later I travelled down south from Yorkshire on business with my husband Keith. It was one of those regular meetings when we met chartered accountants from all over the world. We decided to combine the trip with a few days' holiday so that we could visit friends in Poyntington in Dorset. We set off by car on our long journey south. Usually on these occasions we had a good time: lots of dining out, small talk and trips out for the wives while the men talked business.

After we said goodbye to our business friends, my husband suggested we extend our stay and visit Lyme Regis on the west coast. We had never been to this part of the country before; it would make a nice change. We would then tour the rest of southern England for the next few days.

It was very warm and we had been driving all day, enjoying the beautiful countryside. I had no idea where we were. We started to drive downhill into a town. My husband suggested we have some refreshments there and then find somewhere to stay for the night.

We were just turning the bend at the bottom of the road when the hair at the back of my neck literally stood on end and my skin became covered in goose lumps. I couldn't understand what was happening to me; I had never experienced these feelings before.

I knew this place, I knew what was around the next bend and yet I had never been here before in this life. I looked up and there was the small shop I had seen when I was meditating, right on the cliffside. My heart began thumping as I looked at the pier and the fishing boats directly below me. I turned to Keith and said, 'Keith, where are we, what place is this?'

'It's Lyme Regis, we're here at last. Shall we park up here and have a walk on the pier before we eat?'

'Yes, all right,' I said feeling a little unsure. I didn't tell Keith what I had seen or anything about my thoughts of a previous life; he wouldn't have understood. But he sensed something, and asked if I was OK.

'Yes I'm just fine, just a case of *déjà vu*, nothing to worry about.'

We parked the car next to the pier, and as we got out I reached for Keith's hand. I felt very strange as I relived the scene, knowing that I would not be able to walk with him onto the jetty. I suddenly knew that I had drowned there when I fell into the sea years ago. I couldn't believe it, I was speechless.

Keith said to me as we stepped up onto the jetty, 'Come on, love, stop dragging your heels.'

'I'm not, I'm just a bit tired,' I said as I felt my heart thumping. I couldn't walk with him onto those small planks of wood that made up the jetty leading out to sea.

'What's holding you back? You like walking by the sea and it'll blow the cobwebs away after being cooped up all day in the car.'

'Oh! Look at these small boats,' I said, trying to change

74

the subject.

Then: 'Good day,' said a man who was repairing his fishing boat. The relief I felt as Keith started chatting to the fisherman! I glanced up towards the little shop, hoping it had disappeared and I had imagined everything. But it was still there and from what I could see it hadn't changed at all. We stood talking with this friendly man for a while, then I told Keith we'd better go and find a room.

For a time after that I wanted to find out if a young girl had in fact died under the awful circumstances I have described. It would have been possible back then that a relative was still alive. But I was silly, I never did anything about it as there always seemed to be more important things to do. I think by now it is too late.

The last incarnation I know about is when I was a born as a male. The experience was very short, but I knew it was I.

I was about 12 years old, dressed in a tweed suit whose trousers came down to just below my knee. On my head I wore a flat cap, also made of tweed. It was bitterly cold and dark when I found myself walking down a street of stone-built terraced houses, which looked to be three storeys high with skylight windows at the top. I think there are still some houses around like that now.

As I looked up into the star-filled sky I could see smoke billowing out of all the chimney pots. The pavement and road were cobbled, not like we have today. About halfway down the left side of the street I opened the door of one of the houses and disappeared inside. I was home. That was that.

I came back to reality without any hint of how I had died. I was never shown any other past lives, but I do wonder how many incarnations I have endured, or in fact still have to.

CHAPTER SEVEN

Healing Experiences

Many people wish to know how they can become healers. Those who have succeeded in developing the gift continue to find out how they can become better channels. Healers willingly give their time to the sick, because they possess the divine attributes of love and compassion, a longing to restore health and happiness to those who are suffering in pain and misery.

Spiritual healing is God's gift to all his children, irrespective of race or creed. It is the Divine Plan to encourage the spiritual progress of the human family. Healing is the greatest gift that can be bestowed on anyone. It is certainly the most spiritual one.

I became a healer long before my other psychic faculties developed. I must admit I didn't want to heal. I was only 16 when healing showed itself as a gift to be used, but I wanted to be a clairvoyant. I didn't want to spend my time around sick people; I felt I was too young for that. But though I tried and I tried to develop my clairvoyance, it was no use. I could give sittings, but they were poor in quality. Always a perfectionist, that wasn't good enough for me. I had to be one of the best.

It was only when I became a mother and felt all the attendant emotions of love, caring and understanding that I really started to care about those who were sick.

I didn't start healing in earnest until I was 25. How strange it was! I was doing what I always did: cooking, cleaning etc, and was just finishing the dusting in the dining room, later to be my sanctuary. My hands suddenly became really hot, they felt so big and strange I couldn't understand it. I paced up and down, looking down at my hands, not knowing what to do. I knew it must have been healing power, but why now for no apparent reason? The feeling must have lasted about three hours; it just wouldn't go away.

76

I rang several friends and relatives, asking if they were ill. Those I could tell about this strange power, I did, hoping that someone would offer an explanation for this sudden flow of healing energy.

I must have sat in the dining room for hours wondering what I should do. Obviously someone from the invisible world was trying to tell me something. The only possible explanation could be that those spirit doctors wanted me to use this gift to heal the sick. I couldn't stop thinking about it all evening. The following day, just like a bull at a gate, I rang the newspaper and advertised my healing gift. All I could do now was wait and see what response I would get. It was strange how the hot power disappeared as soon as I put the phone down.

That was the start of my full-time healing career.

Soon the phone started to ring and I was booking appointments. I must admit I was rather worried that I would make a fool of myself. However, I thought that, since spirit had encouraged me do something about the healing gift, they would not let me down. Yet, despite my strong faith, I was still nervous.

It was a few months later, during healing sessions, that my clairvoyance came to the fore. I gave sittings during healing to start with. Then, when I found out that I gave 100% accurate messages, I knew this was for me. I had always wanted to be a good clairvoyant and medium, had waited a long time for spirit to allow me to follow this path. It was obvious looking back, I couldn't choose, it was up to the Great Spirit to decide when the right time would be.

A lady from Ilkley once came to see me for healing. She had a growth in her foot that looked like an extra anklebone. Her doctor had told her she must have surgery to remove it so they could find out what it was. She was most upset, as she dreaded the thought of surgery. During the healing act she told me she saw my fingers physically enter her foot. By the time she left some 30 minutes later, the lump had disappeared altogether. Spontaneous healing had taken place.

Spontaneous healing is a common experience amongst healers. I believe that the power behind all spontaneous healing is that of spirit and it is planned in a methodical fashion. Such change must be a planned act requiring intelligence but it cannot arise from a human mind, because the human mind does not know how to do it, otherwise medical specialists would have derived a form of treatment by now. It is obvious that the intelligence responsible for this possesses a superior knowledge of healing energy. There are far too many cases to be dismissed as coincidental. Healing intelligence from spirit must exist.

A professional rugby player came to see me from Leeds, asking if I might be able to help him through contact healing. One of the opposing team's players had stamped on his lower back, the lumbar region, causing considerable damage. The doctors and specialists did all they could for him, but told him he would never play rugby again.

He was in a great deal of pain when he arrived, though he told me he was learning to live with it. After a few minutes of healing he told me that the pain had lifted and he felt comfortable for the first time in years. He had not been able to play rugby since his injury, but following healing he began to feel more positive. He said that when he had made the appointment, he'd thought it would be a waste of time but decided to come anyway. I had been recommended to him and he thought he had nothing to lose.

After that first time, he came to see me every week for three months, and during that time he started to play his beloved rugby once again.

It is such a pity that spiritual healing is usually only a last resort for people for whom all other methods have failed. Spirit healing ministers are able, in their advanced state of being, to acquire that greater knowledge of spiritual laws and forces that can be directed to heal the sick on earth. These healing ministers have the ability to heal the sick within the scope of their knowledge and within the total laws that govern us all. This is the only logical way to account for supernormal healing.

I have several healing guides. Doctor Panner was the very first to make himself known to me. He lived in Germany during his earthly life and was a practising neurosurgeon. He has shown himself to me clairvoyantly, and has worked with me while I was in trance. What a wonderful spirit person he is, but he never stands any nonsense. Dr Panner had to learn a little patience with people I was training in the development of their healing gift. There are many other healing guides who work behind the scenes, hand in hand, helping the sick. The other names I have been given so far are Dr Johannes Ryder. He prefers to be called a bone specialist rather than an orthopaedic surgeon. Dr Moyo Shima specialises in cancer conditions.

To describe Doctor Panner I would have to say he looks very modern in his dress, wearing the white coat that doctors wear today. He is about five foot eight inches tall, slender and wears gold-metal-framed glasses. His very straight, fair hair is worn in a side parting and swept back at the front and sides, and he has lovely blue eyes. He has a very abrupt manner, wanting only to get on with the work in hand, and has no time for matters other than the healing process.

I remember when I lived in Johannesburg in the 1970s, Dr Panner told a friend of mine she had a condition of the breast. Her response was that, as far as she was concerned, there was nothing wrong with her, but I advised her to see a doctor and get her breasts examined. Years later I found out she'd had a mastectomy but unfortunately she died anyway. If only she had heeded Dr Panner immediately, perhaps this dreadful operation may not have been necessary.

The body is a temple of the soul – the overcoat – and it is up to us to look after it. We need to exercise, keep fit and eat the right foods. Our body is very important; it is not a machine. If we overstretch it in any way, for example by not having enough sleep or rest, expecting it to perform endless tasks, pushing it to its limits, it can break down and collapse altogether. Looking after ourselves is the first aspect of healing. Fortunately, these days most people exercise and eat healthier.

A medium should never say to a patient, 'You will be cured', as there are no guarantees. When our time is up we will leave this world and receive our promotion, no matter how much healing we receive.

A good example of this was Jean, a lady in her 40s diagnosed with a brain tumour, who came to see me for healing. She had gone through all the usual treatment and drugs prescribed by her doctors, including the terrible side-effects of chemotherapy. She was in a very bad state of health when she arrived at my home. Through healing at regular weekly intervals, and check-ups at the hospital, she was told the tumour was shrinking. We were over the moon, thrilled to bits. At last she had a ray of hope to help her over the next few months. I continued with healing and eventually no further medical treatment was necessary.

However, several weeks later I was told Jean had died in a car accident. Although the healing process had worked for her, her time had come to go on to her final destination, the wonderful world of spirit.

Another example is a patient who suffered from a brain tumour. He was a young man of 32 with a wife and three children, and his wife was carrying their fourth child. My heart went out to them all when I saw what a bad way he was in when he arrived on my doorstep for healing. He was rather sceptical and had only come because his wife was a believer in the healing energy and he wanted to please her. He told me he had suffered a brain tumour years earlier and had an operation to remove the cancer, but this time it was inoperable.

The specialist at the hospital had given him only a short time to live, and understandably his family was devastated. No treatment was given except tablets to control the patient's epileptic fits; he was just left to endure the cancer and wait to die.

We talked for a while, and I tried to explain how the healing process worked, and how those spirit doctors wanted to continue with their work from the next world. I told him that these doctors were able to use a healing energy unknown to the doctors in this world, and they had at their disposal the means to operate and treat patients more successfully.

Week after week he came to see me for healing, and during that time there were definite signs of improvement. Dr Panner, my healing doctor, showed me mental pictures each week of how the tumour was changing. We were very positive and looked forward to the time when the doctors would tell us some good news.

Approximately three months after the start of the healing my patient went to see his specialist and insisted on a brain scan to see if there was any change in the tumour. Following the scan the specialist said he would give the young man chemotherapy treatment. It seemed strange to us; he had spent all these months waiting to die and now the hospital was prepared to do something. I wonder what they saw that was different, and why treatment was possible now. I was pleased to hear this news, but I will never forget a peculiar feeling of disappointment deep inside. I couldn't understand why, as it seemed this young man might recover and have a future with his family.

When he came to see me after his chemotherapy treatment I felt something was wrong. I couldn't understand what it was except the healing was different. Usually Dr Panner would show me pictures of the tumour but this time I saw nothing. I didn't know what to say to my patient; all I could do was to tell him the truth, but also explain that this did not mean the tumour had gone. During the next few weeks I continued to give contact and absent healing, but pictures of the tumour were no longer shown to me. For whatever reason I was being kept in the dark. But I trusted spirit implicitly, knowing they had good reason.

I was shocked to hear two weeks later that the young man had died peacefully at home.

Several months have now elapsed since his passing and at last I think I may have found an answer in a book I have just finished reading. The book is about a spirit guide talking through his medium to Harry Edwards, a very well known and respected healer. Harry has also passed into the spirit world since the book was written.

The spirit guide explained that if the patient receives treatment in the form of chemotherapy or radiotherapy, then the cells have been killed and healing of the cells cannot take place. I wonder!

Elsie, a circle of light member and very dear friend of mine, approached me to ask if I would give her son Martin spiritual healing. She was very worried after hearing he had developed cancer of the testicle, and had been taken into hospital for an operation to remove it. I offered to give him contact healing but his wife refused. She was a non-believer and insisted I left him alone. However, I did send him absent healing each day and prayed it would help. Unfortunately we found out later that the cancer had spread to other parts of his body. Martin had received the usual treatment, including chemotherapy, but he was deteriorating rapidly. In desperation, and against his wife's wishes, he asked his mother if she would contact me once again to go along to the hospital to give him contact healing. I agreed, but by this time he was very poorly and ready to receive his promotion to the spirit world.

As I walked through the hospital wards and saw all the suffering, it broke my heart. I was told there was a shortage of equipment, especially the machines that administered chemotherapy. These machines enable the patient to move around the ward while the dose is given, which is better than remaining in bed during the treatment, which can take hours to complete. The machines are called Volume Infusion Pumps (VIPs) I did give healing to Martin but I'm afraid he died. I was left with an awful feeling of having failed. However, I am sure he would have gained some knowledge of life after death, which must have helped him when he finally reached his destination.

I decided the time was right to raise funds for this long overdue equipment the hospital so desperately needed. Cancer was bad enough, and if I could make life a little easier for sufferers of the disease, I would do it.

Elsie, my other dear friend Joan and I started the hard work of trying to raise enough money to buy a VIP machine, which cost around £2000 each. We organised coffee mornings and bring-and-buy stalls, collecting goods for sale. Joan, with nothing more than a state pension to live on, bought unclothed dolls and knitted them beautiful clothing. Her hands eventually ached from all the hard work, but she received many orders and raised quite a lot of money. My mother and I gave clairvoyance – ten minutes per person. The venues we had were not ideal for this, to say the least. We were in two small rooms, no bigger than a closet. But the ventures were successful and spirit worked very well for both of us.

I soon found a charitable organisation which, after hearing my story, decided to fund one VIP machine for us. The end result was two machines and £500 left over for Martin House Hospice. Though I advertised for donations in *Psychic News*, a weekly newspaper for those interested in spiritualism, I received only two donations of £5. It was a very disappointing response.

Healing also works for less serious afflictions than cancer, such as skin conditions. With skin afflictions of all types, there will invariably be a psychosomatic cause: fear, anxiety, frustration and so on. Chronic skin problems are often the easiest afflictions to heal, yet medical practitioners usually direct their attention to the symptoms rather than the causes, prescribing ointments and lotions and in some cases even giving radiation treatment. These may be helpful for some patients, but for the majority they are of little use, because the cause has not been treated.

Some skin diseases are infectious. When a healer comes into contact with a patient suffering from such a disease, she/he must take every precaution to prevent passing on any contamination to another person.

One of my patients, a small child around the age of two, was covered with small warts all over her body. Her parents were very distressed, they had taken her to all the skin specialists hoping for a cure, but she did not improve. The child enjoyed visiting my healing sanctuary, and following several healing sessions the warts started to disappear, until one day they were no longer there. The parents were so thrilled, the whole family eventually came for contact healing when they were ill.

A great many skin conditions are suffered by children, and they are invariably cured through the wonderful spiritual healing energies.

When a healer does not see all the progress he would wish for, he should not blame the patient, the guide or himself. He should not think he is to blame or that the healing gift is not strong enough. We are unable to see or understand the workings of the Great Spirit, but we should trust and know spirit healing is brought about through the knowledge of spirit science and can only operate within the holistic laws that govern human existence.

Roger was a young man of 33 who had cancer. I knew him personally, so I was in a better position to talk to him about spiritual healing and self-healing. He chose the latter. I taught him how to use his mind to heal his body; it was up to him what pictures he imagined in his mind for this purpose. He chose an army of soldiers who fought against the bad cells, killing them. While he slept he had soldiers standing on guard duty.

I gave him a simple example of how the mind works, giving instructions to the brain to send messages to the affected area of the physical body. To explain in simple terms: if you slice an orange in half, the brain immediately tells the mouth to water. Therefore, whatever message the brain sends out, the body immediately reacts to that particular thought.

It is now nine years since Roger received treatment for cancer and was given the all clear. He is at the moment very healthy, fit and well so one can assume that self-healing, along with absent healing, did work for him. Now he is convinced that spiritual healing does work, and talks about spiritualism and life after death to the point of boring people!

I believe in self-healing in conjunction with the power of prayer. Prayer can indeed move mountains or, in my case, a breast tumour.

I was diagnosed with a tumour of the breast, which my doctor told me should be removed by surgery. While I waited to go into hospital I went through hell, believing that I had cancer. Even the best of us can look on the black side when we are ill, which doesn't help the situation at all. You must always be positive in your outlook.

Before the operation I had to sign a document to say that if cancer was found and the tumour was malignant, the surgeon could perform a mastectomy. I remember going down to the operating theatre not wanting to wake up, thinking I might well be without one of my breasts when I come round from the anaesthetic. The first thing I did when I woke up was to remove the padding to find out if I was still intact. What a relief when I found that I still had my breast and that the cyst wasn't malignant.

A few years later I found another cyst had appeared in the same place as the one that had been removed. I felt my other breast and there was another. This time I was not going to go through the trauma of surgery. I would heal myself.

Remember the case of Roger, who pictured something in his mind that could destroy the enemy? I chose the image of 'Pack Man', a computer game which consisted of a round head with a large mouth that gobbled up the enemy. The enemy in my case were the cysts. Naturally I also

85

prayed and asked spirit to help me. Within days the lumps grew smaller and smaller and finally disappeared. They have come back on occasion over the years, but I have no worries now because I know how to disperse them.

Divine law governs all human life and although we may endure pain when in the physical body, we must do so with courage. This will enable us to accept problems that we can challenge, learning the art of mastery which establishes discipline, the strength that is given from the Great Spirit to all. Love is the law, it is life, and when the law is in operation everything works together for good in your life.

Women all over the world fear the dreaded cancer of the uterus and the breast. My advice is to seek medical help, but also give yourself healing. It does work with most people.

We are spirit. The real 'we' are clothed in a body, and the consciousness is spirit. We can realise and strengthen this through meditation. We must believe in an invisible life, a spirit life, an invisible power which we can touch at any time. It will heal us of aches and pains and disharmonies; disharmonies brings disease.

Absent healing can be proved when there is no other possible explanation for a sick person who recovers from a physical or mental illness following healing intercessions on the patient's behalf.

Spiritual love, which everyone can respond to, is pure divine love. To love one another is perfection.

CHAPTER EIGHT

Spirit Knows Best

Although I loved our house in Ilkley and had so many happy memories of my time there, including some wonderful psychic experiences, it was time to move on. All the children were grown up, and Keith had decided to leave his accountancy partnership and set up on his own. I too needed a change, and had been toying with the idea of going into business myself. This was an ideal time to look ahead and reshape my life.

The more I thought about it, the more excited I became. I didn't let the grass grow under my feet; off I went to the local estate agents. A display in the window advertised a health farm for sale. Wow! The thought of all those beauty treatments, saunas, massages, etc – every woman's dream!

I rushed inside and asked the receptionist where the health farm was and how much the owners wanted for it. To my surprise, it was just up the road from where I was already living. This was wonderful news as I loved Ilkley and didn't really want to move away. I made an appointment to view the property, though I knew it would be torture if I fell in love with the place and couldn't afford it.

Three of my five children had left home. Penny was happily married, Victoria was working in London and Paul had found a place of his own. I had it all worked out. Stephanie could help me run the health farm and Rod could help out in the gym, leaving Keith to continue with his accountancy practice. It would be an ideal place to give demonstrations of healing and clairvoyance. My mind was running riot, making all these mental plans before I had even seen the place!

The health farm was situated on the famous Ilkley Moors, overlooking the whole of Ilkley. What a breathtaking view there would be, day or at night! I couldn't ask for a better place to carry on my psychic work, in a health and

87

fitness environment.

I drove up the steep winding driveway to the old country house which housed the health farm. On both sides of the driveway were beautiful gardens. Finally the drive widened out to a large parking area. As I got out of my car I noticed ahead of me a large swimming pool surrounded by more beautiful gardens. At the same time as I was thinking 'wow!', a sinking feeling hit me in the pit of my stomach and I realised that buying this place was far beyond my means. I decided to have a look around anyway, I couldn't wait to see inside the beautiful house. Everything was how I had imagined it to be. A solid oak front door led to the lovely, welcoming reception area. The sitting area had beautiful gold dralon furniture with flower arrangements all around the room. The decor was superb.

After being introduced to the owner I was shown into the dining room. Beautiful tables had already been laid for dinner with gold-coloured linen cloths and the whitest lace tablecloths I had ever seen. In the centre of each table was a lovely display of flowers, all carefully selected in autumn colours of gold, orange and brown. At the other end of the dining room was more gold dralon furniture; this was where the guests had coffee. In the corner of this magnificent room stood a lovely grand piano. My mind ran riot once again; I could imagine the wonderful musical evenings we would have. I had to have it, it was just what I had hoped for, and the rest of the property was just as wonderful.

When Keith got home from work that evening I told him where I had been, and we arranged an appointment the next day to view the place together. It took us only half an hour to decide this was just what we were looking for. The valuation of our home was much more than we anticipated. This meant we could proceed with the purchase of the beautiful health hotel.

Six months later we had sold our home and moved into the health farm. The first thing we did after unpacking was to try out all the equipment: the steam baths, jacuzzi, then the sauna and beauty treatments. What a wonderful way to relax and make a living at the same time! This was a place of beauty where I could practise my spiritual gifts.

It wasn't long before I gave demonstrations of clairvoyance to my old clients and to new ones. I continued with my healing work, and found that healing and clairvoyance were in demand as part of the health farm 'package'.

A young couple, Andrew and Mandy, had booked a two-week break to help them stop smoking and drinking, get fit and lose weight. We all got on well, and on the last evening of their stay they asked me to join them in the lounge for a drink. We talked about everything under the sun. I discovered Andrew and Mandy were about to get married, and Mandy had treated Andrew to this break as a pre-wedding present. It turned out to be a very enjoyable evening. They left the following morning after Mandy had booked a day of beauty treatments with us on the eve of her wedding day, to which Keith and I were invited.

We kept in touch, meeting occasionally for a meal or a drink. Andrew would always leave us with the words: 'I would like a sitting with you some time Barbara'. He didn't exactly believe in spiritualism, but was fascinated by it all. I never believed for one minute that I would see him professionally, but about a year after their wedding he rang me and asked for a sitting. I agreed.

Contrary to what most people think, clairvoyance is not a form of fortune-telling, although this is what Andrew was looking for. I explained to him that we are in control of our own destiny and can change the way things happen to us by our own actions. It is entirely our fault if things don't work out for us, there is no point in blaming other people. Spirit are allowed to help us sometimes, giving us guidance when we need it, but it is up to us whether we take notice of what has been said. The following story will show you what can happen when spiritual guidance is ignored.

Sadly, my husband Keith departed this world after suffering from cancer. I sold the health farm, moved to Halifax and bought a nursing home, which I had for six years, looking after the old folk and watching some of them struggle to remain on this heavy plane of existence, not wanting to let go. Owning the nursing home and working with old people was a good learning process for me, and I don't regret it for one moment. I even found time to give sittings in my office.

I had also bought a small non-working farm just a few miles away, and found it was a real treat to spend my leisure hours there. Fields and trees surrounded the farmhouse, and I could look right across the valley for miles – a true haven for my psychic work. I have been very lucky from that point of view, always finding the most beautiful properties at the right price. If one believes in fate, perhaps I was guided there. I never made any real money but I lived in some wonderful places.

While I was at Halifax, Andrew and Mandy came for their sitting. They were very apprehensive about what was going to happen. I suppose they thought I would turn out the lights and sit in the dark saying, 'Is there anybody there?' Even so, I did think at the time they were going to take heed of what spirit had to say, especially when I gave them information about their business problems – detailed information about certain contracts they should and should not sign, who and who not to do business with, who to watch out for etc. I told them how they should reorganise their finances to accommodate their needs and also gave information about family and friends in this world and the next. It was quite funny watching the expressions on their faces as I relayed the messages from spirit, which came fast and furious, giving me little time to catch my breath.

Andrew and Mandy's faces bore expressions of disbelief and wonder. How on earth could I possibly know all about their private lives? I explained that the information I receive comes from spirit helpers who wish to be of service, trying to prevent people from making errors.

After the sitting we chatted for quite some time over coffee. I think they found the idea of coming to see a medium rather amusing, despite the evidence of survival I had given them, and when they left it seemed to be with an attitude of 'Let's wait and see'.

Several months later I received a phone call from Andrew asking me if I would see him again for a clairvoyant sitting. It was short notice, but by the tone of his voice I knew something was wrong and I had to try and help him. I had no idea what had happened during the past few months as I had not seen him and Mandy for some time.

When I 'tuned in' to spirit once again for them it soon became evident what the problem was. All that I'd told them last time was correct.

'You've no idea what we've been going through,' Andrew said. 'We wish we'd taken notice of you. We never really thought at the time that all this would happen to us, it seemed too far-fetched. We were too secure. Obviously you knew more than us, and it's too late now.'

I reassured him. 'No, Andrew, it's never too late. Making the effort to come and see me is a step in the right direction. First let's see what spirit have to say. I'm sure if there's anything they can do to help, they will.'

Andrew's relatives soon made themselves known to us, and gave him an enormous amount of help. He and Mandy looked relieved and said this time they would do exactly what spirit had told them. They stayed just long enough to quickly catch up on all the news.

It must have been about a year later that I received a call at the nursing home. It was Andrew. 'Hello Andrew, you don't usually ring me at work. What's wrong?'

'Hi, Barbara, everything. Do you remember what spirit told us when you gave us that sitting?'

'I remember they said you could go bankrupt if you weren't careful,' I said.

'Oh dear, it's terrible news. We've lost everything: the

business, our home, the cars. We're totally broke, and I don't know what we're going to do.'

'Oh, I'm so sorry! Didn't you do what spirit advised you to do? They did warn you.'

'I know they did, and I thought we'd been careful. But not careful enough, it's all gone. I thought I should let you know what's happened, and ask your advice. What do you think we should do now?'

'I don't know. Let me think about it and give me a ring later at home.' We said goodbye.

He never rang me back, and the last I heard Andrew and Mandy were separated. One thing I do remember spirit saying was that the couple could avoid disaster if they heeded spirit's words. We all think it will never happen to us, even when we are warned about it. I, for example, should know better, yet I have ignored spirit many times, only to find out they were right all along. Now that I have reached my dreaded 50s I do take notice, but how stupid of me to have left it so long. I could have saved myself a lot of anguish over the years.

My diary was overflowing with appointments, and I had been working day and night. I hadn't been out of the house in weeks and the walls were beginning to close in on me. Tonight at last I had an evening off, so I decided to ring my daughter Stephanie and ask her if she would like to go out. Fine, she said, and I told her I'd be over in half an hour. We would drive somewhere and have a nice relaxing drink. I changed, put some lipstick on and set off to Stephanie's. She had a pub of her own just a couple of miles away, worked long hours, and I thought a break would do her good too.

Soon we had set off in my car. It was now almost 8.30 and dark. Relaxed and looking forward to my night out, I just pointed the car in the direction of the outskirts of the town and drove, not knowing where we would end up. I think it's more exciting to go somewhere new, wondering what is around the next corner.

But I never expected the night to turn out as it did.

We had been driving for about an hour, more or less in silence, only talking when there was something to say. We had travelled quite a distance, the roads were very quiet and we were now out in the country, though we still hadn't found a nice pub. I wasn't bothered as I was enjoying the drive. We decided to stop at the next pub and Stephanie said she would drive home if I wanted to drink alcohol.

It was a chilly winter's night, and the leaves on the trees were now long gone. The country lanes were beautiful but rather eerie; there were no other cars to be seen. It was also beginning to look as though we would not find a place to have that welcome drink. The trees spread their barren branches outward and upwards towards the snow-covered sky.

'I hope it doesn't snow before we get home,' I said, not really too concerned. The heater was working overtime, the car was warm and I felt good. We were travelling reasonably slowly, looking for somewhere to stop; we could see lights just round the next bend. 'Looks like we may have found somewhere,' I said.

We were just turning the next bend when I saw a car coming straight towards us. I could see by its shape that it was an old Ford or maybe an Austin. The lights were very dim, and I dipped my headlights for the benefit of the oncoming driver, which made the road very dark and difficult to see. I remember thinking: why on earth doesn't the driver put on his dipped headlights? I could feel the panic inside me as Stephanie and I watched the car head straight for us. We both said out loud at the same time, 'Oh my God!'

'Watch out, Mum!' Stephanie screamed.

At that moment we hit the car, I can still feel the impact now. But it was rather strange, to put it mildly; we seemed to drive straight through the oncoming car, which was still intact as though it was a mirage. Stephanie looked at me,

93

I looked at Stephanie, both of us pale and shaken.

'Are we dead? We must be. Or are we seeing things? You did see it, Mum, and feel the crash, didn't you?' Stephanie said, very unsure of herself.

'Yes, I did,' I answered, confused. I couldn't believe I was still driving down the road. 'I think you're right, love. God help us.'

I stopped the car at the side of the road, trying to gather my thoughts. We were not injured, but then if we were dead it would have been our spirit bodies we were looking at, and they would not have been damaged. We sat for a minute or two, looking at each other and wondering what to do next. Was this how it happened when one was taken quickly? I tried to remember all that I had learnt over the years about sudden deaths. It was so real; we must be in the next life, suffering from shock.

I got out of the car and looked over it for damage. Nothing at all, which was astonishing.

'Steph, there's nothing wrong with the car, not a scratch. This is impossible, I can't believe it. Do you feel any different?'

'No I don't, are we dreaming? Come on, Mum, you're the medium talk to me,' she said.

Could both of us be dreaming? I didn't think so, although I did think we should feel something. I turned the car around and slowly drove back down the road to find the other car. We had travelled about half a mile when I said, 'Surely by now we would have seen this car.'

'Let's go on for a while, we must have driven further than we thought,' Stephanie said.

But two miles on, still nothing. By this time I was wondering if we were both mad. 'Let's go to the next pub, order a drink each and if we're ignored then we're dead.'

We had both calmed down a little by now, although I did expect to wake up in my bed to find it was only a bad dream.

Not far down the road we came across a country pub

and, judging by the number of cars parked outside, it looked very busy. We got out of the car and checked each other to see if we were presentable. Everything in order, not a hair out of place, we went in and walked up to the bar. I ordered a large brandy for myself; Stephanie wanted a glass of wine.

'Are you all right?' said the barman. 'You both look as though you've seen a ghost.'

We laughed with relief, our hands trembling as we took our drinks. 'Yes, we just had a narrow escape with another car down the road, but we're OK.'

Weaving our way across the room, we found an empty table and sat down. My legs and hands still shaking like jelly, I felt as though every eye was on us. They probably were looking at us, but only because we were strangers.

Stephanie and I raised glasses. 'Cheers, here's to our tomorrows, whichever world we're in.'

We were silent on the way home, deep in thought. What on earth had happened to us? The car we had collided with had to be a 'ghost' car – if there are such things.

The following day we still couldn't believe what had happened. We bought all the newspapers to see if there had been an accident, but nothing was mentioned. We never told anyone of our hair-raising experience, it was too unbelievable. We did go back each week for a month, parked the car at the scene of our 'imaginary' accident and watched and waited for our 'ghost' car to turn up.

It never came back while we were there. Whether it ever did, we will never know.

It is several years since that extraordinary incident, but I am still very careful when driving. Perhaps it was a warning of things to come. I can only hope nothing like that will ever happen. Sometimes I wonder: if I hadn't been psychic, would this have happened to us?

I was planning to move back to South Africa. Stephanie and her husband Roger had already left England and were living in Cape Town. I promised to join them when I had sold my home and business.

Before I left, a young man called James came to see me. I had never met him before but I had spoken to him on the phone briefly when he rang to make an appointment. Pam, a lady who'd had several sittings with me, had given him my number. He was tall and slender with dark curly hair, looked in his mid-30s and was unshaven. As he sat down he told me he'd never had a sitting before. I explained to him that I would give all the information, and all I expected from him was to acknowledge spirit and answer with a yes or a no.

Since I always 'tune in' before a sitter arrives, I had a lady in spirit waiting for James, ready to help. She had already told me she was his wife, so I started the sitting with, 'I have your wife here, she's been waiting for you and says she's glad you came. She is saying Angel, I'm not sure what she means, do you?'

'Yes, my wife's name was Angela and I always called her Angel. She was my angel.' Tears appeared in his eyes as he remembered his lovely wife. 'I'm sorry,' he said, wiping the tears away.

'She said she died of cancer of the womb, leaving you and her two little girls behind.'

'Yes, it was terrible. Why did she have to die so young, and suffer the way she did? Why did she leave us all alone?'

'Because it was her time to go, to get her promotion. She says you mustn't worry, she's well and happy, and try not to be depressed. You're coping very well with the girls. She says, "I will be waiting for you, my darling, I love you".' I relayed everything she said word for word. 'She's telling me you must get the car checked out, it's the brakes. Take it into a garage as soon as possible.'

'The brakes on the car are OK, I think.'

'She's very insistent about it, will you do as she says?'

'Yes. Will you tell her I love her too?' he said, looking a little happier.

'She already knows that, she can hear you, you know.'

After the sitting James looked in need of a cup of tea. He wanted to know more about clairvoyance and spiritualism, so we talked and talked, with him asking intelligent questions I was only too happy to answer.

About two months later the phone rang. It was Pam, the lady who had recommended me to James. She wanted a sitting, so I made an appointment for her.

'By the way,' Pam said, 'I nearly forgot. Do you remember that young man who came to see you a few weeks ago, the one I sent to you?'

'Oh yes, James. Shame about his wife and having to bring those two children up on his own. It can't be easy for him. But he seems to be doing a good job, and when he left here he seemed much happier.'

'Terrible news, he was in a car accident last week, apparently the brakes failed. He was taking his children to see his mother-in-law. It was an awful mess, the car was written off.'

I was shocked. 'Are they all right?'

'No, that's what I'm trying to tell you, the three of them were killed outright. Poor souls.'

It was such sad news, yet I knew they would all be together now, united and, I'm sure, much happier. I remembered James's wife warning him to get his brakes checked, and wondered how the children's grandmother would cope with losing her daughter and then her granddaughters.

I often wonder how I would cope under the same circumstances. Of course I would also have to go through the same grieving process. It is very hard to celebrate a loved one's spiritual promotion, as we would if they were promoted here on the earth plane.

So in August 1991 I returned to South Africa after 20 years, to the beautiful Western Cape. Stephanie had given birth to her first child there, my second granddaughter, whom she named Corrin. Penny already had a little girl

Charlotte aged three and it broke my heart to leave her.

Stephanie and Roger lived just down the road from me at Spanish Farm, Somerset West. I had been living there for about six months when Roger came to see me with Steph. He had a brother who had died in a car accident in his teens.

Quite out of the blue, Stephanie asked me if I would give Roger a sitting. I asked her if he had asked for one. 'No, Mum, but I want you to prove to him about life after death.'

'He doesn't believe in spiritualism. When he's ready, he'll ask me himself.'

'You know what Roger's like, he'll never ask and I know he really wants to know about spiritualism. Please, Mum, do it for me.'

I agreed that, if I could get Roger to sit long enough to prove survival, and if his spirit relatives came to visit when we were talking, then I would pass on everything I was given. But it was entirely up to him what he thought, I could not make him believe.

I don't know what Stephanie wanted to hear, but she didn't look very happy. Her beliefs are so strong – after all she had lived with my work all her life – and I think she wanted Roger to feel the same way.

In terms of scepticism, he is one of the most difficult people I have ever met, and I have had quite a number of awkward people during my life as a medium. These obstreperous people always turn up at public venues and shout horrible things to you. He wasn't quite as bad as that, but not far off. Because my daughter lived with him, he thought she had told me all about his family – understandable, I would have thought the same, but she hadn't.

Roger said to me, 'If you can give me information that even Stephanie couldn't possibly know then I may give spiritualism some thought.'

I knew it wouldn't work and told him that if he wanted

me to link with his relatives later I would do so, but only when he was ready. I didn't want to feel I was thrusting spiritualism down his throat.

About a year later Stephanie, Roger and Corrin were visiting me and, as we sat in the lounge talking, I suddenly saw Roger's brother.

'Roger, I have your brother Angus here.'

Grinning, he said, 'You can't have, he's dead.'

'I know he is, stupid,' I said, thinking he was taking the Mickey before I had time to start. We could talk to each other like that in a joking fashion and neither of us took offence. But I still asked him to be serious and listen to me.

'OK then.'

'He tells me that he was in a car with friends. He put his head out of the window, hit his head on a lamp-post and died instantly from head injuries. Is this correct, Roger?'

'Yes it is, but Stephanie might have known that and told you.'

I felt like packing it in. We wouldn't get anywhere with this attitude; it didn't matter what I was going to say, he would have a contradictory answer. I wasn't in the mood for banging my head against a brick wall. However, his brother had come to visit and it was my duty to pass on all the information. So I decided to continue and take no notice of what Roger had to say. The sooner I got on with it the sooner they would leave me in peace.

Although I was very impatient by then, wishing I had never started, I continued giving him more and more information about his brother, the dog they had and so on.

'I have your mother here now, she's telling me about a watch you bought for her birthday.'

'Yes that's right and I know you couldn't know about that. My family never bought presents for one another, so I kept it quiet.'

I went on to talk of a pet dog he used to have.

'I never told Steph about the dog either. Perhaps you're

reading my mind.'

'Were you thinking about your mother and the dog just now?'

'No, but subconsciously I might have been.'

'Oh Roger, I give up, you're impossible!'

They finally left, Roger muttering all the way out of the door, as he usually did.

Later Stephanie rang me, telling me Roger had not stopped talking about the sitting, asking her questions about spiritualism, life after death, and whether I could read minds. Stephanie told him he would have to ask me, as her knowledge was limited. I remember thinking: Oh no, Roger is the worst person to talk to! Yet I liked a challenge and preferred people to question me and not take everything I said as gospel.

It took time, but Roger finally agreed that 'there must be something in this spiritualism thing', as he put it.

There are several spirit guides who take me into trance. My voice, gestures and facial expressions change and the communications vary considerably in content. I have a wonderful control known as Grey Buffalo, who I have already told you about, and a guide called Daniel. The latter is very wise. He told me that he goes back thousands of years. He has difficulty communicating through me, for some reason he is unable just yet to make his voice clear enough for those listening to understand all that he wishes to teach us. It is hard to believe when you hear Grey Buffalo and Daniel, both with different but very deep, strong voices, that they are coming from the same vessel.

Anna, a young lady who belonged to the Quaker religion when she was on this earth plane in the 18th century, and who died when she was 35, leaving two children aged seven and nine, speaks through me in a gentle, caring and compassionate way. In the past I was reluctant to let her communicate, as her voice sounded like mine with a foreign accent, which I wasn't happy with.

100

Spirit guides are wonderful companions and friends. Their company is enhanced by the knowledge they show of the medium's deeper character, and a wonderful ability to read his or her thoughts. They are always ready to help, bringing knowledge and understanding to comfort and sustain those who need help.

When a medium enters a trance state and willingly surrenders control of her body to a spirit guide (the medium is the mistress of her physical being), she must have trust and respect for her guides. This, as you can imagine, takes time. Consenting is an act of surrender, appreciating the love and affection between the controlling guide and medium. The process is like falling asleep and the preparation for it is meditation, relaxation of the physical and the mental. If the medium has been in a deep trance condition for a long period of time, she usually feels as though she has travelled from some distant place and the sensation of travelling is evident.

A medium must always make sure she is not disturbed in any way. I will never forget a time when my boxer dog Sam came bounding into the room and jumped up onto my lap. I was in a deep trance state at the time and the suddenness of the dog pouncing on me made my spirit body return to my physical body at great speed, leaving me with a feeling of shock. My chest hurt and for a short time I felt very ill. It took me a long time to feel comfortable enough to allow myself to be taken into trance again. However, accidents will happen and I made sure this never happened again.

Usually when I come out of a trance state I feel so much better, renewed and fulfilled, but without training it can have a detrimental effect on the health.

There are many mediums who can listen to the communication that is coming through, as though they are standing some distance from themselves. Some occupy a position above or to one side of their own physical body.

Unconscious trance mediumship is closely linked to

automatic writing, while a controlled medium is much more relaxed. The success rate is about the same in both cases. There is a large percentage of subconscious activity in trance and inspired speaking which can, by training, be turned into a valuable asset.

Spirit writing is produced without the conscious participation of the writer and there are plenty of examples of someone in spirit communicating through a medium in this way. The writing is the same as when the communicator was on the earth plane, the style and character are sometimes identical. Automatic writing, like automatic art, is by its very nature not consciously produced.

Automatic writing in my case is achieved in a semi-trance state and only one of my guides uses this way of communicating. He brings wisdom and knowledge to those who have come to see me or written to me.

I wasted a lot of time as a developing medium by being impatient. I tried years ago to develop this gift of automatic writing and gave up because it started with the usual meaningless scribble and I didn't exercise patience. It was only years later and quite out of the blue that I found I was being used for automatic writing. It is certain that a force other than my own will was causing the hand to move. After all these years I still find it hard to relax because of all the daily problems shooting in and out of my mind. I have always been a person who worries and I don't think I will ever change. I have produced the best writings from spirit, dare I say it, when I have had a brandy as a nightcap!

My first writings started after I experienced a tremendous amount of pain through a personal relationship. My heart was broken; all I seemed to be able to do was walk around like a zombie for several months. I was so depressed I wanted to curl up and die. I prayed quietly over and over again, asking for help from spirit. I needed spirit to intervene, to bring me back to a life free from all the hurt. I had been destroyed emotionally and I couldn't pull myself back to normality. Not only had I lost the man

I loved dearly, I also lost my business, my home and valued possessions that I had worked so hard for all my life. I would have thought by this time that I had suffered enough, but it wasn't to be. During this terrible period I also lost my three boxer dogs, which were bitten in the garden by a puff adder snake. Even with veterinary help, all three died within 24 hours, leaving me totally numb. Alone in a foreign country with very little money, I thanked God my daughter was around. She was wonderful; I don't know what I would have done without her. It wasn't far for her to travel, so she was able to call and see me every day.

I had worked professionally as a medium for many years, helping people with their problems, and I should have taken a bit of my own advice and done something sooner. Spirit warned me often enough, but like most people I didn't want to believe the worst. They did on one occasion tell me I would experience this loss when I reached the age of 50 and sure enough it happened in the September before my fiftieth birthday in January. Why didn't I listen to them?

I had moved to a rented house just down the road from where I had lived. One night, as I sat alone praying, a wonderful thing happened. I still don't know how it came about that I was sitting with pen and paper in my hand. However, after a short time feeling sorry for myself and desperately alone, I felt myself slip into a dreamlike trance state. That was when spirit wrote the following for me:

'Suffering is a test of strength only for the strong, as some souls can take only a fraction of despair. To have faith, to have blind faith in the Great Spirit, to take the strength within thyself, which the Great Spirit gives to all those who deliver themselves totally into his care, can take on the whole materialistic world of matter and survive in greatness. This does not mean greatness of material things, but of infinite beauty and illumination.

'It is also a time to shed tears of sorrow and of joy in the knowledge that in the end a freedom which is earned in true love of spirit, within and beyond the grey world of matter, will indeed be within reach.

'You have gone through a testing period, withdrawn from spiritual thoughts and actions. Now is the time to bring all things together and once again be thy true spiritual self in greatness and truth, without the barriers of those who hold you back from the goodness you are and will always be. To have grown in the knowledge of spirit is a wonderful gift, and will never leave you.

'You have had time to rest and become stagnant, this has been your choice for some time, the lack of involvement, the lack of drive to reach what is yours, to have been deprived by confusion and emotions has now been lifted for you.

'Dwell on these words, and meditate on what has to come in time. But remember one must survive on the earth plane, to exist, to feed the spirit and body enabling the work of the Great Spirit to be registered on the minds and souls of man through true channels of the chosen few.

'Take each step carefully and with great thought, as your actions now are crucial to your future path. Look, for it will be shown to you.

'Take care, dear child as we have given you a great task and burden to carry. Heal thyself and call on the greatness of the healing power to embrace you. Remember what has gone, and what spiritual healing power can and will do to obtain a pure channel in which to work. Remember also the power of prayer. We are with you, you are not alone in your sorrow, call on us at any time, we will uphold and sustain you in this difficult time of your growth towards the freedom of spirit self.'

When I 'woke up' I was astonished to see what was on the piece of paper, and read it over and over. By this time I was beginning to feel much better, and thanked God for the help I had received.

This new experience had given me comfort in the quiet hours, but I had to find some reason amid the chaos and confusion whirling inside my mind. I tried to make sense of what had happened to me over a period of four weeks that had destroyed my life. I clung to all that spirit gave me and was eager to receive more. This was forthcoming:

'Just a fleeting moment, an illusion as the magician makes the magic happen to the eyes of the unknowing. To discover a brief time of love in the eternity of living is a precious moment, a true utopia, and a glimpse of heaven. Fleeting it may seem, for that is what it is, as time is but a dream which lasts for just a second of the true eternal life span of the universe, a memorable experience of the life we should all know and treasure. To make it last for eternity is a great task for only the few. Never let the disappointments turn and decay as some would do. This would be destruction of all that is good.

'Turn that moment to create a world of knowledge and understanding of the unity that had to be, even if once was spoiled by the unknowlegeable, the unspiritual, the unfeeling. A pot of gold, to be shared unselfishly, and given freely to those who care. The magic of a rainbow, that spans the Earth with a natural beauty, the gift of God.

'Experience all that is around, feel the earth under your feet, the movement, the womb of God's creation ready to give birth to the growth of the unborn, the spring of life, a life of love from the Great Spirit. A magician, of the truest kind. A creation, of life and love. This is the only reality.'

Once again, a few days later spirit wrote this for me:

'A wall of silence envelopes those who sit still and dwell in the past. To become, and to make use of the silence within the depths of knowing thyself, is a hard task, a task of self-development, and to understand one's own divine existence is within the reach of self-esteem.

'The doing of great things, the embryo of rebirth, growing in strength and vitality, which is within us all to develop and regenerate, is within our psyche. To heal thyself and to heal all who pass by. Our, living growth. Take only that which belongs to thee in goodness and kindliness. To

105

reach out to those in need and forget self.

'The power which is within can only express itself to those who are receptive and all that is acceptable within the intelligence of what is acceptable to ones development. For what we once knew, and what we know now is difficult to comprehend.

'To approach the unknown, the grief, the impossible, incomprehensible, the development of a soul in turmoil is questionable of the greatness of what will be eventually in the great divine of life.

'Life is but a dream of the past the present and the future of great expectations. One can pretend the magic of the playing cards, but dealt in the most simple of ways they can cause havoc in the real world of materialism.

'Now is the time to look beyond the great divide and spread the wings of growth and look to thee in depth and wisdom. Why are we, why is it so, to be, to do, what is it all for?'

I managed to get through the following few weeks, remembering what spirit had said to me in the writings. Unfortunately I soon fell into a depression again and one day I was having a particularly bad time, not knowing which way to turn. I decided to turn to my spirit helpers again and ask for guidance. This is what they wrote for me:

'My world is yours, you can touch it any time if you try to reach out to us more often. The greatness, which is already there, the experience you have let go for a time can be brought into action.

'Remember the difficult times you have overcome with our help and guidance. Tomorrow will bring you an even greater insight to the vast universe of opportunities. We will help you if you allow us to draw near, as we once did.

'Hold on to the reality within the shadows of your life, take away the veil of despondency and rejoice in what will come, given chance. Hold close the nearness of those who are with you and are attracted to you from this world.

'Break through the barrier of negativity, and open the

door of progression to perfection. Time moves quickly, share each moment with a positive approach to life. Never to repeat the loss of humility, this you already know.

'The struggles are over for you, do the work of the Great Spirit, work with a light heart and a soul of goodness. Remember to bring into its own the power which you know you can touch and use to your advantage.

'Meditate a little, and see the light shine on you in splendour. Awaken to the spirit within you, just waiting to escape the bounds of self-incarceration. Free the true you so you can go forth with the plan of life.

'Break the chains of stagnation and cleanse the soul of burdens you had to carry. It is over.

'Take heed of the words of the knowledgeable, those who see with a clear vision of what will be for you. You have waited a long time to reach your goal in life. Even though once you thought you had arrived.

'I can speak to you with truth and love, and tell you to come forth in greatness at all that you do. For it is within your power of achievement to do all things that have been planned for you since you were born on this earth plane, never failing to respond to our direction, only at times wandering away from the path set out for you.

'You will go from strength to strength. Have courage, tomorrow is almost here, when you will develop the structure for your plan of action to build a better place for the weak at heart. Have confidence in your good will and welcome the future with open arms. Take my hand, I will give you the strength you need to proceed.

'We have been watching and waiting for the right moment to guide you, and to motivate you to be who you are – not what you were made to be by others without conscience or knowledge of the true life of eternal growth.

'Bring your mind close to us, so that we can give you the help you need to continue through the next few weeks of struggle and worry. Fear not, dear child, listen to us and know we only speak the truth as it is, and will be. The path is clear for you, and the sun doth shine down the avenue of expectations.

'Put together the words of the book slowly as we instruct you. Do not struggle to understand how this will come to you, it will. Remember in the silence much is received.

'We will place on your lap the map of life ahead, so you can fulfil all your dreams within the Law of Cause and Effect. The jigsaw remains unbroken, and only a few pieces are needed for a complete picture.'

My faith, my belief in spiritual friends and helpers has kept me going during these past few years. When I am feeling down, I read the words from my spirit friends and I can then cope with all that life throws at me.

These few words were also given to me:

'The majesty of life is a wonderful creation, derived from all the emotions of lovingness, to be distributed amongst the ready. The real seed of life is the magic of insight into what is great and powerful. For this seed grows with knowledge, and knowledge maketh the true you.

'Stand naked and show the world the beauty of the soul within, to express the growth of the unborn mechanics within, waiting to unfold in the spring of rebirth, gently removing the cloak of materialism.

'Strive to create a world of spiritual insight and goodness and understanding of what is there for all you people of the dark material world of matter. An unseen breeze can bring a storm of gifts to those who can receive in humility and selflessness.'

I find that some mediums like myself are rather silly at times. We give advice and guidance to those in trouble, yet very rarely take notice ourselves of what spirit are saying to us, especially if it's something we don't want to hear. My guides had warned me of this traumatic time ahead, yet I put it down to my imagination, or negative thoughts. How wrong I was! Spirit told me this would happen and I could have avoided a lot of heartbreak if only I had taken notice.

CHAPTER NINE

Station Strangler

I stayed for a while in Cape Town in my rented house, wondering how long my little bit of money would last before I had to succumb to the reality of having to return to England. I was still living in a beautiful place in the Western Cape, writing this book. I wasn't to know that my book would be delayed due to the intervention of my spirit helpers prompting me to help the South African Police seek the serial killer of the Western Cape Flatts.

It all started when my daughter Stephanie came to visit me on 30 January 1994. During our conversation that day she asked me what I thought about the terrible serial killings at Mitchell's Plain, a coloured area 10 km from where we both lived and about 22 km from the city of Cape Town. The surrounding area is known as the Cape Flatts, which is where most of the children were being abducted from, sodomised and strangled.

Years ago I gave up reading newspapers because I found it much too depressing reading about all the hurt, pain and unnecessary suffering in the world. I couldn't sleep at nights thinking about what I had read, and what made it worse was the fact that there was nothing I could do to change this sorry, depraved world of ours. I also hadn't watched the news for quite some time; straight after breakfast I always went into my office to write my book.

So I was taken by surprise when Stephanie asked me about the murders; I didn't know what she was talking about. She explained that someone had been abducting young black boys, sodomising and killing them. I was shocked and upset, but never dreamed that I would soon be involved in the case.

Two days later, and for the first time in months, I was sitting in my dressing gown watching television. When the news bulletin began I heard the colonel in charge of the murder case at Mitchell's Plain tell the interviewer his thoughts about these terrible killings, and that they had no leads as to who the killer might be.

Within five minutes of watching the news, I heard my spirit guide tell me that I would be involved in this case. She gave me the name of the killer, and at the same time I was shown his face very clearly. I was stunned and must admit, knowing who the man was made me quite sick. I didn't want to get involved, but knew I hadn't any choice in the matter. I had a responsibility to my spirit friends and to the dead children who obviously wanted me to help solve these awful crimes. With this in mind, I felt it my duty to talk to the authorities.

My spirit guide Anna gave me this information and was to work with me throughout the case. She was a new guide, and had taken me into trance only a few times. Anna urged me to inform the authorities, saying she would help the police to catch the killer. But how does a clairvoyant approach the police and prove to them she is not a crank? It isn't easy.

When I next saw Stephanie, I explained to her what had happened and she agreed that I should inform the police. I plucked up the courage eventually, as I knew my spirit friends would not let me rest until I had contacted the officers in charge of the case. So I rang the police and was put through to the emergency caravans that had been set up as a temporary base for the investigation, located in the grounds of the Mitchell's Plain Police Station. I asked to speak to the officer in charge of the case, telling them I was a medium from the UK with information regarding the murders of the young children.

I was very apprehensive because South Africans on the whole are very religious people who regard mediums as witches with broomsticks. That said, there are many satanic cults practising in the most unlikely places. One, my doctor informed me, was just down the road from where I was staying, a beautiful place on the coast of the western cape.

110

I was referred to a Detective Sergeant Khan, who arranged to see me the following day. He and another detective arrived at my home in Somerset West on 1 February 1994. I was worried how to start the conversation and my heart was pounding as I explained what had happened and how I had received the information, wondering how I must have sounded. I hoped I would come across as a sane, normal human being.

The detectives looked at me, puzzled. Psychic things were alien to them. However, they treated me with the greatest respect and listened to what I had to say with interest. When they asked if I had anything else to add, I was about to say no but at that very moment spirit came through again, showing me pictures of a particular place.

I said, 'Spirit are showing me pictures of a place, I don't know if it's relevant or not.'

'Can you draw this place for us?'

I am useless at drawing, but said I'd give it a try. Spirit had shown me clairvoyantly a place I had never been to before, so I drew this for them. It was a plan of a certain area in Mitchell's Plain.

I drew a T-junction with a row of neat little houses along the bottom. A church was at the top right-hand side of the road with a shebeen (a place where people can buy alcoholic drink after hours) on the left-hand side and a warehouse or something similar on the right.

They exchanged surprised glances.

I asked, ' Do you recognise this area?'

'Yes, your drawing is very good. If it's the place we're thinking of, then it's correct in every detail.'

They were quite amazed at what I had drawn for them, knowing I had never visited the area before. Mitchell's Plain, like all other coloured and black areas, is not a place white people usually venture. It is a residential area, mainly for coloured people, with a population of about one and a half million. Most live in poverty. Extended family boundaries exist, which means that a child could be living with parents, grandparents or other relatives. Mitchell's Plain, like other such areas, is rife with crime.

The detectives then asked me if I would be prepared to direct them from my home to the area I had drawn for them. I suppose they were looking for some sort of proof that I was who I said I was, and indeed able to see clairvoyantly. I agreed to this, crossing my fingers. If spirit wanted me to help the police they would show me the way.

It turned out to be more than satisfactory.

My daughter, both the detectives and I set off in the police car for Mitchell's Plain. We travelled along the N2 motorway towards Cape Town, and as we were passing one of the exits I suddenly knew that this was the one we had to take. I told the detectives to take the exit, then continued with spirit direction: left here, then right, through the robots (traffic lights) and so on until we arrived at the exact location I had drawn. Even I was surprised at how accurate my drawing had been.

I thought that once I had proved the drawing was from spirit, the police would take me back home as they would be able to deal with the information I had given them regarding the killer in their own time at the police station. However, they wanted more information from me. Closing my eyes, I 'tuned in' to my spirit friends. Within seconds I could see the burial grounds where the bodies of the children were found. I had an awful sick feeling in the pit of my stomach, and my head started to ache. I felt very ill; the more information I received the worse my headache became. I wasn't to know that this would happen every time I received information that took me close to the murderer. I tried to describe the wasteland where I could see sand dunes and bushes, and pointed in the direction where I felt the graves were, including a second area that I could see clairvoyantly. This picture was of a derelict building with what looked like railway lines running along the back of it. I pointed again in its direction, trying to describe the areas of the burial grounds. But all I could see

112

was wasteland made up of dense bushes and sand dunes.

Later I found out this was known as the Weltevredebos area off Vanguard Drive. The other derelict building was adjacent to Eleventh Avenue, backing onto the railway lines just before Lentegeur station. I was again asked to direct the police to the areas I had seen clairvoyantly, and we finally arrived at the derelict building.

I received a strong feeling that several bodies were still missing, and I felt we were near to the place where the police would find them. They were amazed.

'We don't know how you did this, but you are correct. You couldn't possibly have known about this, it's not public knowledge. Well done.' According to them I was 100% correct, right down to my statement that several bodies were still missing.

We all tried hard to find the missing bodies, searching the area without success. I felt very nauseated at the stench of human excreta, and the thought that children could be buried here under the concrete beneath me. From what I could see, the homeless must have frequented this place. There were bits of clothing scattered around, shoes and rubbish dumped everywhere. It did cross my mind that any of these shoes could have belonged to one of the dead boys, and my skin began to crawl at the thought.

The bush area of Mitchell's Plain resembles the remote moorlands of Britain, except for the 90 degree-plus heat and the sand dunes, with their unwelcoming atmosphere. The area is very flat. From what I could see these areas had very nice schools and recreation facilities for children, so naturally they were used by young children playing on their own – an ideal spot for the killer to watch and plan his next abduction.

As soon as we entered this dreadful place of crime and my feet touched the soil, I could feel Mitchell's Plain pulsating with death and evil. I became quite ill, as though all this evil was being absorbed into my whole being like a killer virus. I felt the eyes of people staring, piercing through

113

me. They must have been wondering what a white woman was doing, daring to trespass. I had the feeling that the killer was watching every move I made, knowing why I was there, and he was going to stop me, no matter what.

The area where the bodies were found is characterised by dense shrubs and dunes, with bushes growing on the sand. Cars can go so far, but to get to the places where the bodies were found the killer would have had to approach on foot. These areas are mostly desolate, although some destitute people may frequent them. The bodies were found in shallow graves, some only covered with branches. Rapid decomposition had occurred due to the heat. All of them were lying face down, and some had their faces buried in the sand, which had been swept from under them to structure a raised mound under the buttocks. Some of the boys' hands were tied behind their backs.

Where possible the cause of death was established as strangulation, with the boys' own clothing used as murder weapons. A number of similarities showed that the same person must have been responsible for all the murders: the way the children had disappeared, the murder method, the position and condition in which the bodies were found, the victims' ages, the fact that they could be traced to the same area. All the children had been indecently assaulted. It was strange that there was only one black victim; the rest were all coloured.

Earlier the police had asked me if I could 'pick up' the killer psychically if I found myself close to him. I said I thought I could, and was convinced at the time that I would be able to. It didn't take me long to realise that, with all the vibrations of evil and crime in the area, it would be near impossible to 'pick up' this particular person.

We returned home. I felt very tired, sick and I still had a terrible headache. I was hoping this was the end, and the police would soon find the killer from the information I had given them. I never dreamed for one moment that I would be working alongside them most days for the next few months.

Following my first visit to Mitchell's Plain, the detectives were convinced that I had something to offer the South African Police Department. Spirit helpers and the police never let me rest and I became deeply involved in the case. I was able to see the killer clairvoyantly, in his home sitting in a chair or on the move looking for innocent young boys on the streets of Mitchell's Plain.

I found as soon as I relaxed, I could 'pick up' his thoughts and feelings, and knew when he was anxious to find another victim. I could follow him mentally through the streets of Mitchell's Plain; it was a dreadful experience. The responsibility of knowing where he was at a particular moment had a terrible effect on me. All I could do was try to explain the areas I could see to the police, a very difficult task for me as most of Mitchell's Plain looked the same.

A few days later, at about 4pm, I clairvoyantly saw the 'Strangler'. I rang the police and told DS Khan that I could see the killer parking his car and walking through the bush. I said I knew he would walk for ten to 15 minutes through the bush, and described how he eventually came to a long road where he would look for a victim. I felt very strongly that his back was towards the sea, and hoped this would point DS Khan in the right direction.

The detective arrived at my home within minutes, ushered me into his car and drove me to where he thought I was describing, along the beach road past False Bay and right at the robots towards Mitchell's Plain. Under different circumstances it would have been a lovely drive. The beautiful clean white sands and blue sea, the view of the coastline spreading for miles were breathtaking.

We drove through the streets, hoping I would set eyes on the killer. It was a terrible feeling, not knowing if I would be able to recognise this man, or whether I would be correct if and when I saw him. Even though I have a psychic gift, I am still only human and can make mistakes like anyone else.

115

Finally we turned into Vanguard Street where the main burial grounds were. I later found out the first victim was found in the bushes at False Bay in 1987. I mentally followed the killer's car, taking DS Khan with me, or should I say he took me, following my directions. We arrived at a place called Woodlands, Mitchell's Plain. This was a more select residential area, with some nice expensive houses. Most of the residential parts had bush lands adjacent to and close to the streets.

As we drove I could feel the killer to my left. I asked DS Khan to stop the car. To my surprise this was alongside wasteland and bushes with sand dunes. It was not the burial ground known to the police on Vanguard Street but a little further up the road. We got out of the car to find that there was evidence of fresh tyre tracks and adult and child footprints.

We proceeded to investigate further into the bushes. I knew the strangler was in this area, I could feel him watching us and could 'pick up' his thoughts. The traces of fresh footprints continued through the bush and sand dunes and I thought at last we would be able to catch this madman in the act.

In desperation I ran through the wasteland, crying inside as I fought against time to save a child's life. My mouth was dry with fear, and my heart pounded as we walked and ran for what seemed like an eternity. I knew the killer wasn't far away and was probably watching us from behind a bush. I looked frantically at my watch, wondering how long it would take before he showed himself to us. Eventually, to my disappointment, the detective told me we had to turn back. 'I don't have any back up,' he said.

'Never mind the back up, we can't leave now, we're too close!' I cried.

But it was no use. I fell to the ground crying bitter tears. We had failed. I felt so helpless and ill, and as I walked away I could feel the killer's eyes burning into the back of my head. I knew a child had been killed that day.

The problem with Mitchell's Plain is that, like most places where there is extreme poverty, lots of children are homeless and ramble through the streets alone. Therefore, so many children are not reported missing within the Cape Flatts area and the true total of children who have been killed over the years is anyone's guess. I hope eventually they will all be found and laid to rest.

A total of 22 bodies were found during the period from 1986 to 1994. The names of these poor boys, and how they died are listed at the end of the chapter.

As far as the police are aware there were no further murders until 1992.

Mitchell's Plain is relatively up-market when one looks at the rest of the Cape Flatts area for coloureds and blacks. Cape Flatts, as its name suggests, is a flat area that surrounds Cape Town, and includes all of the black townships such as Kkayelitsha and Cross Roads. These are, I think, the worst areas for people to live in. Most of the houses are made of corrugated iron and some of cardboard boxes. There is no sanitation or running water, with only stand pipes available to collect water.

Driving past, one can see from the main road that the only means of light is candlelight. Therefore, there must be no heating either, and during the winter months it must be very cold for the residents. I have driven past and seen these so-called homes under water after a heavy rainfall. The conditions are worst than most people could imagine and no caring person would allow their pets to live like that. No wonder the crime rate is so rife. Although one cannot condone crime, it is understandable to a degree. These poor souls have to find a way of providing enough income to feed their families. It would be sheer luxury for them to have a proper home with the basics of heating, lighting, sanitation and running water, which most of us take for granted. Things are at last changing since the blacks have taken control of their country, but now it seems there is apartheid in reverse. If you stand on the top of a hill and

117

look around you, you can see these very poor townships stretching for miles.

Some of the children were taken from other places within the Cape Flatts, mostly from the railway stations as this was the only way they travelled back and forth from one black area to another. Several things made life difficult for the police, such as not knowing where the killer was from (although it did look as though the children knew him) Also, they were inundated with calls from the residents of these areas wanting to 'help' with information regarding some unsuspecting character that they thought might be the killer, simply because he looked down and out. Imagine how many poor souls fitted that description and were taken in for questioning when they were perfectly innocent!

Day by day the information given to me by spirit started to fit together like a jigsaw. Eventually it was placed correctly in the right order for evidential reasons only. The more information I gave, the more the police became interested. Most of what I told them, even though it was not to trap the killer, was not public knowledge but relevant to the case. For example, the killer wrote letters to the police colonel and left a trademark, the initials TSB. This was classified information. I took Sergeant Khan to a place where these initials were painted on the walls, and other areas where the killer had been, without knowing at the time that it was significant.

On one of my visits to Mitchell's Plain the police took me to a place where I could get a better view of the whole area. I stood on the top of a hill overlooking Rocklands and the surrounding areas of Mitchell's Plain. What a beautiful sight, just like the rest of the Western Cape. On this particular occasion I was 'drawn' like a magnet to an area just below the Kapteinsklip Railway Station, by the signal box. I was told later the so-called killer had arranged to meet someone at that particular spot. The police set up watch but to their disappointment he never turned up. This was also one of the stations where the strangler had abducted some of his victims.

A few days later when I was at home relaxing I saw the killer again clairvoyantly. He was walking down a long road, and I could see a library nearby. He then turned left; I could see a playing field and children kicking a football. I knew he was there waiting for an unsuspecting boy. I informed Sergeant Khan of what I had just seen; he told me there were lots of areas fitting that description. He asked me if I would go with him to see if I could find the area I had described, and I agreed. After driving around Mitchell's Plain for some time, I began to understand what he meant. Eventually we gave up. I felt as though I was time-wasting and that was the last thing I wanted to do. I felt very inadequate, dreading the thought that perhaps I could have done more to help.

Back home I tried to carry on with my daily routine of cleaning, cooking and writing my book. My work had been neglected, including my church demonstrations and private sittings of clairvoyance. It became embarrassing cancelling my appointments time and time again, so I finally gave up and decided not to book any more appointments.

Every day I found out something new about the killer through my mediumship. It had got to the stage that I dreaded relaxing, as this was the time when pictures of him flooded in. Receiving information clairvoyantly at the exact time he was on the prowl made my quiet moments a nightmare. I was at a loss what to do as the information I received usually came to me in the evening, when my police contacts were off-duty. I needed to be in a police car describing the roads as they were given to me. When I felt his presence, I was clairvoyantly taken in the directions he was moving. I found it impossible to be at home and direct a police car as I needed to see with my physical eyes where I was going.

As I worked most of the time with one particular detective, when he was off duty I had to phone his home with any information I had for him. His wife was not very happy with this arrangement. Since he sometimes worked 16-hour days, and occasionally all through the night, I could understand her annoyance, especially when he had to ring me during the night for my advice on the case.

On a couple of occasions, and without notice, the lieutenant in charge of the case asked me to come in to the caravan to identify a particular suspect. I even saw the post-mortem video of the children who were found, it was sickening. The police had no leads, so I felt duty-bound to help if I could. Who else was there to give information, however insignificant it might have been? I wanted to come off the case, but at the same time I didn't want to let those poor children down. What if another child had died without me at least trying? It didn't bear thinking about.

Time and time again I told the police I'd had enough, especially when I had given information to them and they had not followed it up. Sometimes the excuse was that the computers did not carry that particular information, or that they were 'down'. I felt at times that I was banging my head against a brick wall, as some of the police did not agree with the idea of working with a 'psychic' and only accepted me reluctantly. When I knew the 'station strangler' was on the move again, I wondered what I should do if I couldn't get hold of a detective.

Stephanie and I decided we would investigate ourselves if no one was available. Sometimes we would go into the coloured area of Mitchell's Plain with guns in our handbags. I didn't want to be a nuisance, involving the police when I wasn't sure of a good result. Sometimes I didn't even know the names of roads, as they were not given to me by spirit friends.

To add to the burden, each time I saw the killer 'on the move', the body of a young boy was found shortly afterwards. The frustration almost killed me; I had a constant headache, stomach pains and I became depressed. I wanted to take all the children into my safekeeping and protect them. However hard I tried, I never seemed to prevent a death taking place. My life became a constant nightmare.

On 24 February 1994 I told the police to investigate Prestwich Street, Cape Town. I was given the number 13, though I wasn't sure if this was the number of a building or not. I was afraid for the safety of the street children who lived there. But the police did nothing because I was unable to give them a specific date or time.

Then *The Cape Times* of 1 March 1994 published a small article with the headline 'WOMAN "KIDNAPS" TWO BOYS'. They were abducted from Prestwich Street, Cape Town on 13 January 1994 and had been missing for more than a month. My information had been passed on to the police five days prior to the public announcement that the children were missing, the number 13 being the date when they disappeared. As it happens, I could have done nothing to save those children; I didn't start working on the case until February of that year. I must have received the information that the serial killer was responsible, even though it was stated in the newspaper article that 'a police spokesman said detectives investigating the station strangler have ruled out the possibility that the boys could be victims of the notorious Cape Flatts serial killer.' From the information I received, I certainly beg to differ.

One day Sergeant Khan asked me if I would give sittings to the victims' relatives, to find out if the boys would give any information about their murderer through clairvoyance. I was happy to oblige. Even if Sergeant Khan did not get what he wanted, at least I might be able to bring some comfort to the boys' families.

The first home I visited was the home of nine-year-old Marchelino from Eastridge, Mitchell's Plain. His body was so badly decomposed that the head had detached from the body. He was found fully clothed, and due to the advanced state of decomposition it was impossible to tell if he had been sodomised. He was last seen alive at a game parlour in Mitchell's Plain Shopping Centre on 20 December 1993.

I had never entered a coloured or black person's home

121

before, so I didn't know what to expect. We were invited into Marchelino's home, and to my surprise it was immaculate, despite the poverty of the area. The attractive furniture and ornaments were highly polished; in fact the whole house was spotless. The family greeted me rather awkwardly. Even though the police had tried explaining to them what I did, they still had no idea what was going to happen. All they knew was that I was a medium trying to help the police catch their son's killer.

After I had talked to them and Sergeant Khan had explained, with his limited knowledge, about spiritualism, they agreed I should stay. I thought it best to start my sitting by giving information and proof of survival after death from their dead relatives. This I proceeded to do with success. Marchelino's mother had now become more relaxed, so I continued with information from her dead son.

'Marchelino tells me that he broke his toe just before he died.'

'That's right, he broke his big toe not long before he was murdered,' she said in surprise.

'He is also talking to me about a brooch he bought for you, not too long ago.'

'Yes he did.' She went on to tell me about the brooch, believing by then that I was able to link with her son. Marchelino went on to describe the place he was taken to before he was killed. The worst part of the sitting happened when he took me through his murder, and I actually felt the death process as he had suffered it. By this time tears were rolling down my face but I continued, with his parents' permission.

My second sitting was in a very poor area in Woodlands. As we drove up to the tiny house, all the neighbours were outside, wondering what was going on. I had a very bad feeling about this place, unlike the time when I visited Marchelino's home. I felt as though the station strangler was watching me. The state of the run-down houses and cars was enough to put anyone off. It definitely looked like a place that bred crime and violence. I reluctantly got out of the car and was quickly ushered into the victim's house by the police, who seemed to occupy every inch of the downstairs and staircase. The room was very sparse, like a ground-level cellar with a stone floor and stairs, and cushions placed on the floor and settee, which looked more like a park bench. The mother of the 13-year-old victim, Neville, could not speak English so a detective explained to her what I was about to do. She agreed and sat down next to me.

Neville had gone missing from Woodlands, Mitchell's Plain on 1 January 1994. He was found fully clothed, lying on his back, and had been strangled with a nylon cord. The same cord had been used to tie his hands behind his back. His underpants were lying nearby and he had been sodomised.

I started the sitting as before, first giving information from the boy's relatives who were now in the spirit world. I told Neville's mother about her own mother, who had passed from a heart attack, and described her. I went on to describe her husband who had died from diabetes and had a stomach condition. She confirmed all of this.

Neville then took over. He described the clothes the killer was wearing, how he was killed, and said he knew the killer as he had seen him at school. 'Everybody knows him,' he told me.

Before the sitting ended, Neville told his mother that he was happy and was with his family. He also explained he was with the other boys who had died, and went on to say in Afrikaans: 'I love you.' I asked the police if what I had said made sense, as I could not speak or understand that language. They confirmed it did make sense. Neville talked about other children this man had killed whom the police had no knowledge of. Like Marchelino, he gave directions as to where his killer had taken him.

After giving my condolences and a hug to Neville's

mother, we left and set off with a long stream of police cars, trying to find the house from Neville's directions. By this time it was very dark and too difficult to see the 'tower' described by Neville, so we abandoned the exercise until another day. Since that evening Neville has told me clairaudiantly about a bike he either got or wanted for Christmas – a little more evidence for his mum.

I came home that night a little disappointed, even though the sitting had gone well. I had hoped we would have been able to find the killer's house from the directions the boys had given us.

During the time I spent on the case I gave the police the killer's name and what I thought he did for a living. I also gave them a registration number of the car he was driving: CA 73-9. I was told later this was a very old number, and the computer could not go back that far. I was desperate to find this maniac; so many poor children had already lost their lives and I wanted to prevent further tragedies.

On 27 October 1992 the body of an 11-year-old boy, later identified as Jacobus from Beacon Valley, Mitchell's Plain, was found in the bush near Mnandi Beach, Mitchell's Plain. The cause of death was strangulation. He was last seen alive on 23 October 1992 at the town centre, Mitchell's Plain.

There seems to be a gap of two years before the strangler struck again.

There were several bodies found on the Weltevreden Bush known as the strangler's 'burial ground'. This is next to Weltevreden Road, and also near Vanguard Drive, Mitchell's Plain. They were all found in January 1994 when the murderer must have gone on a killing spree.

Detective Sergeant Khan approached me one day and said he would like to 'sit in' on one of my clairvoyant evenings. He was not sure how I worked, or how I received information from spirit. On 26 February 1994 I phoned him and invited him to my home so he could ask questions directly from my spirit guide while I was in a trance state.

It was nine o'clock in the evening by the time we started our meditation and soon Anna my guide came through. 'The man you are looking for has two children with him at the moment, and a child will join me tonight.'

'Where is he, can you describe the area?' Sergeant Khan asked, sounding distressed.

'I can see him in an old disused factory made of concrete – a concrete factory perhaps. Opposite this building is bush land and the factory is on the main road. He will take a child's life.'

'What else can you see? Please describe it to me.'

'The sign on the factory is green, the vehicles were green when in use,' Anna continued.

Sergeant Khan said, 'I know exactly the place you're describing. Can you tell me more?'

'He is driving a cream and blue combi [a large van].'

At 9.20 Sergeant Khan interrupted the trance sitting and got on the phone to ask for back-up. I was still in a light trance state when he asked me to come and direct him to the place I had seen. Naturally I agreed, hoping we would catch the killer. All hell had broken out at this new information, and my feet hardly touched the ground. There was radio contact with the police at Mitchell's Plain as we drove through Somerset West down the N2 towards the factory.

Racing down the roads was a hair-raising experience. We swerved in and out of traffic, driving through red lights onto the motorway. Most of the time I was in a sort of dream state, trying hard to stay 'tuned in' to spirit. I had to continue the best I could giving clairvoyance as I received it: describing what the killer was doing and where he was going. It was difficult for me to remain 'tuned in' to spirit for such a long time. I opened my eyes only a couple of times during the journey, closing them quickly again because of the speed in which we were travelling.

We finally arrived at Mitchell's Plain in one piece at

about ten o'clock. The uniformed police were already waiting for us on the corner of the main road near the disused factory. I was exhausted from trying to retain the link I had with spirit, but the thought of bringing about the arrest of this madman kept me going.

We had arrived at the exact place I had described to the police while in my semi-trance state. My head and chest hurt, and I began to feel faint, worried I might lose my clairvoyant pictures. I rushed out of the car, running across the road towards the bushes shouting, 'Hurry up, he's here in the bushes.'

The police followed me and had begun searching the area when suddenly my spirit guide told me we were on the wrong side of the road. We immediately ran across the road, through the unlocked gates of the factory, and around the back of the building. By this time I was panting and puffing, feeling very weak at the knees.

When I had first arrived on the scene I couldn't see the bushy area behind the building, so we searched in the wrong place. This wasted a lot of valuable time, but I am only human, I had made a mistake.

When we reached the bushes a policewoman said to me, 'Look, there are fresh tyre tracks and footprints. See, this is a man's footprint and there's the print of a small child leading into the bush'.

Sergeant Khan, the policewoman and I followed the tracks. The policewoman kept saying, 'Oh my God, look at the tracks!' as she held my hand. She looked very upset.

'Hurry, he's about to get into his van and drive off!' I screamed, relaying the information from spirit.

As we reached the top of the hill I pointed to the road below. A van was moving off at great speed, and it was impossible to reach it from where we were standing. So the policewoman called on the radio for back-up to go in the direction of the van, giving them a street name.

Radio contact between the police continued throughout the next few hours. They spoke in Afrikaans to each other, so I wasn't sure if what I was telling them was correctly translated. And they had difficulty understanding my Yorkshire accent, though Sergeant Khan had got used to it as we had been working together for quite some time by then.

We jumped into the sergeant's car and set off again at speed, other police cars following close behind. We had only travelled about a mile when the car broke down. The atmosphere was very tense and I was devastated, as time was vital if we were to apprehend the killer. When Sergeant Khan managed to find someone who could understand what I was saying, I was transferred to another car, leaving a disappointed sergeant behind with his vehicle.

I suddenly felt lost and alone in a car with strangers. These plain-clothed policemen didn't know who I was or what I was trying to do, which made things even more difficult than they already were. All I could do was make the best of a bad situation. I tried to direct them through the streets of Mitchell's Plain, following the pictures given to me by spirit. They looked at me very strangely as I sat there with my eyes closed, describing buildings and road signs. I must have looked pretty silly to them, and they must have thought: how can this woman see with her eyes shut?

'Are you psychic?' asked the driver.

'Yes I am,' I said very abruptly. I thought this had been explained to the men when I changed cars. 'I can see the van parked up.'

'Where, where?' the driver asked.

I screamed, 'Oh no, please God, don't let him do this!' I turned to the detectives. 'He knows you're after him, and he doesn't seem to care. I can see the word "something-lands".

'Woodlands, Rocklands? Which?' I didn't know.

'Can you see this place?'

'Yes.' The driver asked me to describe it as we headed down the road. I tried the best I could.

We set off for Woodlands, as this was nearer to where we were at the time. But when we got there I knew this was not the place.

'Describe it to me again,' said the driver.

'There's a school and behind the school is a narrow dirt road, which is where he's parked. The school is next to a shopping complex with a parking area.'

'Right, I think I know where it is. Keep talking to me.'

I went on to describe how I was in the van with the killer now. 'Oh God, one child is already dead. Please don't hurt that boy! Oh no, no, he's going to kill the other boy! He's putting a cord around his neck, he's twisting the cord and pulling the child towards him. Please God, don't let this happen. Hurry, hurry, it's going to be too late. Oh my God! Oh my God, he's murdered him!' I sobbed, my heart breaking. We were too late.

For some reason I had to experience this terrible deed, yet I could do nothing to stop it. That will be imprinted on my mind for the rest of my life, a real living hell.

'He's turned on the van lights and he's setting off again,' I sobbed.

'Tell me where he is,' the driver asked.

I was in a bad way, tears were running down my face and I couldn't think straight.

'He's passing a building for animals, an animal home or clinic. It's on the right-hand side of the road; he's approaching a set of robots. He's going through and I know he's going to turn left at the next set of lights. Can you place this, and would the road lead onto the N2 motorway?'

'Yes it would and yes, there is a veterinary surgery on the right,' the driver said, as he proceeded to inform the police ahead by radio. Yes, they could see a van answering that description, a voice on the other end of the radio said.

I was having great difficulty remaining 'tuned in' to spirit. It was hours now since I had first set off with Detective Khan. The pictures were fading, and I was feeling

128

terribly ill. My chest was tight, and my head and stomach hurt badly. I had set off on the 'chase' with a chest infection and had received medication that day from my doctor. As we drove out of Mitchell's Plain following spirit direction, the ordeal of the night's activities were having an awful effect on me.

'I can see the motorway, he's crossing over the road, a bridge. I can see a railway line to the right of the road, he's heading for Kuils River,' I explained.

All this time the uniformed police were wonderful, getting us through the traffic, escorting us down the N2 motorway. I had my eyes closed, trying desperately to follow this killer mentally.

'I'm losing him, I'm losing him,' I kept on telling the driver. 'Please hurry.' I opened my eyes. 'What the hell are you doing? I said Kuils River, not Cape Town.' I could see the signs for Cape Town and the city lights were just ahead in the distance. I felt sick at this lack of understanding, the difficulty in communicating with the officer. Sergeant Khan would have understood. I was losing my concentration now, and feared the worst.

'Kuils River?'

'Yes! I snapped at him.

He picked up the radio and asked permission to take a U-turn across the motorway. By this time we were 15 minutes away from Kuils River and time was against us. We sped back up the motorway in the direction we had just come. Incredibly, the motorway police tried to flag us down for speeding and our driver had to get on the radio to ask the speed cops to leave us alone.

We finally arrived at Kuils River, where the Kuils River police were waiting at the roadside for us. I could see the murderer in his van, turning left by a church on the main road going into Kuils River. He was driving around the back of the church, now taking a right turn and then a left. Then I lost him.

In Afrikaans my driver spoke to the Kuils River police,

who didn't know who I was either, or what I was doing.

'They tell me that there is no church on the roadside,' my driver told me.

I opened the car door and said to the police, 'Yes there is, you're wrong. I'm positive, it's set back from the road. It's a stone church with grass in front, and a fence around the grounds. It's on the main road,' I insisted.

'No, no I can't place a church like that. There is one on the other side of the road, but it's not like the one you've described,' the policeman said.

But I knew I was not wrong, I could see this church as clear as day.' How stupid they must be, I thought as they talked and laughed among themselves in Afrikaans. I was wondering what they were saying – possibly some rude remarks about me.

One of the policemen said suddenly, 'Look, there is a church like that, it's just here on the left.' He poked his head into the car and said, 'Turn left at the next set of robots.'

True enough, 100 yards further down the road was the church I had described. I was furious and had now lost contact with the station strangler. But having come this far, I was not prepared to give up. At least we could try to find the killer's vehicle parked up somewhere.

Following the directions I'd seen earlier, we turned left behind the church, then right, but there were no signs of the van anywhere. We drove around for some time without success; finally we gave up, and headed back to Mitchell's Plain. The occupants of our car sat in silence as we drove back. I felt numb, to say the least.

We pulled into Mitchell's Plain police station at around one o'clock in the morning. As I got out of the car the driver said. 'Thank you for your efforts, Detective Sergeant Khan is over there in the caravan.'

As I walked towards the caravan I could see the look on Sergeant Khan's face – a desperate, disappointed look. I couldn't see any tears, but they were there. He said to me, 'Never mind, Barbara, you did your best. I was with you all the way, listening on the radio. We'll get him another time. You look terribly ill, but would you mind if we went back to Kuils River and tried one last time tonight to find him?'

My heart sank as I heard those words. I was exhausted and could have cried; all I wanted to do was go home to bed. After all, I had been on the road a long time and I was feeling very feverish. But I could see that this poor man was totally devastated, so though I was dehydrated and felt terrible, I couldn't say no.

We set off once again for Kuils River, but had no more success.

One week later, on a Saturday afternoon, a young boy called Alroy was found murdered in dense bushes at Kleinvlei, Eerst River, behind the Kleinvlei Cemetery – about 3 km from where I had taken the police on that terrible night, and where the chase had ended. Alroy had gone missing one week earlier from the Strand Railway Station near where I lived in Somerset West.

It is believed that the murders of 1987, 1992 and 1994 were committed by the same man. The previous sets of murders remain unsolved, and previous suspects were brought in once again for questioning by the police.

The 1994 bodies were found by wood-hackers. Thousands of uniformed police were brought in to search the bushes for more bodies. The community set up a neighbourhood watch, and also hacked out the bushes in one of the areas. This particular area happened to be a nature reserve. The community had become hysterical and any suspicious character was chased through the veldt. Some members believe that the strangler used underground drainpipes to come in and out of the area without being seen. The community had already searched the pipes for more bodies, and the person leading the search was even regarded as a suspect. The people burnt cars, besieged houses and police stations if they suspected that the killer was there.

131

The victims would have been easily lured by the promise of food, money or a ride. From the facts, it seems the boys went voluntarily with the strangler, which also gives rise to the theory that he was disguised as someone in authority whom they knew and trusted: a social worker, priest or teacher.

For example, a lot of so-called social workers often took food to the school children, so such a person would immediately have an audience of hundreds of children who would know him as a man who brought them food. The next day he could have approached his victim, who would willingly accompany him, since this man had given him food the previous day.

The extended family environment in South Africa means that a boy may inform his mother, whom he usually lives with, that he wishes to live with his grandmother for a while. The mother will allow the boy to go to the grandmother's house without later checking if he has arrived safely. It is not strange for boys to be absent from home for a few nights; their mothers assume they are visiting friends or relatives. Boys hang out in video game parlours, often travel by train alone or sometimes assist owners by washing taxis and then riding along. These children can be out at all hours of the night.

Since the killing fields are so desolate, this killer could spend plenty of time with his victim without being found. He might also have had an accomplice who could warn him or restrain the children. This was the case, according to one of the victims, who appeared when I gave a sitting to his mother. He confirmed that another person was in the vicinity while he was being murdered.

Once it became public knowledge that a serial killer was on the loose, the killings became less frequent. However, during December 1993 and January 1994 the killings escalated to one every few days. To my knowledge very few lives were taken in February. However, the station Strangler did threaten that another 14 boys would be killed.

I think this killer was or is very organised. He took no weapons and left behind no clues such as fingerprints. There seems to be no motive, no connection between the boys, except for race, sex and age. They are not all from the same school or religion; the only connection could be that the children remind him of the boy he used to be. One motive could be that he himself was sexually assaulted and this was his revenge upon the community. Sexual fantasies could also have played a role in motivation. The killer must have expected at least one of the victims to be found as he left a note in the child's pocket for the police, inviting them to participate in his own game.

Since I arrived back in Britain in June 1994, several other boys have been murdered. The headline of a report in *The Cape Times* dated 19 July read: 'BOY'S NAKED BODY FOUND IN CITY QUARRY.' Another boy, about 12 years old, had been found dead, this time in the Bo-Kaap. His partially naked body, found on a rubbish dump in the old quarry near the intersection of Strand and Buitengracht Streets, had not been identified. His blue jersey was wound tightly around his neck and his blue tracksuit pants had been pulled down. It was not yet known whether he had been sodomised. He was not wearing a shirt or shoes, and a mattress had been dumped on the lower part of his body. Police were investigating the strong likelihood that the boy had been murdered, but had not ruled out the possibility that he may have died of exposure. A post-mortem was to be conducted to determine the cause of death. A police spokesman said police were investigating the possibility, amongst others, that the death was linked to the station strangler dossier.

If it were found that the boy was strangled and sodomised, it would bring the number of boys found killed in this way in the Peninsular since 1986 up to 22.

At the time of this boy's death, the police had in custody a suspect for the serial killings. This man has now been charged with the murder of one of the boys and been found

133

guilty. He has not been charged with the other murders.

Two years later, I was back in England when, quite out of the blue, I received a phone call from South Africa.

'Hello, Barbara, this is Detective Inspector Khan, Cape Town.' He had been promoted a couple of months earlier. I congratulated him, and he went on: 'Remember the station strangler case?' How could I forget it? 'We've uncovered several bodies of the boys you told us about, the boys you said were buried underneath concrete. You were right. I just thought you'd like to know. It makes me wonder how much more of the information you gave us will eventually prove to be correct.'

I have not been able to give all the details of the case, because in my opinion, for what it's worth, the station strangler is still out there.

A total of 22 bodies were found from the period 1986 to 1994. The first boy, Jonathan, was from Elsies River, 15 to 20 km outside of Mitchell's Plain, but within the Cape Flatts area. He was 14 years old, and was found on 3 October 1986 between the University of Western Cape and the Modderdam Railway Station, Belhar. His body was found fully clothed in the attire he was last seen in, and his hands were tied behind his back. He was last seen alive on 30 September 1986 at Bonteheuwel Railway Station. When the body was discovered it was partly decomposed.

The second boy was called Yusaf, he was also 14 and was found in a bush next to Spine Road, Rocklands, Mitchell's Plain on 7 January 1987. Yusaf also came from Elsies River, Cape Flatts. He was dressed only in a pair of dark blue pants, and there were signs of strangulation. Neither the cause of death or whether he had been sodomised could be established, as his body was badly decomposed. His hands were tied behind his back with a blue rag, and he was lying on his stomach with his face in the sand. He was last seen alive on 29 December 1986 at the Kapteinsklip Railway Station, Mitchell's Plain.

134

On 23 January 1987 the body of a 13-year-old boy was discovered in the bushes near Serepta, Kuils River, Cape Flatts, next to the R300 highway. Dressed in shorts and a T-shirt, the boy was found on his stomach with his face buried in the sand. Due to the advanced state of decomposition, it could not be established whether his hands were tied, if he had been sodomised, or how he had died. He was later identified as Mario, from Manenburg was.

On 9 April 1987 the body of a 14-year-old boy was found in the bush near Modderdam Railway Station, Belhar. He was also found lying on his stomach with his head in the sand, and had died of strangulation while being assaulted. He had suffered a stab wound to the left of his neck, and his hands were tied behind his back with his own belt. He was fully clothed, although his pants had been lowered. His identity is unknown.

In the bushes close to Belhar Railway Station, Freddie was found on 26 June 1987. He was 12 years old, another victim from Elsies River. The cause of death was established as strangulation. He was lying on his back with his hands tied behind him with his own pullover. He was wearing shorts that had been pulled down slightly and had been strangled with his T-shirt, part of which had been forced down his throat. He had been sodomised, and was last seen alive on 25 June 1987 at Belhar Railway Station.

Samuel's body was found on 25 August 1987 in the bushes near Belhar Railway Station. He was from Nyanga East. Samuel was found lying on his stomach with his face in the sand, and he was fully clothed. His left shoe and sock had been removed, and his hands were tied behind his back with his own pullover. He had been strangled with his own tie and had been sodomised. He was last seen alive on 24 August 1987 when he got into a car in Modderdam Road, Bishop Lavis. The driver of the car remains unidentified.

The seventh child's body was found on 1 October 1987.

He was about 14 years old and was found in the bushes between the University of the Western Cape and Modderdam Railway Station. The cause of death could not be determined due to the advanced state of decomposition. He has not been identified.

Nine-year-old Calvin from Belhar was found on February 1988 in the bush near Unibel Railway Station, Belhar. He was lying on his stomach with his hands tied behind his back with his own pullover. He was fully dressed, although part of his shirt had been torn off and used to strangle him. He was last seen alive on 5 February 1988 when he left his home to go to the station.

On 11 November 1989 the body of 11-year-old Denver from Athlone was found in the bushes near Sarepta Railway Station, Bellville South. This is also within the Cape Flatts area. Denver was last seen alive on 28 March 1989, and due to the advanced state of decomposition the cause of his death could not be ascertained.

On 13 January 1994, a boy was found lying on his stomach, dead from strangulation. Because of the advanced state of decomposition it is impossible to tell if he had been sodomised. He has never been identified.

On 20 January that same year, the body of an 11-year-old boy by the name of Elino from Lenteguer, Mitchell's Plain, was found. He was lying on his stomach, face downwards in the sand. His T-shirt was around his neck and he was still wearing his pants, which had a big tear or cut in the seat. His underpants were found close to him. Sodomy is suspected. This boy's hands were not tied. He was last seen at a video and games parlour at Lenteguer Shopping Centre, Mitchell's Plain.

Two young boys' bodies were found on 25 January, about 20 metres apart. One of the boys was identified as Donovan, ten, from Beacon Valley, Mitchell's Plain. The cause of death was established as strangulation and assault. He was lying on his stomach with his hands tied behind his back; his pants and underpants had been removed. He had suffered a fracture to the skull and was last seen alive on 11 January 1994.

The other boy was identified as 12-year-old Jeremy from Westridge, Mitchell's Plain. His hands were tied behind his back with his shirt, his pants, underpants and shoes had been removed. He was last seen alive on his way to the shopping centre in Westridge on 1 December 1993. A penknife was found next to his body. Both bodies were badly decomposed, making it impossible to ascertain if Jeremy had been sodomised.

On 26 January the body of 13-year-old Jeremy from Rocklands, Mitchell's Plain was found. He was covered with branches and was lying on his stomach with his face in the sand. He had been sodomised and strangled with the cord of his pants. His ear was severed and the reason for this is unknown. The cause of death was established as strangulation and assault. He was last seen alive on 24 January when he went to Mitchell's Plain Railway Station to meet someone.

In January 1994 the bodies of a further six young boys were found in the bush near Weltevreden Road, Mitchell's Plain. The badly decomposed body of an unidentified boy was found wearing only a shirt. His hands were not tied. Grey pants, presumably part of a school uniform, were found next to the body. In the right pocket a note was written in pencil in English: 'Many more in store'. On the back of the note was written: NR 14 Station Strangler, then a sign and a face were drawn. A set of upper dentures was found next to the body, owner not known.

Nine-year-old Marchelino from East Ridge, Mitchell's Plain, whom I have already spoken of, was another of these six victims.

The body of an unidentified boy was found wearing only his pants. His underpants were found close to him. He was face down, his hands were untied and he had been strangled with his pullover.

Two bodies were found lying close to each other, and

both boys were found lying on their stomachs with their hands tied behind their backs and their pants removed. Both had been sodomised. One boy was identified as eight-year-old Fabian from Lentegeur, Mitchell's Plain. The other was 11-year-old Owen from Heideveld, who was visiting Fabian at the time. Fabian's underpants were used to strangle Owen, and Fabian was strangled with Owen's undervest. They were last seen alive on 1 January on their way to Lentegeur Railway Station to take a train to Heideveld. Fabian had a neighbour's phone number written on a piece of paper in his pocket; he was supposed to phone them when he and Owen reached their destination. They never did, and it is not known if they ever even got on the train.

An unknown boy of about 14, fully clothed and lying on his back, was found strangled with a nylon cord. The same cord had been used to tie his hands behind his back. His underpants were lying nearby and he had been sodomised. The boy was identified later as Neville, last seen alive on 7 January 1994.

Perhaps the station strangler was possessed by a discarnate entity that drove him to carry out these atrocities. There are such inferior spirits who are obsessed with having a hold over certain human beings, always working to keep them under their power.

Spirit people on a higher plane of existence have no desire to use such influence. They are content to give good advice and speak only the truth. They continually fight the evil influence of spirits in the lower realms. If we ignore these lower entities they will eventually leave us alone.

Very rarely, bad spirits do attach themselves to human beings and obtain a hold over them, blending with their spirit and therefore influencing that person against their will. The preoccupied spirit is able to restrain and have an effect over that person, ruling their lives, preventing the medium from communicating with other spirit friends, pretending to be a loved one and substituting itself for the loved one who is near, giving false information.

Because mediums are open to spirit influence they must be extra careful that an inferior spirit does not impose itself upon them. Early in their development, inexperienced mediums can be deceived and lied to, because they leave themselves wide open to such lies. That doesn't mean to say that the medium is possessed by this type of spirit person, as most mediums at some point in their mediumistic careers go through some kind of test by inferior spirits. A medium may be deceived without being possessed; possession consists of the hold of the person that has been taken by the spirit, making it difficult or impossible to get rid of that spirit person.

Usually a medium is aware that they have a spirit who is trying to deceive them, as it doesn't try to conceal its evil intentions. The medium can generally recognise the deceit, and is always on guard against deceptive spirit entities. This sort of person is disagreeable and inconvenient, to say the least, obstructing communications from loving spirit friends and relatives who wish to give messages to their loved ones on the earth plane.

In some cases the bad spirits annoy and try to frighten us with sounds of blows and other noises, but a more serious case of evil intent is direct action of a spirit on a medium's thoughts, which can paralyse the judgement with regard to the communication they receive. The problem with this is that a medium cannot believe they are being deceived, as the spirit inspires the medium with confidence that the information is from their guides and helpers. Intellectual and educated people are not exempt from this. The bad spirit leads his victims along as though they were blind, making them accept the most ridiculous statements and theories as truth, and in some cases getting them to undertake dangerous actions.

Spirit people are not created for evil or to perform evil acts. They exist at different levels of advancement and can improve themselves when they are ready. This type of spirit possession is one of the worst stumbling blocks a medium has to overcome, so we must do our utmost to be aware and combat it. Therefore, every communication transmitted by a possessed medium is impaired and undeserving of confidence.

There are several ways to recognise the existence of this kind of possessed medium. The spirit has control and persists in communicating, whether it is wanted or not, and its persistence prevents other spirit beings from communicating with the medium. The spirit can also deceive the medium by preventing them from seeing the falseness and absurdity of the communications they are receiving, making them believe in the absolute identity and infallibility of the communicator, who pretends to be a highly respected spirit. These bad spirits use famous, venerated names and give false and ridiculous information.

An example of this type of possession was when a spirit was wooing a young woman. She came to see me, wanting to join one of my development circles and told me about the automatic writing she was doing with great enthusiasm. She told me the controlling spirit told her he was in love with her, and in a previous life they were husband and wife living in France. She believed everything he told her, and was taken in by his lies. Following lengthy discussions with this entity I started to challenge him regarding his past life with this lady. For a while he tried to convince me that he was genuine but when questioned he was unable to give me satisfactory or correct answers. When he realised he had been found out he became very angry, saying he would never let the young woman communicate with any other spirit beings, or allow her to come to my development circle. By this time she had grown to love this being and was not prepared to let me send him away.

We must always consider the dangers, but do not be put off. It is not a misfortune to be a medium but a wonderful experience; it is not this faculty which makes possession possible. Neither mediums nor spiritualism created spirit or the spirit world; it is spirit who has made both spiritualism and mediums. Spirit beings are only souls of men and women, and have existed as long as souls of men and women have existed. The mediumistic faculty is for spirits to use to manifest themselves and bring messages of love and knowledge to those of us in this world. It would therefore be an error to suppose that spirits only influence us through verbal, written or other manifestations. Their influence upon us is continual and those who do not work with spirit people or do not even believe in their existence are still exposed to their influence, just as we are.

Being a medium gives us the means of assuring ourselves of the nature and character of the spirits who act upon us, understanding their motives and repelling them if they prove to be from the lower realms. Possession can sometimes be vengeance exercised on someone, who may have wronged spirit during their last earthly life or other previous existence. It could be that a spirit suffered and enjoys making others suffer by tormenting them in this way.

There are some spirits who persecute you through sheer hatred and jealousy of what is good and attach themselves like limpets. Other bad spirits like to take advantage of weakness in a person they know is incapable of resisting them.

Those who play with ouija boards or glass and alphabet are opening the door to these spirits, just as if they left their houses open, letting anyone come in, good or bad.

Book Two

Chapter Ten

What Is A Medium?

There is a difference between a psychic and a medium. Unfortunately it seems that most people group us all together and call us all clairvoyants. Therefore, I feel that it is time that the difference is explained.

A psychic is an individual who is sufficiently sensitive to react to psychic influences around them from the energy of places and people. Those who are sensitive learn to 'sense' people's reactions to a more refined extent than normal. The brain then learns to 'interpret' the signals of information and vibrational waves of energy, which are then impressed on their mind, their normal consciousness. The psychic is not necessarily a medium, although every medium is a psychic.

As you may already know, everything vibrates, and the psychic receives or draws his information from the *living* vibrations of energy around him, at earthly levels. Whereas the medium, unconsciously in the beginning, and later deliberately, adjusts his level of consciousness, paying acute attention mentally to higher, faster vibrations of energy. By doing this, he receives information from sources outside the normal communication levels used by humankind. He is a far more highly sensitive individual, whose heightened sense of awareness can be used to form links between the dead and the living.

The methods used are many and various. It is like tuning from MW to VHF on a radio tuner. The medium changes his mental consciousness frequency so that, when attuned, communication received from the spirit world can be passed on verbally. The medium then becomes a receiving transmitting station. But he has to learn how to control the frequency, vibrations in use in order to maintain control of any possible 'atmospheric' interference of any kind.

The beings that communicate with you are called spirits, which are the souls of men and women who have lived upon the Earth. They make up the spirit world, as we do during our Earthly life. The spirit world is the normal, eternal world surviving everything else. It is where we came from and where we will return on our death.

The corporeal world (the Earth plane) is secondary. There are different species of Earth life but God chose human beings for the incarnation of spirits that have arrived at a certain degree of development. Their morality and intelligence are superior to all other species'.

Spirits belong to different classes and are not equal to one another either in power, intelligence, knowledge or morality. Spirits of the highest order are distinguished from those below them by superior purity and knowledge. They are all goodness. Angels, for example, are pure spirits. The other classes are more distant from this perfection; those of the lower ranks are inclined to most of our passions, hatred, envy, jealousy, pride, etc; they take pleasure in evil. Among them are some who are neither very good nor very bad, and can be troublesome rather than malicious, often mischievous and unreasonable and may be classed as foolish spirits.

We are all destined to attain perfection by learning and passing through different layers of the spirit hierarchy. This is effected by reincarnation. How fast we attain this depends on what we learn in this life on Earth. When we leave this world and quit our bodies, the soul returns to the world of spirits from where it came, and will re-enter upon a new material life, after a longer or shorter period of time. Reincarnation is not possible in animals.

Spirit beings that are not reincarnated do not occupy any specific region. They are everywhere – in space, around us, seeing us, mixing with us in an invisible world as tangible to them as our world is to us.

143

Good spirits lead us onto the right road and sustain us when we are experiencing trials in life. The bad try to tempt us to evil acts.

Spirits are attracted to us by their sympathy to our moral quality. Superior spirits take pleasure in meeting us by the love of all that is good and the desire to improve us. Their presence of light and love repels the spirits of those who are at an inferior stage of development.

Our spirit body radiates in all directions and can hold communications with other spirits, which they warm to and are in sympathy with. The soul is an incarnated spirit that inhabits a material body, this being the envelope, the clothing.

There are three things in man:

1) A body, or material being, animated by

2) A soul, or immaterial being, a spirit residing in a body.

3) A link that unites the soul with the body is known as an intermediary, that joins matter with spirit. This is called the perispirit, the 'ethereal body', that unites the body and the spirit, a sort of semi-material envelope. (I have explained this in more detail in the section on auras) This is invisible to us in its normal state but can be visible occasionally, and tangible in the case of apparitions (explained in more detail in the section on physical phenomena)

Eg Man has two natures:

1) He has the instincts and nature of animals.

2) His soul participates in the nature of spirits.

We are human beings with a brain, a mind, and over the years we have created our own characteristics, habits, desires and ideas. These are so vital that they rule the way in which we think and behave.

It's not easy meditating or linking with spirit, because most of us are lazy, allowing our minds to take the line of least resistance. We can't be bothered to force a new line of thought. We look for the easiest way. Most individuals find it very difficult, as the mind wanders back to all the problems

144

of everyday life. But with patience and careful training, the mind can be diverted so that whenever an idea is suggested, it will respond and dismiss all negative thinking.

A medium is really a telephone line: the clearer the line the clearer the communication. If you want to become a medium you will need to work very hard to achieve the clarity that is required. I always tell my development class to be patient. This applies to all types of mediumistic faculties: good mediumship has to be worked for.

There is nothing worse than having to listen to 'inspired' speakers giving long drawn out, poor quality messages of little substance. Excellence is what you should aspire to; this is essential to good public speaking. What a pity that there are very few good mediums. This can only be corrected in one way, and that is to improve your mind by increasing your learning, not rushing onto the platform before you are ready.

When you start your mediumistic training you will soon be aware of spirit helpers around you. Your control, the general communicator, is the most common type. He or she is there to pass on information and impressions first obtained from the sitter's dead relatives and friends, then they pass this on to the recipient through your mediumship. They do this because they are familiar with the process of working with you. This enables them to do a better job than the relatives can do for themselves. Their role is limited but specialised, giving evidence on behalf of those unable to communicate satisfactorily by themselves. Their duty is to make sure order prevails during the communication process. Those who have recently passed to the next world give excellent evidence of who they are, proving they are the close relatives of Mr and Mrs so and so.

Guides have a different role, much wider than that of the general control. They bring spiritual wisdom, and are wonderful teachers of importance. Their mediumistic presentation is excellent and in no way limited. They work behind the scenes of every human being, linking with each individual.

It's amazing when you think that they possess a spiritual plan or pattern for you, assisting you to fulfil your own spiritual opportunities within this plan, enabling you to carry out on the earth plane the tasks that you came here to do. They have insight into your character, and with their advanced knowledge the guides occasionally discuss your future, though this does not necessarily intimate prophecy. The insight of a guide to his charge does at times seem to extend a little into his or her future. If you, the medium, are aware of this, it gradually prepares you for heavy duties ahead, which you might otherwise find yourself most unwilling to face. Helping you with a challenge or entanglement, which normally would put stress upon you.

Working with the guides is a long-term process, very rarely consisting of specific instructions to act in this way or that, but gently guiding you and gradually widening and deepening your consciousness. A responsible guide will always respect the free will of his medium, never imposing his beliefs upon you or making you dependent upon him.

There are various types of mediums: clairvoyants, clairaudients, sensitives or impressionables, trance and physical mediums.

A clairvoyant is a person who is endowed with the gift of 'second sight', the faculty of seeing spirit even when perfectly awake. 'Seeing' mediums see with their soul, their spirit eyes, and can see just as well with their eyes closed as open.

This form of mediumship has been and still is practised more than any other form of supernatural power in many countries throughout the world; it has been proved to spiritualists and psychical investigators that human beings do survive bodily death. Clairvoyance is the most popular current method of communicating with those who have gone on to the next life. Thank goodness it is not quite so frowned upon these days as it once was. Even so, in this modern day and age there are some that think we are devil worshippers, which is quite ridiculous. Many years ago, clairvoyant mediums would have been burned at the stake as witches and it's only recently that the witchcraft act has been changed, otherwise who knows what would have become of people like me!

Contrary to what some people think, we do not see spirit people as 'ghosts' with our physical eyes. We see them with our 'third' eye, or 'psychic' eye, which is located at the centre of our forehead. Therefore, what we see may appear to be superimposed as a solid object and seen when the eye is closed or open. For example: If we stare at an object and then close our eyes we will be able to see clearly that same object has been imprinted in front of our eyes. Some mediums see spirit forms as solid beings, but there are other clairvoyants who see them when they are in a relaxed state and the ordinary consciousness is at rest.

Spirit usually appear to us as they would have been remembered, so that we can describe them to those they have left behind in this world. If we were to describe the spirit visitor in their spirit form, the sitter would not recognise them. For example: If a man was deformed, or had an artificial limb when he was on the earth plane, this would automatically be rectified when he reached the spirit world, as it is only a physical condition, not a spiritual one. On reaching the next world the spirit body would be made whole once again and all pain removed.

Some clairvoyants can see things that have happened miles and miles away, beyond their usual range of vision, and are later proved to have actually occurred. Some are able to penetrate into the past, the present and receive glimpses of the future, although this does not mean that clairvoyant's are 'fortune tellers'.

It saddens me that the majority of people who come for sittings are looking for a glimpse of the future. I believe that proving life continues in another existence is much more important than who we are going to meet next year,

147

or if we are going to win the Lottery. If only people would give their relatives in spirit a chance to communicate, they would find that even though these spirits are on a different level of existence, they still want to help and guide those they have left behind and still love.

I can only tell you what I believe to be the truth and can only speak for myself, putting forward the general idea of spirit – a state of being totally separate and distinct from the material world and the material body.

To be able to see friends and family in the next world is a privilege and pleasure for me and I wouldn't change a thing, except of course to improve this wonderful gift.

I hope that after you have read what I have to say, you will at least give spiritualism some thought. It's a wonderful way of life that brings love, truth, peace, knowledge and a more sensitive and caring outlook to life in general. It removes all fear of death and brings a new insight to what this life is all about, why you are here and what you have to learn, so that you can grow and improve yourselves as you are supposed to do. Your schooling is very important to you, and now is the time to start and understand.

So far I have talked about my clairvoyance, but I also hear spirit voices, which is called clairaudience: the ability to hear messages from someone without a physical body. There are some mediums that can hear spirit as if the voice has come from inside their head, their interior consciousness, but it is quite possible to hear it from outside as though the voice is coming from across the room. I am sure some of you have at times heard your name being called and when you turn round there is no one there.

It is possible to have quiet conversations with more than one spirit person or guide at a time, mentally inside your head. Mediums with this faculty hear the voices of spirit people as distinctly as if the person is in the flesh. When a medium is in the habit of talking to one particular communicator they immediately recognise the characteristics of that voice.

Daniel, one of my spirit guides, always clears his throat before he speaks to us and has a way of not pronouncing his Rs, so we always know it is he. Sometimes in the spirit world this faculty can be used by communicators through a second spirit person, an intermediary (medium), who then plays the part of an interpreter by relaying this information to the clairaudient, the same way as a medium in this world acts as an intermediary between the two worlds, passing on information from spirit friends and relatives.

Spiritual clairaudience is a power which enables mediums to be receptive to sounds or vibrations from the world of spirit. To be able to achieve this you must relax and listen to the stillness, that voice within, the voice of conscience. I find it is helpful to concentrate on my throat chakra (explained in the part of the book on chakras)

This is how to develop clairaudience or clear hearing.

Your inner voice, the voice of conscience, can be heard. Just listen and respond to the vibrations from the higher world. Your mind can interpret a sound within that silence, which comes to you from your spirit friends. Spiritual things are not heard with the physical ear, but the spirit ear. It is possible for you, whilst you are still in your body, to raise your consciousness to higher planes of existence and in this state you can be deaf to the noises of the physical plane.

I have during meditation heard loud cracks and bangs, raps and even spirit music. During the silence it's possible to hear a pin drop onto the surface of a carpet. This is because your hearing faculty is heightened during meditation. With patience, everyone can develop this and experience different spiritual noises. Even whispering in the room of spirit friends is so real and not a bit frightening.

Thoughts can actually be heard, because they make vibrations at a mental level, as in the spirit world a thought is sent forward and instantly received by a particular person. So a thought from a particular guide or sprit person can actually be heard.

All our thoughts are registered in the next world!

In the beginning a medium expects to hear somebody shout to him in a loud voice, hear voices that are clear as earthly voices, or music as clearly as if it had come from a radio. It would be nice if it were that easy, but first a student would have to learn to attune to the conscious so that he can interpret impressions which come into his mind. I know this sounds impossible, but with patience it can happen. Don't give up, spirit will not use those who are easily put off. Dedication and perseverance are a must if you want to become a good medium or healer.

How do you distinguish hearing from spirit and what is coming from your own mind? During early stages of development this can prove to be a real problem. But as you become increasingly sensitive, you should develop a distinct feeling of something coming into your consciousness. When you carefully analyse it you will be able to tell the difference between impressions and what arrives in your mind suddenly when spirit influence you. It can be in the form of psychic sensing, when you feel as if someone has actually spoken to you.

My daughter Stephanie often tries to give me information from spirit, always saying to me beforehand, 'I'm not sure, but...' This is because she cannot yet distinguish between what is given to her from spirit, and what she herself is thinking. One day, with a little help, she will be able to give clairaudience and clairvoyance.

Tension must be avoided at all times in mediumship, as this creates a barrier for spirit communication. You should relax mentally and physically and wait for answers, not be tense and hurry them along. Patience must be practised. It's a long hard journey becoming a good instrument for spirit to use.

When you give sittings clairaudiently, one correct name is far better than half a dozen you are not sure about. The message should be totally accurate. It is much better to spend less time with someone and give 100% accurate messages to the sitter than to spend twice as long and give disappointing information.

There are so many mediums who work in halls and churches and give name after name, without quietly and mentally asking spirit to repeat the name or information so that they can be sure they have received correctly. This would enable them to receive complete and positive proof, and to receive perfect impressions transmitted from spirit helpers.

You must never ask too many questions at once, otherwise, it could cause confusion. Always wait for a reply before going on to the next question.

This can also happen in automatic writing, when the words are heard in the physical mind. Your mind can interpret a sound within the silence, as I have already said, which comes to you from spirit.

I have always thought clairaudience is essential, as it is impossible to hold a conversation with someone you can see clairvoyantly and describe, but whom you cannot hear. I told you the story in the first part of the book when this happened to me. Ideally, it is better if both are operating in unison, and then you have a good instrument that is able to give good evidential messages.

My clairaudience is spirit communicating direct to my conscience. Only on very rare occasions do I feel they are speaking to me from across the room, from a physical body. However, for me clairvoyance and clairaudience have to go hand in hand, otherwise I would not be able to give good accurate messages.

Sensitives, or impressionables, are people who can recognise the presence of spirit by vague impression. This type of mediumship has no specific characteristic. All mediums are impressionable but this must be regarded as general rather than special. It is vital in all other mediumistic faculties. This faculty may become so subtle that a person can recognise the presence of a particular spirit.

In the case of trance mediums, changes come about as we progress. Today, however, being a trance medium doesn't always mean that we go to sleep (as was expected years ago) and don't remember what we are doing. Sometimes all of what is said and expressed is heard.

There are degrees of trance, from total insensibility when nothing comes from the subconscious mind of the medium, to a much lighter stage of trance, called over-shadowing. Therefore, allowance must be made, however small, for messages and information that can be a result of the medium's own subconscious mind.

These days we approach a mediumistic trance quite differently from the way we used to. Mediums used to have to make many preparations before hand, but now we can simply sit and allow it to happen, provided we have taken necessary precautions and approached this in the right and proper frame of mind. Relaxation helps and training is essential.

Those of you who are experienced and want to develop trance mediumship should sit comfortably in a chair and try to imagine your spine merging into the back of the chair, as though it is fluid. You will have a sensation of falling backwards, yet know that you are completely safe and protected, with a wonderful feeling of love from the spirit guides as they draw nearer to you.

I have at times imagined rocking my spirit body out of my physical body. In the early days of my development for trance, I also used to imagine myself spinning so fast that my spirit body was thrown out of my physical body and pulled upwards in the reverse of the whirl pool. When you are able to trust in your own spirit guides you will know they will protect and look after you. Remember this is true.

During the years I had my private development circle, I had to learn to trust spirit if I wanted them to take me into trance. It is not easy giving yourself over totally to an unseen influence, even though I had worked many years with my spirit friends and guides.

I found that at the last minute, just before I felt myself going off into trance, I would suddenly feel apprehensive and bring myself back. I believe now that this is normal if you care enough about your physical and spiritual well being.

You must be absolutely sure that your spirit helpers are genuine, which is why time, patience and working with your guides are essential. These things cannot be rushed. It took me several years before I was ready to say, 'Here I am, use me.'

I was a very difficult instrument for spirit to use, and had to learn to relax fully. However, the wonders that finally came from spirit communicating made me feel very humble and insignificant. I will always feel very privileged and honoured to be able to do this work.

Spirit brought wisdom, knowledge and laughter. On many occasions the upliftment and love reduced us to tears of joy and we couldn't wait for Fridays to come when we gathered for our weekly development circle and spirit teachings.

As I have said, total trance control mediumship is not recommended until the medium is fully aware of the implications. This deep trance state can be dangerous for those who do not know what they are doing.

The depth of trance depends very much on your spiritual state and also the power and energy of the guide. When I am taken into a deep trance state, my spirit body temporarily leaves my physical body and stands to one side, while a spirit guide controls my physical body to deliver messages. With deep trance control it is quite normal for the guide to use his own particular mannerisms, gestures and words.

Sometimes I feel as though I am standing behind myself, and at others I seem to travel to different places, or I simply feel that I have completely merged into the whole of creation and everything is part of me. It is very hard to explain but I will try. It's like when I am in meditation and reach a particularly high level of consciousness – I feel as if I am just a speck in the vast universe.

Very few mediums have attained a high degree of proficiency along this line, although many have aspired to it. I have been trying for 30 years and still haven't got it right to my satisfaction. The main problem is a lack of knowledge as to the best method of development; for many, as for me, it has been down to trial and error.

I am very good at giving advice and the worst person I know at putting it into practice. For example: During a light trance state, when a medium speaks in her own voice, I personally find that unacceptable. I would hate for the recipients of the message to think I was passing on information from my own subconscious mind. That is why I have always held back in the past, allowing spirit only to take me into a deep unconscious trance state, speaking with their voice and mannerisms. This has made life very difficult for me, as I know that in most cases, when you have a trance sitting, the voice that comes through the medium's lips is his or her voice, even though the communication comes from a spirit control. After all, spirit are using the medium's voice box.

All controlling spirit entities wanting to transmit spiritual knowledge and ideas through a medium find themselves just as much under the control of the medium as the medium is under theirs. The consequence is that the content of the information given will only be as good as the instrument that is being used. So if the medium is ignorant and has an untrained mind, the information will reflect this. Conversely, an educated medium with a well-trained mind will produce much better results. Although there have been exceptions to this rule, they are very rare. All mediums should therefore try to acquire more knowledge, thus bringing our mediumship to its highest efficiency.. We are here to learn. The more we learn, the more we should want to, that's what this life is all about.

When a medium is unconscious they are of course

unable to control what passes through their lips. Nevertheless, his or her mind does influence the control, advantageously or detrimentally. This applies even more to the consciously controlled medium, the medium that is overshadowed. By the content of the communication, and the language used, we will know whether it is from the consciousness of the medium or from spirit.

Automatic writing is usually produced through trance. In the early stages of developing this gift, the sensation you may feel is usually like a very small electric shock, a tingling sensation down the arm. The correct way is to let the hand go on moving until the power has been exhausted, even though you may be writing nonsense at first. You should always try to fix your mind on something apart from writing, though I must admit this is not easy.

Spirit usually experiment with your hand and pen, drawing loops and circles before commencing the difficult task of writing. You should accept this patiently. A person who can produce such work is often called an automist.

During automatic writing, some mediums are completely unaware of their surroundings, their actions and are often surprised to see the work they have put on canvas or produced on paper. Some become drowsy when they work and only become vaguely aware of their hands and what is going on, whether it is drawing, painting or writing. Others are totally conscious of allowing someone to use their hands to create something under spirit guidance. Automatic writing often develops a particular style, a consistency of expression, after much practice and perseverance.

Inspirational writing is quite different because each word or sentence is known in the mind before it is transmitted through the hand, as though the words are being dictated. The link between the hand, brain and spirit operator can become so perfect that a medium may find it very difficult to distinguish where the communication is coming from.

I have also had some experience of physical phenomena,

which I will tell you about. The rest I can only tell you from reading many books on this subject.

Physical phenomenon is a type of mediumship which is completely under the direction of spirit operators. The most important part of physical phenomena is that the medium should be comfortable at all times, and healthy. Mind and body should be free from tension as any emotional problems will inhibit the release of the ectoplasmic force and prohibit the success of the sitting.

While the sitting is in progress, the medium should to be allowed to fall into trance or go to sleep. The circle members should not expect or wait for materialisation raps to transpire during the sitting; they will occur if everybody is patient and in harmony. The medium will sense any agitation or impatience from other sitters in the circle, which will cause him anxiety and put pressure on him for some phenomena to happen.

It is very important that the members of the circle trust each other. If a member has the thought that another sitter is untrustworthy, then the whole circle must break down and a new circle of sitters that are able to trust each other should be assembled. If anyone feels that any manifestation is suspicious then the true experience of physical phenomena cannot take place.

In some cases the sitting may begin with a slight breeze in the air and/or rappings on tables. The sitters may feel a gentle touch of a spirit hand on the face or body. These signs should always be accepted and the circle members must thank the spirit operators for what they are receiving.

I was in my teens when I first experienced table tilting. I had gone to visit my grandmother, an established medium, and there were six of us all sitting around a small table in a darkened room. (Physical psychic force is very sensitive to light and the room should be made dim, a red or blue light is preferable for this purpose, though having said that, I have since heard of spirit creating physical phenomena in daylight.)

We started the sitting with hymn singing and then said one or two prayers. I wasn't sure what to expect, and was a little dubious. Within a couple of minutes the table started to rock and at the same time I felt a power pulsating through it. The power grew in strength and the table tilted backwards and forwards, from side to side. I sat there watching the other sitters' hands to see if they were moving the table; initially I thought this possible, but after a while the table really tilted with force. I could hardly keep my hands on it and it eventually almost landing on my knee. My grandmother said they had a message for me, and encouraged the spirit communicator to spell it out alphabetically. We counted as the table was tilted, spelling out each word, with someone taking notes as soon as the communication started.

It makes life easier and the sitting quicker if the medium of the circle asks questions such as 'Are you such and such a person's wife?' rather than wait until the whole name has been spelt out, which takes time and uses a lot of energy.

I must admit, I wasn't sure what to think, although the message was very clear and accurate, but my outlook and knowledge about such things was very limited in those days.

When indulging in table tilting or rapping, care must be taken to see that the phenomena are not caused by conscious or unconscious muscular action on the part of the sitters. One must gently rest one's fingers on the table for this phenomenon, the only way to obtain results. It is usually better if the little finger is touching the little finger of the sitter next to you, although this is not imperative.

Table tilting and table wrapping are the most common forms of physical phenomena, which are responsive to collective action. The first signs of the table moving are generally a faint trembling and they end in powerful movements deliberately made by an invisible intelligence.

Rappings are much rarer and usually begin with faint creaks or taps resembling a pencil being dropped on a table. These may increase in volume until they resemble the sound of someone striking a table with something very heavy. Sometimes it can sound like a whip being cracked. Other sounds are also simulated.

'Parakinesis' is a term used to describe any form of physical phenomena when the medium and members of the group are in actual contact with the object, which is effected by no normal means. Table tilting and table rapping when the sitters' hands are resting on the table, are well known examples of this. One should always limit the time spent with this type of sitting as it may cause nervous exhaustion.

Most mediums who use this form of physical phenomena use certain codes to understand the messages they receive, such as one for no, two for unsure and three times for yes. This must be agreed before the sitting takes place so that the spirit operators know exactly what they are doing. This gives us more time to receive information.

The energy used for this sort of manifestation is the same or allied to normal nerve energies. Singing and music are, I feel, very important, for the creative action of spirit operators to bring about good psychic phenomena and plays a part in all mediumistic faculties, including supernormal manifestations. How many times have people said laughter is good for the soul? So is singing, it is known to bring a feeling of upliftment. It is always good to sing, it doesn't matter if it is a hymn or not, but a cheerful hearty song heightens the vibrations and it is good for producing supernormal phenomena, especially of the physical kind and will often work wonders.

With any type of mediumship the best results are achieved if we have the same amount of male and female sitters, sitting alternately, man, woman, man, woman. If this is not possible we take the physical constitution of each individual into account and place the sitters: strong, weak, strong, and weak.

Levitation is often witnessed without anyone being in contact with the table. It is suspended in the air for several

158

minutes without any visible support. This may happen spontaneously without trained mediums.

Infra red photographs have shown ectoplasmic rods supporting the table created by unseen spirit operators. Usually the material used for these phenomena is borrowed from the sitters and then returned afterwards without any adverse effect on them. Spirit operators extract what they require from the medium and to a lesser degree from the sitters. Ectoplasm is explained in more detail later.

Although I have experienced rappings and table tilting, I have not experienced or been successful with the moving of objects and lifting of tables. However, I have never sat in earnest for physical mediumship.

Other forms of physical phenomena other than table tilting and raps should be obtained if the medium is good for physical phenomena. Usually telekinetic phenomena require the presence of a highly qualified medium to be successful.

There is a certain amount of risk incurred by a medium in all physical practices. However, the invisible spirit operators in this kind of mediumship endeavour to make their mediums safe against all danger. One does not know or understand what goes on behind the scenes; it is all within the laws that are governed in the spirit world.

It takes a long time for communicators from the spirit world to produce physical phenomena. They first have to find a medium that suits them, and then the intricate efforts to succeed on their part can be achieved.

Apart from table tilting and rappings the only other physical phenomenon I have personally experienced is transfiguration. This consists of the change in aspects of the living body, which often takes on the appearance of another spirit being, presenting the similarities of their face.

Sometimes transfiguration may be caused by a simple muscular contraction, which changes the expression of the face, making the spirit person more recognisable. In some cases a simple appearance of a young or old person is made by altering or modifying the atomic conditions, which can give temporary visibility and tangibility. The face may even change in its appearance and become luminous, depending on the power of the spirit. This can be caused by the spirit person combining his or her own fluids with that of the medium, substituting their appearance with that of the medium, thus giving the effect that the medium's face has disappeared and is under the direction of spirit operators.

If, for example, the transfiguration assumed the likeness of a small child then the manifesting weight of the size of the face must be lessened accordingly, and then the face becomes smaller.

To see the reactions of the sitters after they have actually met with their loved ones in the spirit world is a rewarding experience.

As I have already said I know very little about materialisation, only what I have read. However, I feel I should explain a little about this extraordinary phenomena.

For materialisations to take place the medium has to sit in a cabinet or some suitable place that shields him from the light, which may inhibit the phenomena. This is usually made of a black material, and generally this type of sitting is held in complete darkness.

Ectoplasm is a substance with which spirit work to enable a materialisation to take place. It is light and very highly sensitive. Spirit operators must agree in advance whether a stronger illumination is necessary or not.

When materialisation takes place one can actually embrace the spirit and feel the warmth of the body. Usually it is a relative or a friend who appears to give us evidence and speak to us as if they were sitting next to us in the same room. They are as real as though they were back in the physical body.

The great materialisation medium was Helen Duncan, and what a wonderful medium she was. I don't think there has ever been anyone who could come close to the marvellous

160

work she did, bringing evidence to the public from those in the world beyond the grave. Helen's ability to materialise deceased people is unequalled. She was noted for her ability to materialise human forms capable of independent thought and speech and able to converse with their loved ones on this earth plane, although they had left their physical bodies.

Helen was a physical medium for over 40 years. Born in Scotland on 25 November 1898, she came from a family of eight. The first time she noticed her psychic gift was when she was at school, aged seven, and the answer to a question she didn't know appeared on the slate on her desk. Helen was destined to become one of the finest physical mediums in psychic history. People were soon talking about her psychic activities and strange behaviour, and she was accused of being a witch. She had the ability to find people who were missing and could see them walking along the road. She told her mother she had seen such and such a person who was missing and that he or she was dead. Such things were classed as witchcraft, as in those days people believed in curses. Helen always seemed to know what was happening and at times told her friends their own secrets that only they could know. She almost knew what people were thinking. Because of this she was very much isolated.

Her mediumship started to develop in the early years but very little phenomena manifested, although spirit people would talk through her when she was in trance. Her guides told her that physical phenomena materialisations would take place in due course.

Helen's first experience of physical manifestation was in 1926 and wasn't pleasant as something evil manifested through her. She and her husband sought protection from this evil force, which had entered the room and all future seances. She opened her meetings with a prayer that proved to be successful. She did eventually organise a circle and had materialisations at which her spirit control told the gatherers to place a black curtain across the room and introduce a red light in front of and above it, explaining

161

that this would help the conditions for future development. As the circle grew in size, a great deal of activity took place behind the curtains but nothing materialised or manifested outside the cabinet for quite some time. They decided that they must be doing something wrong or that something was missing; perhaps it was the number of circle members. So they started to look for special sitters to join the circle and bring it to its correct number of members.

The ectoplasm was tried and tested by spirit operators over the years, then one day Helen's guide Dr Williams explained that ectoplasm was a substance necessary in physical phenomena. It would take time but they would witness it during her development. Eventually Dr Williams was replaced by another control called Albert Stewart, who stayed with Helen and worked as her control for the rest of her life as a medium. She also had another spirit person who worked through her, a small child by the name of Peggy.

Helen didn't have to wait long before materialisations developed. They started with partial materialisations, such as single organs. The object of the spirit entity manifesting is obviously to give evidence of their identity, so the appearance of heads were more frequent, hands and arms were also often materialised, and this method was quite convincing. The reason only partial materialisations were produced was because of a lack of sufficient ectoplasm, a substance extracted from the medium's organism from which the materialisations are then formed. There are other reasons why only partial materialisation can be produced. Climate, temperature, the medium and the sitters' attitudes can all cause this.

Helen's circle developed and the manifestations became complete materialisations of human forms with independent thought and speech. She was soon in demand because of her wonderful ability as a medium, with people coming from all over Britain to see her.

Good materialisation mediums usually have one or more

spirits who regularly manifest at their seances, and who are concerned with the production of these phenomena. These spirit beings are usually able to manifest themselves with great ease when perfect conditions are available.

When people do not understand and are ignorant of supernatural occurrences they can cause havoc and this happened to Helen. Eventually she was accused of trickery, of packing lots and lots of cheesecloth into her mouth, which she was supposed to have regurgitated later during the seance, to make out that materialisation had taken place. The materialisation looked like a white substance joining the medium to the materialised figure by what looked like a rope attached to the medium's mouth or nose.

Ectoplasm is a substance of which materialisations are made. It is ideoplastic in nature, and is capable of being moulded by thought; this conveys its extreme sensitivity. The ectoplasm is derived from the body of the medium by supernormal means, quite unknown to us.

There are hundreds of photographs showing the actual process and scientific experiments have now placed it beyond all reasonable doubt. The photographs have shown varying appearances of psycho-plastic material. It is first shown as what looks like a thread then it gradually expands, forming the appearance of a cobweb. Then it thickens to the consistency of muslin, spreading over the body of the medium until it shows a complete form separated from the medium. These results do vary with different mediums. During the initial stages of materialisation, the formations generally appear to be of a fluid consistency. White luminous flakes varying in size from a pea to a ten pence piece are distributed here and there over the medium. This manifestation is a phenomenon which sometimes precedes more wonderful appearances that will take around one hour to complete.

There can be no doubt whatsoever that the substance itself emanates from the whole body of the medium and is extracted from the physical organs. There seems to be no fixed way, although it seems to emanate especially from the orifices and extremities, from the top of the head, the breasts and the tips of the fingers. The most usual origin is from the mouth. We then see a substance externalising itself from the inner surface of the cheeks, from the gums and roof of the mouth, then falling to the floor by its own weight. The visibility of the substance varies a great deal, and sometimes it disappears like lightning

With some mediums a materialised form can manifest suddenly and just as suddenly vanish. On the other hand they can sometimes be observed gradually appearing and disappearing. Some materialisations are actually formed in the medium's body, in some instances even from between the hands. On other occasions they slowly form at a distance from the medium. Usually this starts with a filmy or cloudy patch of something white or grey observed on the floor in front of the medium. It gradually grows and expands, visibly extending itself as if it were an animated piece of muslin, lying fold upon fold on the floor. It extends to two and a half feet by three feet with a breadth of a few inches. Soon it begins to rise slowly near the centre and looks as though a human head is underneath it. The cloudy film on the floor begins to look more and more like a piece of muslin, falling into several folds about the person mysteriously rising. By the time it has attained two or three feet in height, it looks like a child is underneath a sheet, moving its arms up and down as if manipulating something. It continues to rise and sink until it attains a height of five feet or so. It's as though the entity is arranging the folds of drapery around its figure. Eventually the arms rise above the head and open outwards through a mass of cloudlike spirit drapery as the form displays itself before the sitters.

If materialisations are, as some people suppose, a result of subconscious action on the part of the medium, then they actually demonstrate the possibility of human consciousness acting apart from the physical organism.

When the materialised form is complete, it has the

164

perfect appearance and all biological qualities of a living form. Whatever the formation may be, the phenomena does not always remain in contact with the medium. It is often observed quite separate from her. The structures, therefore, show a certain independence. It is obvious that the human soul does live and act apart from the human organism.

The materialised forms seem to have vitality, as they are alive in the biological sense. It is a temporary living being as sensitive in all parts as a human body. The spirit manifests through its elements exactly as we do through ours. A well-developed hand has the functional capacities of a normal hand.

Materialisations are among the rarest form of psychic phenomena. Conditions required for manifestations are so delicate that even the most trifling circumstances may render their production impossible, or spoil them so that satisfactory results cannot be obtained.

What can be more marvellous than the sudden appearance of a fully developed human form, apparently from nowhere? Especially when this strange visitor exhibits the mental as well as the physical attributes of a human being. It is so natural when these spirit people appear that it is impossible to distinguish them from ordinary folk. They have been known to walk about in daylight, talk and, on rare occasions, eat and drink.

The most troublesome difficulties encountered concern light, which has been regarded as a major problem in the entire field of physical psychic phenomena. White light is a destructive agent and must be dealt with carefully. It is better to use a red or blue light to illuminate, although this has been a sore point with spiritualists for years.

I have already explained about the partial and complete types of materialisations, but there are also the invisible materialisations, which can be felt but not seen. An analogy to help us understand this is that we are able to feel the wind, but unable to see it. These materialisations present themselves by touching, making noises and voices. It is obvious a finer substance has been produced, making finer physical forms. These are not sufficiently dense to be seen, even though the substance is solid and strong enough to lift tables and make loud noises.

During the time I sat for physical phenomena, we used a red light and bought infra-red films for the camera. While I was in trance the circle members took photographs of everybody. When we had the films developed, we could see strange shapes and cords stretching out attached to each member of the circle. It looked like a finer substance of ectoplasm joining us all together.

'Ghostly' apparitions are difficult to recognise though fairly common. If we try to touch them our hand passes through them without any resistance. These materialisations usually appear misty; sometimes they are so transparent that an object can be seen through them.

Spirit people can do marvellous things with the human organism without harming the medium; this is obvious in good physical seances.

Another marvellous phenomena is spirit apports (objects appearing out of thin air), which are theoretically feasible, though how they are produced and transported is a great mystery. One theory is that etheric tubes are created through which any small object can be passed, altering the rate of vibration of the object and the matter it has to pass through, so that they vibrate at the same level, enabling this phenomenon to take place.

What a pity that these days we hear very little of the wonders of this kind of manifestation, or of any wonderful materialisation mediums.

CHAPTER ELEVEN

Healing

'Absent' healing might be more accurately called 'distance' healing, because naturally the healing cannot be 'absent'. Healing from a distance is different from contact healing, where the healer lays on hands and has physical contact with the patient. By whatever name it is called, distance healing works very well when conditions are right for its operation and effectiveness.

Once this form of healing is applied, within a comparatively short period of time the patient's symptoms lessen, the pain fades away and the ill effects are overcome. It all depends on the patient's condition how long the period of healing takes; it could be a matter of weeks or much longer.

It is so wonderful when you think about it. Healing can be given anywhere in the world, and distance creates no problems. It is hard to believe that a patient who suffers from an incurable disease and lives on the other side of the world will receive the healing energies. We have to accept the fact that this contact is made, otherwise absent healing could not take place at all. With the knowledge spirit possess, this is quite possible.

If we live in harmony with natural and divine law, learning to look after our physical bodies, keeping ourselves healthy, this will help us. When the laws are broken then weaknesses appear and the human body suffers disease. The physical body needs to be treated with respect and consideration, we must learn to love ourselves. Do not over-work, over-eat over-indulge your body. Don't forget it is a vehicle for your spirit self.

Spirit healing is a thought process. With distance and contact healing there is a mental request from the healer to the healing doctors, guides, who then set in motion the appropriate healing energy to reach that given patient. There must be a form of thought request before any healing can take place, to attune to spirit during a healing intercession. The attunement means making ourselves comfortable so that there is no bodily stress, forgetting our problems and focusing on the healing process with a happy and loving frame of mind. We must raise our spiritual mind and vibrations, giving thoughts to spiritual pictures. A healer must relay some form of mental picture to their spirit operators so that the healing can take place, linking the healer with spirit doctors and the patient. As I have already said, every thought is registered in the world of spirit. Having received this information the spirit doctor will be able to diagnose the illness of the patient and give specialised treatment.

In healing, nothing is casual; there must be a purpose at all times. It is better if a little time each day is set aside for us to send thoughts out for all those in need. Preparation is important to establishing attunement with spirit through meditation.

If I can remind you about my son-in-law Roger, a non-believer who became very ill with testicular cancer. The cancer spread to other parts of his body, but I'm pleased to say that Roger's illness ended on a happier note due to the power of 'self healing', the power of thought.

God does indeed move in a mysterious way. The Great Spirit performs miracles and uses many ways to heal, to repair and to develop a character of every one's soul. Bodily sickness is the result of disharmony, an imbalance with the body and soul. To restore bodily health we must work through the soul, otherwise our patients will only receive temporary relief.

Spiritual healing works not only on our body but also on our soul and our very life. We must be tolerant, forgiving, patient and truthful, for all these attributes will gradually develop in the soul by trusting in the Great Spirits healing power.

It is important how we deal with our problems, as

sometimes this can cause illness. We must be still, find a place of silence and when the emotions are still and we are linked to the spirit realms, then we will be able to examine our problems in a much calmer way. If we ask for strength and guidance we will receive it and be filled with peace, and better able to overcome our anxieties because there is a spiritual flame within us.

Through prayer and meditation we can seek that contact from the spirit world and receive fuller knowledge and joy from the life of spirit, be at peace totally, let go of all earthly problems and leave ourselves in the hands of the Great Spirit, knowing that the love from spirit will envelop us and sustain us.

The healer's function is to be the communicative link between the absent patient and the healing ministers. The patient helps the healing by their spirit self acting as a receiver and transformer of the healing power, in contact healing as well as distance healing.

The intelligent direction of a healing force originates only from the spirit realms, not the healer, and is able to ascertain the cause of the disease. It knows how to administer the remedial force to induce a state of beneficial change within the patient. The spirit world can change the vibrations of the physical body of matter, and bring about a positive act of healing. Spiritual healing is the result of a law-governed healing force that brings about change. Therefore, to bring about any change there must be intelligent direction, someone to administer these forces to the patient.

The physical and spiritual laws combined are within the definition of the total law. No healing can take place outside the confines of the total law.

It is important for a patient or the patient's relatives to correspond on a regular basis, informing the healer of the progress that has been made. The letter need not be anything more than a simple note, reporting the patient's response to the treatment. These letters are very important both

169

ways as they build a bridge between the healer and the patient, but also between the patient and the healing doctor. However, it has been proved that even those who do not write have in fact continued to improve, and eventually do recover. I can only think that thought waves, vibrations from the healing prayers, are very much like a telephone, reaching out to the homes of those who are sick.

Many people wish to know if they possess the healing gift and how they can develop it. Healing is a natural talent. Generally speaking, all those who inwardly 'feel' for those who are sick and in pain, with a deep inner yearning to help, may well possess the healing potential, which only needs developing. Distance healing is often the best way to start, as it will awaken the gift for the developing medium and can serve as an introductory method to developing any healing potential.

Healing is not a mystery; it is ignorance on our part that makes it mysterious. In fact the practice of spiritual healing started as far back as 100 000 years BC with Palaeolithic man, who used simple herbal remedies and potions. There is evidence to suggest that the Ancient Egyptians regarded spiritual healing as the most advanced therapy, though only the higher priesthood practised it. The priesthood established schools for the training of novice priests in the art of healing.

I find it hard to understand why some people after all these years are still finding spiritual healing difficult to accept. What a wonderful world this would be if all human beings practised or received healing.

Franz Anton Mesmer established himself as a healer from 1733 until he died in 1815. He believed that the healing he achieved was brought about by an energy which he called 'animal magnetism'. I am sure most of you will have heard that expression.

In those days there was extreme poverty and wealth . The wealthy in particular were searching for something new that would replace their previously unquestioned

170

beliefs. Mesmer realised he could not fail and he prospered with his theories of animal magnetism. His cures did not rely on the use of a magnet but on touching the diseased part. However, most of Mesmer's patients were healed from a distance.

Magnetic healing as we know it is a direct inheritance from Mesmer. It is the ability to direct to a patient some of the healer's own abundance of natural vitality or cosmic strength. The word 'magnetic' is a common definition now, but other terms which have described the magnetic force are 'Odic Force' and 'X Force'.

A healer who possesses this excess of energy is able by holding a patient's hands, to direct some of his own strength into the patient, who will often feel all the better by being visited by a person with this magnetic power.

Now we know what has happened when we hear people say, 'He seems to drain all the strength from me.' Magnetic healers possess these energies in abundance and are usually in vibrant and radiant health. When a magnetic healer gives his energy to a number of patients, he will feel a sense of depletion and consciously needs to replenish his vitality. Most healers have this faculty and are able to give this strength to a patient.

If a healer feels at all depleted after treating patients, it may well be that he has given more than he should of his own strength. In this case, the healer should sit relaxed for a few moments and, by characterised breathing, open himself to receive a fresh supply of the cosmic energies he has expended.

Magnetic healing can be very beneficial to a patient who is weak, but this is not spiritual healing. The energies do not come from a spirit source; they are of a physical origin only. However, magnetic healing and spiritual healing can merge.

I have explained only a little of how spirit healing first began, but we have come a long way since then. In 1959, 1500 hospitals in Great Britain agreed to allow healers

171

into their wards to administer the healing power, and doctors were cooperative

We continue to move forward, and the potential to heal any specific condition is within the hands of every spiritual healer. Special kinds of healing force are necessary for different ailments. For example, if a patient is suffering from arthritis and the joints have become calcified, then a healing force to disperse the adhesions is necessary. A different healing force is needed to overcome anaemia or to disperse a tumour. Each case will vary in the length of time necessary to bring about relief. It makes sense that if a patient seeks healing in the early stages then the healing is more likely to very rapid. If the disease is deep-seated the period of time to complete a cure will take longer.

Nutritional disease causes arthritis, which makes the blood system weak so that waste deposits from the cells are left in the joints and tissues instead of being disposed of through the respiratory and excretory system. The healing act is to build up the health and vitality of the patient, which will improve the condition of the blood and through the bodily intelligence this will disperse the adhesions. The dispersal of arthritic substances is the dispersal of the atoms composing it. Therefore, the chemical structures that lock a joint are removed.

As I have said, the healing act is planned, needing the intelligence and direction of a spirit doctor. You can only operate through the great knowledge and wisdom of your spirit doctors. You do not possess the knowledge of how to do this. The degree of knowledge and experience of the spirit doctors varies; some have a wider knowledge than others, just the same as the specialists in our world. Therefore, it makes sense to believe that there must be 'specialists' in the spirit world.

We no longer have to prove spiritual healing; it has already been factually established through the healing of 'incurables', patients who have been told that medical science cannot find a cure for their disease and they will

172

have to either learn to live with it or die. Now, the medical authorities have agreed that spiritual healing does take place, and that it cannot be accounted for. That is why, over the past few years, the medical authorities have been referring patients to reputable healers and complementary therapists. So we have established that spiritual healing is a reality, not a mystery. It is spirit science.

Most healers like myself conduct their work in their free time, carrying on with their full-time occupations and spending their evening hours in their sanctuaries, receiving patients into their home.

Spiritual healing comes from spirit, an act of love and a force that impels it. There is a vital difference between medical science and that of spiritual healing. It is now universally recognised that a very high percentage of physical disease has a psychosomatic origin. There are many cases that can be summed up as 'sickness of the mind and spirit'.

When a patient is ill due to fears, emotional stress and anxiety, doctors are rarely able to reach them clinically, and usually treat only the symptoms by prescribing sedatives and anti-depressants. These types of medication only dope the patient and the effects eventually wear off. The doctor then prescribes a stronger tablet and in the end the patient will have to take them for the rest of his life. Spiritual healing goes to the cause of the problem, the source, and treats these conditions in a positive way, giving a feeling of upliftment that soothes and calms the fears.

Having said that, the medical profession does now refer patients to those who are competent in stress management, counselling and other similar therapies.

The art of attunement means establishing a state of oneness with the spirit guides. For the beginner this is often a problem, but for experienced healers it is second nature. Established healers have the ability to receive thoughts direct from spirit friends, and are able to influence

173

the patients' bodily intelligence, to act in a positive manner.

Unlike the mental concentration needed for spiritual development, one should practise mental abandonment for healing. Gently contemplate, thinking of contact with spirit people with the intention of healing the sick. Do not try to make your mind a blank, as you will not succeed. Tenseness must always be avoided, let your mind dwell on beautiful things. When you feel confident and know what is ailing the patient, spend a few minutes allowing your mind to picture the distress causing the illness. As you are doing this, you are communicating these thoughts to 'someone' who is 'listening in' to you. Try to project the mental image outwards, linking up with the invisible mind of those who are listening, your spirit ministers. Mentally request again that they take the pain or stress away, whatever it may be. This is, of course, the way to develop distance healing.

You must always remember it is the healing guides alone who are the administrators of the healing energies. Therefore, it is the guide who is able to make a correct diagnosis of the character of the healing energies the patient needs. Thus the diagnosis is the responsibility of the guide and not the healer.

There are different ways a healer receives diagnoses, varying according to the manner in which the guides can use the healer. The most common form of diagnosing the area of trouble is when the healer places his hand over the affected part. Both the healer and patient become aware of a strong heat emanating from the healer's hands, which appears to penetrate into the patient's body. When the hand is removed away from the painful area the sensation of heat dies away, only to return as the hand comes back to that part. It has been proven that no healer can create this at will; the heat cannot be physical it has to be a psychic or spiritual power, therefore this cannot be a clinical heat. The heat is a healing force. While heat is generally felt, the opposite effect of extreme cold is, at times, experienced. Therefore, it cannot be ruled out that under the direction of spirit intelligence healing does take place. No human being is capable of increasing the temperature in any one part of the body by will.

You must always seek to change the patient's outlook from hopelessness to expectancy. You will need to make his mind and body receptive so that the healing energies can be absorbed and work as intended. Each healing act, whatever the ailment, is administered and planned by a superior intelligence. Spiritual healing is a divine purpose, simple in its action and one that may be outside the confines of our present way of thinking.

I couldn't talk about spiritual healing without including a few brief words about psychic surgery. This differs from other types of paranormal healing in that the healer actually performs surgical interventions on the human body while in a trance state, under the control of their spirit surgeons. When he wakes up he is unaware of what has taken place.

It may seem strange but we can actually learn and grow through suffering and discomfort. The only way to be able to say to a patient 'I understand how you feel' is to have suffered it first hand. It is always best to add knowledge to the love and compassion you feel, so that you can understand how the body works. If I hadn't read lots of books on healing, I would never have been able to write this on the healing intelligence, or been able to understand some of my patients' illnesses.

It is about 35 years ago that I started to heal. I read all the healing books I could lay my hands on. One of the books I read described psychic surgery. It was fascinating, but the thought of all the blood and gore put me off developing this type of healing. The book was written about healers in Brazil and the Philippines, who were known for the phenomenon of psychic surgery, especially one Brazilian by the name of Jose Arigo and a Filipino Tony Agpaoa.

Arigo had very little schooling and worked as a farm hand, until one day a local spiritualist told him that spirit were trying to work through him. It took time but Arigo became a healer, seeing as many as 300 patients a day. One of the patients, a psychic researcher from America, had a tumour removed from his arm in less than five seconds. There were hundreds of people who stood around to witness the wonderful performance of psychic surgery, including a camera crew who recorded the event. Using a pocket-knife, Arigo cut the skin and it split wide open, revealing the tumour. He just squeezed the tumour and it popped out. After three days the wound had healed.

He performed hundreds of other operations without the use of conventional instruments: sometimes an ordinary kitchen knife, nail scissors or just his hands. He was able to give accurate diagnosis of illnesses. He could also estimate blood pressure accurately without an instrument and gave complex drug remedies. He arrived at his diagnoses by listening to the voice in his right ear, repeating whatever it said. The voice was his spirit guide, a medical doctor by the name of Dr Adolf Fritz.

Eventually Arigo was prosecuted and imprisoned, and he died in 1971.

The conditions for research were much better in the Philippines. Amazing experiences were studied with the psychic surgeon Tony Agpaoa and other healers who worked with him.

Psychic surgery is very hard to accept as normal or even genuine, but there are many who have witnessed this phenomenon and received proof that is does exist, including many doctors in Brazil who would testify to these acts of surgery performed by psychic surgeons.

Several investigations have proved that some practitioners are fraudulent, using chicken blood in a bag. They break this open as they pretend to cut flesh, which makes a very bloody performance. These fraudulent conjurers are very convincing and it takes only a little practice and sleight of hand to convince people that psychic surgery has actually taken place. I assume they still practice surgery undercover and I suspect it would be very hard to find them.

Quite a number of years ago, British television showed a programme about psychic surgery. I'm not sure after so long who the psychic surgeon was, but the actual psychic operation was screened. It was fascinating but at the time I was not at all convinced.

I now believe that psychic surgery is possible, and there are many healers these days who practise psychic surgery without the blood and gore, including myself. Spirit doctors can perform surgery without opening the physical body. The healer is taken into trance, so that the spirit surgeons are able to work using the medium's hands as if they were their own and perform these wonderful operations.

Some of the best healers are on your own doorstep. Look around and find one who suits you, who is known and respected for the work he or she has accomplished.

CHAPTER TWELVE

Chakras And Auras

What are chakras and what is aura? There are seven main psychic centres situated within your body, which are called the chakras.

The seventh chakra is on the top of your head and is called 'the crown'. The sixth, 'the brow', is between the eyes. The fifth, near the hollow of the throat, is called 'the throat centre'. The fourth is 'the heart centre', the third, at the navel, is called 'the solar plexus' or 'the psychic centre'. This is a spontaneous receiver of messages from the unseen world. The second chakra, slightly below the waist, is called 'the sacral', while the first and final of the seven centres is at the pubic area and called 'the kundalini'. This particular centre has great creative power. Correctly used, it can be the greatest most holy power for good but can also be the root of all evil. Therefore, this centre must be used in a proper manner, working with the higher chakras, the heart, throat and head centres. Most students are made aware of the dangers of the kundalini, which in a dormant state is harmless. It is best to leave well alone, as it can be awakened and become active, so you must learn to control and understand its significance.

During meditation the student learns to discipline the emotions and thoughts of the physical body, and with the attitude of love and light the kundalini force can be released with nothing to fear – if the student obeys the rules. If you attend a development circle in the right frame of mind, with the love of God seeking only goodness and truth, then all is well. While in this state the kundalini can be awakened, and the divine qualities will be stimulated and strengthened, opening up a magnificent opportunity for growth and development.

The object of development is to train you in the practice of meditation, bringing all these chakras under the control and direction of the Great Spirit. The chakra centres are the traditional energy centres of our astral bodies. To understand them, we must first realise that there is one life force or energy. The astral body is an energy plane that co-exists with the physical body, and so the chakras are the areas of inter-connection.

Knowledge of the chakra centres has existed for thousands of years, although it's only during the last century that this knowledge has filtered through to the west.

There are many pictures of chakras that depict them as lotus blossoms or spinning wheels (*chakra* is a Sanskrit word that means spinning wheel) It may be simpler for people who are not familiar with metaphysics and Eastern terminology to think of the chakras as computer disks that are imprinted with all sorts of information. Like a hard disc in a computer, the chakras spin and take in data, and can also be tapped to give up that information.

There is one force, the Universal Life Force, and its energy can be stored in all of us in the base chakra or kundalini. We can learn to direct this energy to the higher centres, thereby expanding our consciousness. This is when we begin to realise that we are indeed spiritual beings.

All our chakras absorb life-force, break it up and distribute it to its sympathetic endocrine gland and the rest of the body, using not only the endocrine system, but also the nervous system and the blood.

The endocrine system is the body's hormone system and each chakra roughly corresponds to an endocrine gland that secretes hormones. Hormones, as we know, are chemicals which can control long-term changes in the body, including growth, maturity, rate of activity etc. The health of the body depends on a balanced output from the various glands that form the endocrine system. When a chakra becomes blocked or partially closed, the endocrine glands are unable to function to their full capacity (this can happen due to trauma) and the physical body suffers.

Considering how important the chakras are, let's look

at them in more detail.

The chakras are part of our physical and spiritual make-up and we gain access to them during different phases of our spiritual evolution. By this I mean as we enter each age of evolution. For example, the age of Aquarius is a higher, more positive frequency/vibration than the age of Pisces. Similarly, as each of us grows to adulthood, we activate the chakra energies and also our spiritual lessons in sequence, from the bottom to the top.

The way we perceive the world and ourselves depends upon which chakra we are functioning from. If energy is blocked at any chakra, malfunction will manifest in the corresponding area of the body. This also happens if a chakra is too open, for then we have no control over the amount of energy flowing through it. So we have to learn how to awaken and direct energy through our chakra system to maintain well-being.

All our chakras are open to some degree, but each operate some more than others, therefore one or two will be weaker than the rest.

Clairvoyants are able to see these round circles of light situated in the etheric body; these points are the windows to the soul. Through these you can receive impressions and messages transmitted from the spirit world. As you develop, your spirit helpers can see these centres growing, developing and changing, becoming more beautiful as one progresses.

The spleen/splenic chakra.

I want to mention this chakra even though it is not considered a major chakra. It is located over the spleen (lower ribs, abdomen, left) As I talked about earlier, the chakras take in life force and distribute it through the body. This life force is also absorbed by the splenic chakra.

Universal life force (prana) manifests on the physical, astral and mental levels. Its manifestation on the physical levels depends on the sunlight. Prana radiates/emanates from the sun and enters some of the physical atoms which

180

float about the earth's atmosphere.

On a sunny day, prana is abundant; on a cloudy day, it is greatly reduced. At night we use the prana which has been manufactured the previous day. When we sleep our nerves and muscles relax, and the assimilation of prana takes place. This is why sleep, even a short nap, is so recuperative.

The splenic chakra absorbs the vitality from the atmosphere, and breaks it up into seven variations of prana, each radiating its own colour – the seven colours of the spectrum (contained in sunlight), which are reflected in the seven colours of the chakras, and of course the aura.

There are many minor chakras all around the body, for example in the palms of the hands and soles of the feet, but we will concentrate on the main ones.

Each chakra contains all the colours of the spectrum, but only one colour is dominant in each. I will describe each chakra in turn, its colour and function.

First chakra: the base, root or kundalini.

At the base of the spine, this chakra is the centre of vitality. Its dominant colour is red, and to easily visualise the base chakra, think of a red rose with its petals open. This chakra acts as a storage bank, which means that energy can be drawn up from the Earth (called Earth energy) into the base chakra, and stored for use. The spiritual challenge of this chakra relates to how well we manage our physical world. Will-power comes from this chakra, and the ways in which we bring our creative ideas into fruition.

Second chakra: the sacral.

Located between the navel and the pubis, the colour of the sacral chakra is orange and again it is easy to visualise: think of an orange. The moon (whose effect on libido and fertility has been well documented), interestingly enough rules the sacral chakra. The second chakra is associated with sexual energy (which is the second most powerful energy in a human being. The first is prana.) This centre doesn't awaken until puberty.

The second chakra lessons apply strongly to our sexual relationships, to partnerships, friendships, and all kinds of one-to-one interaction, power struggle, control dramas etc. Two of its higher qualities are wisdom and love.

Third chakra: the solar plexus.

The dominant colour in this chakra is yellow a nice bright daffodil yellow. This is the centre of self esteem, a very vulnerable chakra, for if it is too open, a person will pick up everyone else's issues, whether positive or negative, and then may become anxious and nervous. However, when in balance and not swayed by these emotions, the solar plexus is a valuable intuitive guide.

This is the chakra where upward moving energy from the Earth and downward energy from the universe (cosmic) generally meets. In reflexology, this chakra is known as the triple heater due to the heat generated by the process of digestion. It is related to the emotions, for instance, if we are blocked at the second chakra (sexually), then sexuality cannot be connected to love (fourth or heart chakra) The sun rules this chakra. (Solar = sun, plexus = collection of nerves.)

When two people enter any kind of relationship, cords are formed between their solar plexi. The stronger the relationship, the stronger the cords. If the relationship ends, then the cords are slowly disconnected (hence the saying 'severing the cord'.)

Fourth chakra: the heart.

The dominant colour here is green (grass/nature) and the ruling element of this chakra is air (located in the chest) The heart chakra can be considered the most powerful of all the chakras. It can create or destroy, as it is the centre of love. It is also first of the higher creative centres.

The challenge of this chakra is to learn compassion, the value of forgiveness and conscious love (often referred to as unconditional love) When this chakra is balanced and open we have a great capacity to extend undemanding love; if it is too closed, then we become insensitive to others and unable to love ourselves. The heart chakra is also the bridge over which we cross from the physical to the spiritual realms.

The thyroid chakra.

We are entering Aquarius, which is a more loving age than the age of Pisces, which was very aggressive and selfish (Yuppies etc) Another chakra, not one of the main seven, has recently become activated. This is the thyroid chakra, which is located near the thyroid gland (part of the endocrine system) in the area between the heart chakra and the throat chakra. This chakra has helped to ease our transition, due to its location. It helps us to communicate (throat chakra) from a place of love (heart chakra).

The thyroid chakra is connected to our immune system and electromagnetic waves make us more susceptible to stresses, such as infectious diseases, and what we think of as 'new' diseases such as AIDS, ME, PVS. We are called upon to strengthen our immune systems on a physical or endocrine level, and we can also see how attitudes are changing. For instance, when AIDS was newly discovered, a stigma was attached to the disease. Victims are now treated with much more compassion. The colour of this chakra is aqua.

Fifth chakra: the throat.

This centre is blue (imagine bluebells) and its ruler is Mercury. The throat chakra is associated with hearing. We talk endlessly these days about nothing in particular, we are bombarded with low level noise, and so our sense of hearing has become deadened. The thyroid chakra aligns with the heart chakra, and thereby verbalises our truth and our real needs and feelings.

The challenge of this chakra is not how well we exert our will over others, but how well we can control ourselves. When opened and in balance, this chakra brings the gift of telepathy. When it is closed, we have difficulty expressing ourselves. By being aware that every thought we have is either a potential act of grace or a potential weapon, we

183

learn to direct our life force to the kinds of thoughts and words and deeds which will return positive energy to us.

Sixth chakra: the brow.

Also known as the third eye/psychic gland, this chakra is located between the eyebrows. The colour is indigo (a dusk sky) This chakra is also known as the *anja* chakra, *anja* being the Sanskrit word for command, and it is here that we receive commands from our higher selves. When awakened, this chakra acts as a third eye, with the development of clairvoyance, which is a kind of spiritual awakening. We often use this chakra as a centre for concentration when we meditate; it's a door which leads to deeper and deeper levels of awareness. On a physical level, the brow chakra can help us to increase our powers of intelligence, memory, concentration and visualisation, so it's related to the eyes, ears and brain. Instability here leads to tiredness, irritability, sleeplessness and confusion.

The challenge presented to us by this chakra is to let go of judgement on others, and to accept that life has purpose and meaning far beyond our understanding. In other words, to take the wider view, the larger perspective.

Seventh chakra: the crown.

Its colour is violet /lavender, and it is ruled by Neptune. As a colour, lavender represents dignity and self respect. The crown is situated above/outside the physical body, because it is mainly connected with higher consciousness. When the centre is open, we see spiritually in a very personal way, not tied in with any religion or dogma. It then becomes a conscious experience of divine energy. The energy of this chakra pours into our life whether or not you are aware of it, but when we meditate to receive the energy, we can direct it to change our lives.

The challenge of this chakra is to release fear about any aspect of our lives – from what will become of us tomorrow to when our Earthly lives will close. When nothing feels secure to us it is because our sense of safety is rooted in the physical world. We also hold on to our past, which

184

then continues to adversely affect our lives. This is because in looking backwards, we don't appreciate the grace and guidance we receive each moment. Of all the chakras, the crown chakra requires the least effort to activate. It is our true connection to the universe.

Eighth chakra.

I'll talk about this separately from the others, as the eighth chakra represents our next level of evolution, so does not influence our physical bodies as yet, nor our personal, emotional or psychological selves as directly. The eighth chakra, whose colour is a beautiful magenta, contains universally recognised images, which provide impersonal, symbolic views of our human experience. This dimension of consciousness connects us with others in an impersonal experience of evolution, a kind of warehouse of universal information and consciousness. As we enter more deeply into the age of Aquarius, we will gain access easier to this link between our personal consciousness and the impersonal, greater consciousness of the next dimension.

The eighth chakra does not have a bodily counterpart as the other chakras do and is located above the energy field which surrounds and permeates our bodies. It mostly connects with the seventh chakra, insight, and has always been there, though we are only now beginning to gain access to it as we have been developing the meditative conscious ability to see beyond the visible world and perceive the energy dimensions of our lives. This is because as human consciousness evolves, we become more sensitive to our more refined vibrational field that is part of Aquarius. What this means is that we are developing the ability to interpret our physical being through its symbolic meaning. The physical element in our lives then looks like props on a stage that set off a response from our conscious minds. We are meant to continue to learn more about ourselves, so we can establish direct dialogue with our unconscious.

We can practise using our symbolic sight to detach our

185

emotions from a situation, whether positive or negative.

Thus: Change 'I had an argument with a friend' to 'An argument occurred between two people, the cause of the argument was a power play.' This way of detaching allows us to see what is taking place behind the physical and emotional surroundings of the event itself.

Practice. We can also apply it to the past. Instead of saying, 'My parents always belittled me', say: 'Adults who were disappointed with their own lives chose to make up for it by diminishing those around them'. Then connect with the eighth chakra using this invocation: 'I fully accept divine will as the guiding force in my life.'

We can also see the interconnectedness of the chakra system, as well as our evolution, if we recall the challenge of the third eye chakra to let go of our personal views, and take the wider perspective.

Aura.

What is the aura? The aura, or subtle anatomy, is the electromagnetic field surrounding a person, animal, tree, plant, and rock. Everything has an aura, even the chairs we sit in. With practice and patience, seeing an aura becomes possible. We've all seen the aura surrounding the moon, for instance, street lamps and candles. Some people actually see colours which I will explain about later, and some perceive a subtle movement of light, a bit like a fuzzy image you get around things when the television is not tuned in properly.

Kirlian photography is proof that auras do indeed exist and is another innovation which has opened a promising field of investigation. By the end of the 19th century investigations had shawn that there was a connection between the human psyche and the aura shown in high voltage electrophotography, but it was not until new methods were developed during and after the Second World War, that the possibilities were generally realised.

Kirlian photographs show an amazing aura of light around both leaving and inanimate objects and it is claimed

186

that this aura is partly of non-physical origin and so can be modified by human thought, and has shown that emotions affect the aura of light seen in these high frequency photographs. Kirlian is a form of radionic/x-ray photography.

Hold your hand up about two feet in front of you and study its outline as you gently and slowly stretch and contract your fingers. Then move your fingers apart and shift your focus to a point in the distance. Concentrate on your hand, but look beyond it to your distant focus. Shift your vision back and forth. Rest your eyes now, and repeat the exercise, leaving your eyes focused on the distance. Notice the movement of light or energy around your hand. Practise this. Always remain relaxed, as a relaxed attitude always makes things easier.

To see an aura, we use our peripheral vision. If we stare at someone, we may make him or her feel uncomfortable, and so we look to the side of them.

Sit opposite the person you want to look at, up to three feet away. Take a few deep breaths to help clear the mind of particular thoughts or images. Now very quickly open and close your eyes once, so that you get a quick glimpse of the person in front of you. This makes a sort of frozen photographic image imprint on your mind. Hold the image. Examine it. What stands out? Do you see a glow? Do certain colours stand out? As the image fades, quickly open and close your eyes again to strengthen it. How much detail can you see? Which part fades first? Which linger? All these things tell you about the strengths and weaknesses of a person's aura.

The inner auric space surrounds the body and spreads out up to three feet. The outer auric space, which is a bit like a buffer zone, extends beyond that, up to 15ft, and is often referred to as our 'personal space'. When we are closely involved with someone, and feel familiar and comfortable with them, we feel a warmth when they are within our 'space', but a stranger coming too close can make us feel uncomfortable, and quite often we take a step backwards to protect our space or aura.

The size of auras varies. People who live in areas which are not densely populated have a need for lots of personal space, as this is what they are used to. For instance, in a quiet country pub, groups of friends will distance themselves from another group. In a city, though, people are used to being closely packed together, constantly invading one another's auras, and this is one of the reasons why stress levels are so high in cities: people constantly feel invaded and threatened by the proximity of others. We can find the size of our auric space by walking towards someone until we begin to feel uncomfortable. This is the 'buffer' zone.

Often when healing is taking place, people see colours. This is because as they relax their mind energy expands, and they see into the energy dimensions. It's been proven that colour and light affect people and so healers work with this principle to bring about effective healing.

You will also have noticed how hospital wards are usually painted in a restful colour such as green, never red, reflecting natural colours like grass, flowers and blue sky. Have you ever noticed how uplifting a bright blue sky is?

I mentioned earlier that the aura expands and contracts. Our moods and circumstances also affect this.

If you use this simple meditation you will see how it can work.

Sitting comfortably, close your eyes, concentrate on slowing down your breathing. Take your time. Now imagine a circle of light on the floor in front of you, beautiful white light. Now, think of a time when you felt really happy, full of fun and laughter. Maybe a holiday or a day out, or perhaps good news. Watch now what happens to the circle of light; see how it expands. Take a moment to enjoy the feeling.

Still breathing slowly, think now of a time when you felt sad and depressed, tired, miserable, fed up. Notice now what happens to the energy field this time, see how it shrinks and loses brightness. Concentrate on the circle of

188

light and think again of the happy time, watch the circle expand again. Bring your attention now to your breathing, and return to the room in your own time.

Each gland, body organ, and body system has a vibrational frequency, which is sympathetic to one of the spectrum colours. This means that the cells vibrate in the same rhythm as one of the colour vibrations. Just as we need a variety of foods to provide us with physical nutrition, we need a balance of all the colour vibrations if we are to be healthy, this is could be called spiritual nutrition.

The aura consists of seven layers. Just as there are seven main chakras, these exist beyond the physical body. Each one permeates the physical body, and overlaps the previous one extending outward and relates to one of the chakras, linking the innermost 'etheric' layer of the aura with the body. Thus, each chakra draws in life energy from its matching level of the aura.

The Etheric Body.

this vibrates at a higher rate; which is why we cannot see it unless we raise our physical vibrations. This is done in meditation.

The etheric body is made up of energy pulsing through the body from electrical impulses from the brain travelling through the nervous system. On the Etheric level, this energy can be perceived as a pale red, this reveals the basic life force and permeates out from the base chakra.

This energy is absorbed and maintains the etheric body, so that the physical body is protected from negative/harmful vibrations. This layer is the blueprint for the physical body, and it's in the etheric body that disease starts. It can be seen or felt as an accumulation of energy, which may ultimately manifest as a physical disorder. So the energy from the etheric body can be seen as a band of blue light emanating around the physical body. This layer registers pain, pleasure etc. In a healthy person the colour is a clear light blue.

The Emotional Body.

This layer reflects the electromagnetic vibrations associated with the emotions, and centres around the spleen chakra, which is the main organ for extracting life force from our food and water. It is mainly perceived as orange chakra. This layer is usually filled with a mass of changing colour energy, which indicate our moods and emotions. As our feelings change, so do the colours in this layer of the aura, eg if the colours here are perceived as dark or muddy, this would indicate areas of emotional trauma or repressed feelings. People who have a well balanced heart chakra can let their emotions flow outwards, connecting them to feelings of compassion and love, and the colours of the emotional body will be tinged with rose-pink. The sacral/spleen chakra in a healthy person the colours should be clear and bright.

The Mental Body.

This layer is filled with vibrations from our mind, our thoughts. Every thought the rest of humanity has creates a form. If we think negative thoughts, they attract other negative thoughts, thereby amplifying the original thought. In the same way, positive thoughts will attract more positives.

The mental body is divided into two parts, the first linking with the left side of the brain, which is involved, with the mental process of reason and logic, organisation, language. The lower mind connects to thought patterns and habits taught to us in childhood and reinforced during our life. Yellow is the characteristic colour of the lower mind.

In the aura negative thoughts will dim the yellow, and positive thoughts will look strong and bright. This layer is linked with the solar plexus chakra. In a healthy person the colour is a bright daffodil yellow.

The Astral Body.

This is the other part, our higher mind, and is linked to the right side of our brain, the aspect of the mind which is much more abstract and free to exercise discrimination,

190

empathy, judgement and intuition. Sensitive people such as artists, musicians and poets use their higher mind. The colour relating to the higher mind is green, for the higher mind is closely linked to the heart chakra. The more creative we are, the more we exercise our higher emotions, the lighter and more clear the colours in the astral body become. The colours are lovely shades of turquoise and pale blue. The higher mind connects us with our soul.

This layer registers personality and how we relate to others. In a healthy person the colour is clear sky blue.

The Etheric Template Body. (Causal or Karmic Body.)

This body is the record of all our previous lives, and also contains the reason for our present incarnation. When we incarnate, we bring with us the knowledge of the path we have chosen and all the challenges we have elected to meet our life plan. From the moment of birth, we are subjected to conditioning, which makes us forget our life plan (like finding our way without a map.) The dormant colours of the karmic body are shades of a beautiful, ethereal blue, exquisite and delicate. It is this body which allows us to view the events of our whole life at the point of death.

This layer is linked with the throat chakra and registers speech, listening and all that of the etheric body. In a healthy person the colour is clear and bright.

The Celestial Body. (Spiritual Body).

The spiritual planes embody the intuitional and divine planes. On these planes, we merge with cosmic or universal consciousness, and the higher principles of humans. The spiritual bodies are rarely seen except around great spiritual masters, or saints.

The celestial body represents the true self. The colour energy in this layer takes the form of pastel shades and can extend a long way. It's said that the Buddha's extended for two miles. This layer is linked with the brow chakra (colour indigo blue) and registers love beyond human love, spiritual love. In a healthy person the colour is made up of beautiful

191

pastel shades.

The Ketheric Template Body.

The colour energy in this layer takes the form of brilliant light at the edge of the aura. The divine aura cannot be projected from within. This light comes from a cosmic source, and we take in its vitality through the crown chakra where it is broken down into its constituent colours, which are then absorbed by each energy centre.

This layer is linked with the crown chakra (colour violet) and registers all that is spiritual and physical. The colour is made up of all the other layers and it has golden threads like fingers holding all the rest of the bodies/aura together. (Note: Chakra colours differ from the aura colours.)

Disease or disharmony in the physical body starts in the aura. If it is not dealt with at this level, it will then manifest in the physical body, because the aura interpenetrates the physical. Colour surrounds and fills everyone, so the disharmony is seen or felt as either an absence of colour, or the 'wrong' colour in the 'wrong' places.

The aura acts as a prism through which the white light energy (sunlight) passes. The light is broken down into its component colours, and then sent to energise the individual chakras. As the aura is made up of light and sound vibrations emitted by all our cells, glands and organs, the colours in the aura reveal our general state of health. Bright clear colours show good health, while dull murky colours show an imbalance somewhere in the system. Areas where there are energy blockages will show up as dots and blobs, the position of these indicate areas in your life where energy is blocked. One of the ways of addressing the blockages is to use/introduce the correct colour. Colour can introduce the right frequency into the body, thereby restoring harmony, and we know that colour plays an important part in the healing process.

If you have not yet seen an aura, here is a good meditation for becoming aware. You can also use it for healing, since we know that the transmission of positive life energy into appropriate parts of the aura is the basis of spiritual healing.

Sitting comfortably, close your eyes; bring your attention to your breathing. Begin to consciously slow it down. Breathe in for a count of three then hold for three. Do this three times. Repeat this exercise, increasing by one each time. As you relax more and more, allow your body to spread out, and imagine that it is slithering out over the floor, letting all tension go. Let the chair take your weight fully. Breathe naturally.

Be aware of the limits of your physical body. Sit there and sense where your body ends, and mentally travel all around the outline of your body, beginning with your feet. Up one side, over your head, back down the other side to the feet. Do this slowly and steadily, keep your focus and concentration. Don't rush; better too slowly than too fast.

When you are back at your feet, you now have a good awareness of your body and its area of being. Now let your body become weightless. Bring to mind the fact that your body is made of energy. Sense and feel your life energy within you. Feel its flow and movement over your physical body. It's easy to feel light. Imagine yourself becoming lighter and lighter with each breath you take until you are completely weightless. Imagine yourself floating just a little off your chair, and in your imagination, let your body stretch, first above your head, then below your feet for a distance of about two inches. You actually drift up, then down by a couple of inches.

Feel and sense your response. The object is to move into your aura, above and below. Be aware again of your physical body as it floats above the chair, weightless and motionless. Imagine that this time you move up once more, by a distance of about one foot. Sense how it feels, take your time, and then move back through your body, then below it to a distance of about one foot again. Note your feelings and responses. Moving slowly and gently, taking your time, move up to the edge of your aura, a distance of two to three feet. Move back through your body, then below it, to about two or three feet. Then move slowly back into your body, ready for the next stage.

You can now begin to expand and contract the aura itself. Be very gentle. Become aware of your breathing and don't alter it in any way. As you breathe in, imagine that you are drawing in your aura. Breathe naturally, drawing it in. Little by little your aura is contracting, until it feels quite light over you. Be aware of your response. Continue until you feel your aura is quite close to your physical body. Feel the energy of the aura move in. Remain still like this, aware of your aura close around you. Feel it beneath your feet, above your head and to the sides. Now turn your attention to your breathing out, again don't alter the level of your breathing. As you focus on breathing out, allow your aura to move out. Concentrate on this, letting the aura expand beyond its usual size to the very edges, as far as it can go. As this happens, feel a sense of expansion and space. Breathe your aura out. Pause now and collect your senses, let awareness and sensation return to you. Relax and drift a while if you wish.

Now begin to make your return. Gradually and very gently, return your awareness to your physical body, become aware of your body's weight once more sitting in the chair. Return to the room.

CHAPTER THIRTEEN

Reiki

Reiki (pronounced ray-key) is healing by the laying on of hands, a technique that is thousands of years old. It is thought to have been used by Tibetan Buddhist monks, but was rediscovered in the late 1800s by Dr Mikao Usui, a Japanese Buddhist. The Usui system of Reiki is very simple and a powerful form of healing which is easily given and received.

The accepted definition of the word *rei* is 'universal'. The Japanese characters have seven levels of meaning, which vary from the mundane to the esoteric. So while *rei* can be defined as 'universal', ie present everywhere, research into the more esoteric meaning of the Japanese character for rei shows that it can also be interpreted as 'spiritual consciousness'. This consciousness is of the higher self, which, by definition, is all knowing.

Ki is 'life force'. It has been identified by all cultures, and given many other names. The Chinese call it *chi*, it is *prana* in Sanskrit, *manna* in Hawaiian. Ki is a non-physical energy which flows through and animates all living things. As long as something is alive, it has life-force circulating through and around it, believed to be the energy associated with our thoughts, emotions and spiritual existence.

Martial artists use *ki* to assist their physical and mental development. Shamans use the same energy to aid psychic awareness, manifestation, divination and healing. All healers, regardless of cultural background or discipline, employ *ki*. It is present all around us, and is an energy that can be harnessed by the body and guided by the mind.

Reiki is a special kind of life force that can only be channelled after someone has been attuned to its energy. The attunements (or initiations) are the continuation of an ancient process of tuning the healer's body, both physical and etheric, to a higher vibration. This clears a channel for the energy to flow through. Once attuned, this channel will remain open and the energy is available to be used by the healer for the rest of his/her life.

Rei and *ki* combined can therefore be defined as 'spiritually guided universal life force', which is a good working definition of the word.

The reiki healing energy moves through the healer, working on him before being channelled through the recipient. As it is channelled, the healer's own energies are never depleted. In fact, the more a healer gives of the energy, the more is received. The benefits to the healer through using the energy are that negativity and 'blocks' within himself are removed, and a general cleansing of both body and mind are experienced, leaving a feeling of serenity and well-being.

All healers use life force or *ki* but not all use reiki. The reiki energy works on a different vibration, and is generally only available after a reiki master has given a correct attunement. Of course, it is possible that some healers might be born with the reiki attunement already having taken place, but this would be very rare.

It is widely accepted that people who already do healing work experience an increase of at least 50% in the power of their healing energies after receiving reiki attunements.

Once attuned, the practitioner with the intent to heal simply places their hands on the person to be healed then gives reiki treatments. While a number of easily learned hand positions are used on the recipient's body, the reiki energy has a way of naturally flowing to the area where it is most needed, therefore no conscious direction by the practitioner is required as Reiki communicates with the recipient's higher self.

Every reiki treatment is different and recipients report various effects, such as increased heat or cold, or sensations such as tingling. All seem to report a deep sense of relaxation. The recipient will always receive the correct amount of energy to facilitate and restore balance and to

196

promote healing. When used constantly, reiki facilitates spiritual development within the practitioner and creates beneficial change within the user, dispelling negative thought forms and attitudes to promote a feeling of well being.

Regular practitioners take responsibility for their future development, become more in tune, increasingly aware of their surroundings and the changing world.

May you discover, as I and many others have, that reiki, this ancient healing energy, is a powerful tool with which to assist one's own spiritual progression. It lifts one's vibration, which in turn benefits others and, ultimately, humankind and the Earth.

Dr Mikao Usui was born in Japan in the mid-nineteenth century. He was fascinated by Buddha and his desire to help others, and the unusual metaphysical abilities the Buddha possessed after receiving enlightenment. It was believed that the Buddha was able to heal physical illness and that he taught this ability to his disciples, who also acquired healing abilities after following his teachings.

Dr Usui was aware that there were many people unable to lead happy and productive lives because of illness or physical disability. Feeling compassion for them, he decided to set out on a quest to see if the secret of healing used by the Buddha and Jesus could be found so that he might help the sick and needy.

He travelled through Japan, talking to Buddhist teachers and priests, asking if they had the ability to heal. The answer he was given was always the same: while it may have been possible to heal in the past, the spiritual side was felt to be more important, and the ability to heal the physical body was forgotten and lost.

During his travels, he became friends with the monks in a Zen monastery, and was allowed to stay and study the Buddhist scriptures known as *sutras*. The abbot of the monastery was also interested in physical healing and helped and encouraged Dr Usui in his pursuit. The Japanese translations did not have the answers Usui was looking for, and because he wanted to read the sacred books in their original language, he learned Chinese and eventually Sanskrit. It was in the Indian sutras that he discovered the formula for contacting a higher power, which could give him knowledge of healing himself. He had found the information he had been looking for, but simply knowing the formula did not give him the ability to heal. Having discussed this with the abbott, he decided that he should go to the top of Mount Kori-yama, a sacred mountain, where he fasted and meditated, following the instructions in the formula for 21 days.

To keep track of time on the mountain, he set up 21 stones and each day he threw one stone away. On the twenty-first day, after throwing away all the stones, he had still not received the healing power. It was night, and he stood up, thinking he had failed in his quest.

As he looked out towards the horizon, he saw a point of light coming towards him. Looking at it, he realised it had a consciousness and was in fact communicating with him. He realised the light contained the healing power he was looking for, but he also became aware that the light was so powerful that, if it hit him, it might kill him. He decided that the ability to heal was worth the risk, and although he was afraid, he did not move.

The beam struck him on the forehead, knocking him unconscious. Rising out of his physical body, he saw bubbles of light containing the symbols. He immediately received an attunement, and knowledge of each symbol, and was, as a consequence, initiated into reiki.

Dr Usui hurried down the mountain. In his haste, he fell over, stubbing his big toe and tearing the nail. He placed both hands over the injured area and within minutes the pain and the bleeding had stopped. Shortly after, he was completely healed.

Having fasted for 21 days, he was by then very hungry, so when he reached the foot of the mountain, he stopped at an inn for something to eat. While waiting for his food to be cooked, he heard a young girl crying in a nearby house. Upon investigating, he found the girl had been suffering for days from a bad toothache. He laid his hands upon her face and within minutes, the swelling had receded and the pain had stopped.

The innkeeper, who by now had prepared the meal for Dr Usui, warned him not to eat such a large meal after fasting for so long, but he ate his fill and felt no adverse effects.

Back at the monastery, he discovered that the abbott was ill. He eventually managed to persuade the other monks to allow him to see the abbott, who had been suffering badly from arthritis. Whilst talking to him, Dr Usui placed his hands on the Abbott's body, and the healing energy flowed into the abbott, who was soon healed.

After discussions with the abbott and the other monks, it was agreed that Dr Usui needed to practise and learn how the healing energies worked. To achieve this, he went and worked in a beggar camp in Kyoto, where he remained for seven years, healing the sick. After healing the young and the able, he sent them off to find work.

At a subsequent visit to the beggar camp, he recognised many of those he had healed and had sent off to find work. He asked why they had returned to the beggar camp, and they answered that it was much easier to beg than to work. He realised that they neither valued the healing he had given them, nor appreciated the opportunity to improve their way of life.

Around 1925, Dr Usui gave the master attunement to Dr Chujiro Hayashi, a retired naval officer. In addition, he charged him with the responsibility of preserving reiki so that it would not be lost to future generations. Dr Usui died in 1930 and Chujiro Hayashi opened a reiki clinic in Tokyo, training teams of reiki practitioners, including 16 masters, during his lifetime. In the clinic, healers worked in groups on patients who lived at the clinic during the time of their healing.

Dr Hayashi also kept records of treatments to demonstrate that reiki finds the source of physical symptoms and provides the energy needed to restore the body to wholeness. Using this information, he created the hand positions, the system of three degrees, and the initiation procedure for first degree, second degree and the reiki master.

Realising that a war was coming, he decided to pass on the complete reiki teachings to a woman in order that they might be preserved. Hawayo Takata was chosen for this purpose.

Hawayo Takata (nee Kawamuru) was born on 24 December 1900, on the island on Kauai, Hawaii. Her parents were Japanese immigrants, and her father worked in sugar plantations. Too small and frail for plantation work, she took jobs while still at public school. After school she was offered a servant's job at a large, prosperous plantation owner's house. She eventually became housekeeper and book-keeper, a very responsible position, and finally married the plantation accountant, Saichi Takata, in 1917. They had a happy marriage and were blessed with two daughters. Saichi died aged 34, in 1930, leaving Mrs Takata to raise their children.

In order to provide for her children, she worked very hard, taking little rest. As a consequence of this, she developed nervous exhaustion and was diagnosed with a gall bladder disease which required surgery. Because she had a respiratory condition and difficulty in breathing, anaesthetic was dangerous for her. Her health deteriorated, and she was told that without surgery she might not live, but also that the surgery might kill her.

After her sister died in 1935, she travelled to Japan to tell her parents the sad news. She also felt she could get help with her health problems in Japan. Once there, she entered a hospital in Alaska and was scheduled for surgery after a few weeks, by which time she had been diagnosed with appendicitis and a tumour in addition to her other complaints.

The night before surgery she heard a voice in her head say that the operation was not necessary. She heard it again on the operating table while she was being prepared for anaesthetic so, getting up, she asked the surgeon if there was another way to heal her. The doctor told her about Chujiro Hayashi's reiki clinic. The surgeon's sister, who had been healed by Hayashi's healers and had taken reiki training, took her to the clinic that day.

At the reiki clinic, Mrs Takata began receiving reiki treatments. This was all new to her. Using their reiki hands, the practitioners could sense what was wrong with her. In fact, their diagnosis very closely matched the surgeon's at the hospital. This gave her confidence in what they were doing. She received daily treatments, and became progressively better. After a four-month stay at the clinic, she was completely healed in body, mind and spirit. Impressed with the results she wanted to learn reiki. However, at first she was refused – not because she was a woman, but because she was not Japanese.

Mrs Takata talked to the surgeon at the hospital, who persuaded Dr Hayashi to allow her to learn reiki. She received her Reiki I training in spring 1936, joining the team of healers who worked at the clinic. In 1937, she received Reiki II and, after a two-year stay in Japan, she returned to Hawaii, where she set up a Reiki clinic in Kapaa. In the same winter of 1938, Dr Hayashi visited her in Hawaii, where she received her Reiki III training. On February 22, 1938, Hayashi announced Hawayo Takata as a master/teacher and his successor, insisting that she did not give training away without charge. She was the thirteenth and last reiki master initiated by him.

The Second World War arrived, and Hayashi was drafted into the navy but, as a healer and medic, he vowed not to take life. His solution to the dilemma was to take his own life instead, which he did on May 10, 1941. His wife survived the war, but their house and clinic were taken over by the occupation and, as a consequence, were not able to operate as a healing centre.

Hawayo Takata was the means by which reiki continued. Having brought it first to Hawaii, she then introduced it to mainland United States, Canada, and finally Europe. She lived to a ripe old age and always looked decades younger than her actual age. During her lifetime, she trained hundreds of people in the reiki healing system, and in the last ten years of her life, between 1970 and 1980, she initiated 22 reiki masters.

When introducing reiki to America, she felt it would be difficult for the Western mind to value something that was free, so she decided to charge a large sum of money for the reiki master teachings attunement, feeling this would create appreciation for reiki that was needed. She also created the story that Dr Usui was a Christian monk, as she felt that a Christian background would be more acceptable to the West, given the bad feelings towards Japan as a consequence of the war. According to the story, Dr Usui was the principal of Doshisha University, a Christian school in Kyoto, where he apparently received inspiration by how Jesus had healed the sick. It also said that he studied at the University of Chicago, gaining a degree in theology. Unsurprisingly, the archives at Doshisha University have no record of Dr Usui at all. Likewise, neither has the University of Chicago.

One of the 22 Reiki Masters initiated by Mrs Takata was her granddaughter, Phyllis Furomoto, who succeeded her as grand master, after her death in 1980. Mrs Furomoto remains the current grand master of Usui Shiki Ryoho.

Usui Shiki Ryoho.

Since Mrs Takata's transcendence the form of reiki known as the Usui system has evolved. As previously mentioned, both Hayashi and Takata added to the original system rediscovered by Dr Usui. As Reiki becomes more widespread and available throughout the world, it continues

202

to develop and change as Masters incorporate knowledge learned through experience and/or channelled teachings. This ensures that reiki progresses, whilst honouring the initial teachings of Dr Usui.

As this progression occurs, it is inevitable that there will be a divergence in terms of both emphasis on what is taught, and how much is paid for the attunements.

Reiki is, and always will be a simple system that can be used by everyone. Given the nature of the teachings, one should trust one's own intuition and feelings as to the course of development and time scale.

Reiki attunement.

The process of attunement or initiation is what makes reiki different from every other form of healing. Consequently, it is not taught as other healing techniques are taught. This is what creates the reiki healer. The ability to attune to the reiki frequency is passed from Master to student during the initiation process, which can be made into a beautiful ritual, or performed without ceremony.

This process opens the crown, the heart and palm chakras. Students may experience a variety of things: some perceive colours, some are filled with light or a feeling of serenity, wonder or love, and some become emotional. The sensations are perceptible, but always gentle. The process opens a channel from the 'rei' or 'universal God' force, giving the students exactly the right amount of energy that is appropriate to their needs. This may explain why there are as many reactions to the attunement process as there are students. The process, although orchestrated by the master, is attended by reiki guides and spirit helpers, which may explain the source of the colours, lights, visions, etc, which many students report experiencing.

One attunement is all that is necessary to open the student to the energy. It could be said that the initiation does not give the receiver anything new, but rather that it opens and aligns what is already part of the person. Some masters give more than one attunement, and the value of this may be to strengthen the energy given. In addition, the more a student is attuned, the clearer the channel becomes, with increased benefits to the healer in terms of psychic sensitivity, and a raising of consciousness of the individual. Some students report that their 'third eye' is opened by the process. Traditional Usui reiki first degree uses as part of the attunement four stages, which have the effect of gently opening the channels within the student to the reiki energy.

The first three open the healing chakras, and the fourth seals the energy. Once the student has acquired the ability to give reiki, it remains for life, even if that ability is not used for periods of time.

Reiki attunements could be likened to the first steps in a spiritual journey, which starts with a cleansing of the physical, mental and emotional bodies. It is quite usual for students to go through a release of emotional energy shortly after. This could be described as detoxification, which could include diarrhoea, running nose or increased urination.

What is happening is that more ki energy is entering the student's aura than has been experienced before, and the aura and chakras are clearing and adjusting to enable the new healer to channel the additional energy. After this initial adjustment period, students begin to see a refinement of their belief structures and feelings, along with a release of any pent-up emotional energy; ie they become more 'balanced' individuals.

Once attuned, the reiki practitioner only has to place his or her hands on the subject, with the intent to heal, and the healing energy will flow automatically. After receiving Reiki I, it is important that for, say, the first month, the student gives as many healing sessions as possible, including a daily self-healing. This continues the refinement process started by the attunement.

One of the fundamental differences between reiki and other forms of healing is that reiki knows how much energy is needed. Therefore, from the healer's point of view, the process is automatic and does not require the healer to guide or force it. The healer may or may not know what needs healing, but the energy has intelligence far beyond human understanding.

It is important to remember that the practitioner is a channel for the energy to be given, not the source of healing. This explains why treatments do not drain the giver. It could be said that during a healing session, two people are being healed in that the reiki energy also acts and works upon a healer as well as the person to be healed. The energy heals on all levels, physical, emotional and spiritual.

A treatment will normally last for about an hour, the practitioner should allow a certain amount of time for each hand position. However, with practice, the healer should adopt an approach in terms of time for each hand position based on their intuition. If someone has a visible injury, say on the left leg, it is obviously appropriate to concentrate on that area. During the healing session, the energy may flow to different parts of the body in addition to the mental/emotional levels, where the true source of the illness may be located.

It is important that students do not become too reliant on results and that their own ego is disengaged from the process of healing. After all, you are merely a channel and you must trust that the recipient is receiving the amount of energy to restore harmony, if that is God's will.

It is never ethical to say, 'I healed this person'. You cannot make a mistake with reiki. You cannot give too much of it, or apply it wrongly. It can never do any harm. It is a healing energy which only works for the good of the recipient as well as the healer. You are merely a conduit for the energy to flow, and are not responsible for the results. One need never worry about giving reiki. It will always be helpful.

Reiki first degree works on a physical level: you need to touch to heal.

What can be treated?

During the history of its use, Reiki has aided in the healing of just about every known illness and injury. In addition, it can help to break unwanted habits, eg smoking, drinking, taking drugs etc. It can also assist with weight loss and it is especially beneficial to pregnant women, and has a relaxing and reassuring effect on the unborn child.

Two important aspects for the healer to bear in mind when giving a treatment are that:

(a) He or she must be in the right frame of mind ie relaxed and calm. Stress and healing do not go together.

(b) The treatment itself should be conducted in a relaxed area, where both practitioner and recipient feel warm and comfortable. The practitioner should always see that, for the duration of the healing session, there are no distractions, eg telephone calls or television, radio playing etc. Often, playing soothing instrumental, music (at low volume) during the treatment can aid the relaxation of the person being treated especially if they have come to you for the first time in strange surroundings.

If the recipient wishes to talk with the healer during the session, the energy will not normally be interrupted. However, it is advisable that conversation is kept to a minimum. The reiki is normally found to be so relaxing that the recipient invariably does not want to talk after a few minutes.

The giving of reiki healing is a spiritual process, and it is fairly common for a sensitive practitioner, by psychic or intuitive means, to access information from the recipient during treatment. This occurs due to the interaction of the energy fields between the practitioner and the recipient, and often leads to a greater awareness on the part of the healer of the recipient's condition. Practitioners should, in the main, keep this experience to themselves, as to divulge information gained in this way may force the recipient to become tense or anxious, and they may regard the process as an intrusion.

Charges.

Some students have difficulty with the concept of charging for healing. After all, reiki is a God-given healing energy for the betterment of mankind. However, remember what was written about Dr Usui's experiences in the Kyoto beggar camp. He came to the conclusion that people in a material world only respect those things that have material value, or where payment changes hands.

Natural justice requires that if something is given, something should be received in return. Throughout the ages there has been a long tradition of material goods or services having been offered to spiritual leaders or persons for prayers or spiritual favours. The church collection box and harvest festival are continued evidence of this concept. It is also useful to remember that if you place no value on the treatment given, then the recipient will not either.

It is thought that over 90% of all illnesses originate in the mind. It is therefore important for the recipient to value the process. Positive thoughts and feelings about the healing process will help to restore harmony.

The Reiki Principles

Just for today I will give thanks for my blessings
Just for today I will not worry
Just for today I will not be angry
Just for today I will do my work honestly
Just for today I will be kind to my neighbour and every living thing.

CHAPTER FOURTEEN

Bio-Energy Healing

Bio-energy healing works like reiki on the human life energy force but unlike reiki it is a non-contact form of healing. It also came from the East and was hidden away by the Chinese.

Before 1122BC the Chinese referred to this energy as 'chi'. 'I chi' describes three types of energy: cosmic, Earth and human, human energy being a mixture of the first two. It is possible to manipulate them. Around 300 BC people used breathing techniques to control and manipulate these energies, maintaining health and curing illnesses by changing the quality and quantity of energy levels within the human system, and using them to attain a higher state of consciousness. It was *not* concerned with the health of the masses.

People worked with the life energy, trying to escape the endless cycle of reincarnation. They worked on a deeper level and tried to control the various functions of the body's internal organs as well as slow down the ageing process. Monks lived well over the age of 100, which in those days was unheard of.

The Buddhist monks in 58 AD locked away their secrets behind monastery walls until the Ching Government was overthrown in 1911 and documents became available to India, Korea, Japan and the Middle East. The monks then went on to use the life energy training in martial arts and enhanced fighting techniques.

Many ancient monuments were built on sites where the Earth's magnetic lines are strongest; hence the concentrations of energy are more powerful than those found in other areas. The surface of the Earth has identifiable lines of magnetic force and the Earth is influenced by other heavenly bodies such as the moon and the tides. This interaction of the universal energy influences human behaviour, eg dowsers and how they locate water underground etc.

Today with electric equipment we can measure minute electromagnetic currents. Biosensors can pick up these energy exchanges eg ECGs (electrocardiographs) in the heart, EEGs (Electroencephalogram) in the brain, and lie detectors in the skin.

Dynamic energy is the energy field or what is known as the aura, called Superconducting Quantum Interference Device (SQUID) This actually gives more information about the brain than the EEG does. Some people (usually clairvoyants) can see this colourful aura, or energy field, and can see health or sickness etc in a person.

Psychoanalyst Wilhelm Reich spent years studying the life energy. He called it 'Orgon' energy. He believed there was a unity between human beings and nature and that it was impossible to split this energy without serious repercussions, and that the life energy was all present and its flow changed only in density and concentration. Changing the concentration of energy or regulating it within the body could help those suffering from disease.

Scientists in the USA re-investigated 'Orgonomy' with hundreds across the world, experimenting and investigating psychokinesis, telepathy, psychometry and precognition. The Soviet Union had 20 research institutes trying to understand phenomena beyond the laws of science.

All living things have an electronic field, and scientists now believe that the human energy field may be composed of ions, electrons, neutral particles and strongly ionised substances. This could be considered a fourth state of matter.

How the energy flows.

Circulation of energies inside and outside the body is crucial to the healing process. When both Earth and cosmic energies meet, a new and more powerful energy is created within the human body. This energy is utilised throughout the body, through the seven major and 21 minor energy centres (chakras) These centres take in energy in a spiral motion, which determines health.

Everyone is sensitive and susceptible to these energies, constantly feeding off them. Without it we would not survive. Cosmic energy flows from the crown centre to the base centre of the spine and the Earth energy flows from the base centre to the crown centre. When they meet at the Solar Plexus centre it then changes to Human energy. Standing up is the best position to avail our selves of these energies. When we lie down the energy becomes weaker and the body functions slow down.

Pathways.

These are called meridians where the energy flows. These are closer to the nerves and relate in the same way as a high frequency current relates to an electric conductor. The Earth and the Cosmic energy fuse and form a new type of energy that is within and outside the body.

Vital life force enters these centres in a spiral motion, which looks like a vortex or whirlpool and takes on the characteristics of the living organism and is strongest in the areas of the brain, throat, heart, stomach and intestines. The energy is distributed through the meridians then to the organs and other parts of the body which need it.

The energy in a healthy person is continually flowing and transformed as a result of breathing, circulating of blood and the actions of the nervous system.

It is possible for an individual to direct and manipulate the life energy in themselves and others by using their will. Blood circulation is crucial, as blood is the carrier of the life force and oxygen, and is an active ingredient in the transformation of energy. Blood circulation and the central nervous system could not be carried out without the life energy that sustains us. This is the key to bio-energy therapy.

The Energy Centres.

Energies are contained in our physical body. Energies are generated in our thought process. Changing the way we think and project ourselves can affect our existence, including our health.

210

The seven major energy centres (chakras) take in raw energy and it is changed to a more subtle state. It is then carried to the blood and oxygen, then distributed to other parts of the body which need it.

Our physical and energy bodies (aura) merge and mix together at the energy centres. The seven major centres correspond to the nerve centres of the physical body:

Bio-energy healing is activated at these centres through the will of the healer balancing the entire energy field allowing the patient to heal themselves. Each centre is associated with a particular sense: touch, hearing, smell, taste and sight.

The tips of these five energy centres are joined at what are called the 'roots' and within the roots are 'seals' which control the energy exchange between the seven layers of the human energy field/aura which extends outside the physical body. The size of a person's aura depends on their energy and make-up. The shape also reveals much about a person's state of health, both physically and mentally. In healthy people, it is an oval shape and extends around a person evenly in all directions. When people are ill, this shape is noticeably distorted, in part or in whole.

First layer: the physical or 'etheric' body. This is associated with the physical functions of the body. (Pain, pleasure as well as automatic functions like breathing and the heart beat) It extends from a quarter of an inch to one or two inches from the body. The colour is light blue through to grey and shows the state of a person's health.

Second layer: the 'emotional' body. This is associated with the emotional life of a person. This layer is fluid and in constant motion, and follows the line of the physical body, extending one to four inches beyond the body and into the third layer. When healthy the colours are clear and bright, if a person is ill the colours become dark and muddy.

Third layer: the 'mental' body. This relates to a person's mental life. It extends from four to eight inches, sometimes 12, and radiates outwards like very narrow fingers. It also extends into the fourth layer. The colour is a bright clear yellow, which is a healthy colour. Muddied, it shows signs of mental problems.

Fourth layer: the 'Astral' body. This relates to the individual's personality and how they relate to others, and is associated with the heart and its energy centre. It is composed of a cloud-like substance, made up of the same colours as the second layer. It extends from about six to 12 inches from the body. The colour is a clear sky blue in a healthy person.

The fifth, sixth and seventh layers are associated with higher thought processes.

Fifth layer: This relates to speech and listening, and is called the 'etheric template' body because it contains a copy of everything that is contained in the first or 'etheric' layer. It extends one to two feet from the body.

Sixth layer: the 'celestial' body. This is related to love beyond human love, the spiritual side of a person. It is composed of gentle pastel shades, radiating out to two or three feet beyond the body.

Seventh and outer layer: the 'ketheric template' body. This is associated with the total integration of an individual's physical and spiritual sides. It extends from two and a half to three and a half feet from the body and contains all the other six layers of the aura. It is composed of tiny threads of gold light and appears to hold the entire energy field together.

The open end of each funnel-shaped energy centre is about six inches in diameter and varies from one four inches from the body. The term 'open' means 'working well'. The energy centres, when open, spin to use the energy better for good health with the physical, mental, emotional and spiritual. Therefore, it is necessary for all the centres to be open and balanced. The front and back energy centres balanced are equally important. (Note: If the centres need to be opened, they must first be balanced with each other.)

In sick people, the energy centres are blocked, clogged,

212

torn, collapsed altogether or inverted. Maybe they are spinning in the wrong direction or the flow into them may be erratic or one-sided. The more serious the blockage the more serious the illness. The reopening of the energy centres has to be done slowly and carefully over a number of therapy sessions, so as to allow the energy field time to adjust to the new state.

What the energy centres are responsible for.

Crown to root: This is linked to the quantity of physical energy a person possesses and the will to live. Also it is responsible for sending energy to the following parts of the body: bones, blood, muscles, body tissue, adrenal glands, some internal organs and sex organs. This is an important centre for growth and development.

Blocked or working badly: The person will generally avoid all physical activity. The result can cause the following illnesses: Cancer, leukaemia, arthritis, back pain, blood disorders, allergies and growth problems.

Root to crown: Blocked or working badly: This will lower a person's vitality for life and controls the bladder.

Note: There can be adverse effects if either the throat, head or spinal centres are not working properly.

Sacral: This region is at the back and at the pubic centre at the front (near the spleen) This centre is linked to the sexual energy. At the roots lies the desire for sexual union – one of the most powerful drives of a human being.

Blocked or working badly: Lowers a person's vitality for life. This centre also controls the bladder and can be adversely affected if the throat, head, or spinal centres are not working properly.

Solar plexus. Front: This is related to knowing oneself and one's place in the scheme of things (mutual understanding of the emotions) It has a very important role to play and it controls the following: pancreas, liver, diaphragm, large intestine, appendix and lungs. It acts as a 'clearing house' for the rest of the energy system as higher and lower energies pass through here.

213

Open: A person should have a good orderly and regulated emotional life and a strong desire to keep healthy.

Blocked or working badly: A person is undeveloped emotionally. On a physical level the following may result: diabetes, ulcers, hepatitis or heart disease.

Solar plexus. Back: This is related to a person's desire for good physical health.

Open: It indicates that a person has a strong desire to keep healthy.

Note: There is a link between the solar plexus and the heart centre. (sensitive - emotion - stress) hence the feeling of a 'knot in the stomach'.

The entire body can be re-energised at this point if there is a lack in the energy field.

Heart: The expression of love. The more open, the more compassionate and caring. This is the most important of all centres in bio-energy healing. All energies circulating in the body are utilised through the hands of the healer and have to pass through this energy centre. Therefore, what happens to the life energy at this point is very important.

Front: Physically this energy centre controls the following: thymus glands and the circulation system.

Blocked or working badly: A difficulty in giving love. This may cause the following; Heart and circulation related disease.

Heart. Back: Located between the shoulder blades. This is related to the will.

Open: A good attitude to getting things done.

Blocked or working badly: Negativity. This centre controls the lungs and to a lesser extent the heart. The following problems may arise; lung disorders.

Note: Putting energy into the back centre will help the heart and the entire body can be energised.

The solar plexus has an effect on the heart centre, so if there is a problem in the solar plexus, this may show in the heart centre.

214

Throat. Front: This is related to taking care of ones needs and not blaming others when things go wrong.

Blocked or working badly: Low esteem of others, regarding helping them when they are in trouble.

Throat. Back: this is related to how people see themselves in society and in their profession or trade.

Open: Satisfied and contented.

Blocked or working badly: Unfulfilled and do not give of their best. On the physical level it controls the thyroid and parathyroid glands. The following disorders may arise: goitre, sore throat, asthma and loss of voice.

Brow. Front: Understanding of concepts and creative instincts. Physically, it controls the following: Pineal gland, nervous system, pituitary and endocrine glands and various other vital organs.

Blocked or working badly: A confused picture of reality and how the world works. The following disorders may arise: loss of memory, paralysis and epilepsy.

Brow. Back: Deals with the ability to implement creative ideas thought of at the front. Ideas will follow through with action.

Note: This centre has a great influence over all the other major energy centres. The entire energy system can be energised from here very quickly.

Crown: This is related to the whole health of a person. Spiritually, emotionally, mentally and physically.

Blocked or working badly: Great difficulty relating to spiritual matters. Not related to:

Religion, but more to a sense of contentment and purpose. Physically, it controls the following: Pineal glands and the brain, in fact the entire body.

The Detection of Energy Imbalances.

There are various ways to find blocked or malfunctioning centres. The main way is to sense these centres through the hands. You can read the interaction of the patients' energy and your energy through your fingers and palms. It is possible to tell by feel alone if the energy is flowing freely or if it is blocked. Bio-energy therapists monitor the response in their hands differently.

When you diagnose what is wrong with a person on an energy level, you pass your hands along the energy centres both back and front with the hands as close to the body as possible without touching the patient. You can then feel the excess of energy as heat and a tingling flowing through your outstretched fingers (like sand running through them) You can feel the energy going into the energy centres. If the energy is flowing correctly, all is well. If the centre is closed, you can feel this in your hands. Patients may feel heat, tingling or a strong sensation of pulling in the directions of your hands. The larger the vortex which the energy enters, the greater the energy centre itself and the greater the energy flows into it.

A comparison must be made between all the various energy centres in order to ensure they are in balance with each other. If one is out of balance, sweeping motions must be made so as to balance it with all the others. Then the entire energy field is balanced.

The more distorted the movement of energy into a particular centre, the more of a problem the patient has. The speed in which the energy enters is a good indicator. A fast moving energy flow means that energy is being processed quickly through that particular centre. Whilst a slow moving energy flow indicates slow processing. With practice you then are better able to interpret an accurate diagnosis.

Who can do bio- energy therapy?

Everyone can become a bio-energy healer with training. Intention is very important. A completely healthy person can only undertake the healing process. A sick person could do more harm than good. People emotionally linked with the patient should not be present during treatment or anyone who is negative to the therapy. They can effect the outcome. Negativity can be picked up on an energy level and you are dealing with subtle energies.

As far as the healing process is concerned, exclusively the healer does determining the energy imbalances and directing the healing energy. Initial diagnosis on an energy level is important. The exact locations where blockages need to be released and healing energy put in have to be found.

Therapists are trained to spot the energy imbalances and to know how they can be rectified. This is done mainly through changes in the temperature of your hands as you travel over the patients' energy field. Varying from warm, hot, ice cold or tingling sensations.

The length of treatment varies with each patient from five minutes plus per session, and can continue for months.

The human energy field or aura is a subtle imprint around your physical body. An energy image of the body contains our complete genetic make-up. Kirlian photography shows the bio-energy condition of the human energy field.

Each tiny part of the universe is linked to every other part, including ourselves. Disease is a perfectly natural part of being alive. Energy flowing properly lessens the risk of disease and sickness. Blocked or imbalance of the energy field will cause a chemical disturbance in the body, causing illness. Negative attitudes and emotional stress have the effect of weakening the immunity systems causing blockages and depletion of the energy field and open to disease. Stress is a good example of this. Energy blockages are particularly noticeable in the energy field of those who are stressed. First reaction is alarm, followed by the secretion of adrenaline to cope with the stress. Responding to the stress uses up energy that could be used in other ways bringing energy depletion, so disease is likely to set in.

What we eat, where we live and a sense of purpose in our lives are all important. These are the underlying causes of the problems dealt with. A positive attitude towards life and harmony helps in overall health. Look at your lifestyle and values. Be positive.

217

Things that cause havoc with our lives: 1) synthetic clothing. 2) additives in food (practise healthy eating) 3) chemicals and electromagnetic waves and other things. Human beings get diseases that are unknown in the animal and plant world.

Relationships between human beings and nature lies at the heart of bio-energy therapy. Emotions play a major part in healing and can cause blockages or impair the whole process. Disharmony may have resulted from prolonged illness and has left a psychic imprint on the mind and this will take time to remove.

Energy centres vary according to age. As we grow and mature, our energy centres develop accordingly. This is not always the case, eg with a child rejected at a young age. Such a child's heart energy centre can be under-developed as a result of the experience. Similarly, other blocked energy centres effects the activity associated with it and will be diminished.

There are direct links to various organs and rapport. In this sense, both patient and healer actively participate in the healing with the patient's own inherent ability to heal himself, eventually stabilising and restoring the original condition.

The time a healer takes depends on the individual condition. The treatment involves reopening the centre so that the energy can flow and restore balance.

1) Make a criss-cross motion with your hands down the seven chakras near to the patient to find the blockage, illness or imbalance.

2) Anticlockwise motion with the hand takes out energy, shake this off up to fifteen feet away.

3) Clockwise motion with the hands replaces energy up to fifteen feet away.

4) As number one. Criss-cross motion to smooth the aura.

Usually three days after a treatment a patient can feel worse. It takes this length of time for the condition to be brought to the surface for the natural healing energies to start working.

Energy blockages must be directed away from the patient and the healer. If a healer were to absorb these energies into his energy field, he would then need treatment himself. The same applies to a patient with major energy depletion; the healer would be totally exhausted. Once the released energy is outside the patient and the healer's combined energy field then it goes back into the vast pool of energy all around you and is no threat to others. Therapists know this because of their sensitive hands and know exactly where it goes.

Planes of Reality in, which exist. (As related to the layers of the aura)

Spiritual Plane

7.   Ketheric Template
6.   Celestial Level
5.   Etheric Template

Primary creative force moves into higher layers of manifestation.
Finer substance = Higher energy = Denser 'vibrations'.

4.   Astral Plane

Graduation of light

Physical Plane

3.   Mental Level
2.   Emotional Level
1.   Etheric Level

Physical Level

The physic plane is composed of 4 levels: Physical, Etheric, Emotinal and Mental.
The astral is the Bridge between the Spiritual and Physical, and the spiritual is above it and has graduations of enlightenment whithin it. We have at least three layers in our spiritual bodies - the Ethical Template, Celestial and Katheric Template.

What takes place in the lower levels effects the higher levels.

Expressions of Consciousness in the Auric Levels

Level	Expression of Consciousness	Statement Consciousness Makes
7. Ketheric level	Higher concepts	I know I am
6. Celestial level	Higher feelings	I love universally
5. Etheric Template level	Higher will	I will
4. Astral level	I. Thou emotions	I love humanity
3. Mental level	Thinking	I think
2. Emotional level emotionally	Personal emotions	I feel
1. Etheric level	Physical sensations	I feel physically
Physical level	Physical functioning	I exist. I am becoming

The Creative Process of Health

Ketheric Template Body — Divine knowing.
I know I am one with God.

Celestial Body — Divine loving.
I love life universally.

Etheric Template Body — Divine will.
Thy will and mine are one

Astral Body — Loving.
I love humanity.

Mental Body — Clear thinking.
Clear thinking used to implement love and will.

Emotional body — Real feeling.
Natural unbloked flow of feelings corresponding with divine reality.
Creates: Love.

Etheric Body — I exist.
Natural metabolism of energy, which maintains the structure and function of the Etheric body. Yin/Yang balanced, Creates: We're OK.

Physical Body — Being ness.
Natural metabolism of chemical energies, balanced physical systems.
Creates: Physical health.

Working with universal law. Energy flowing=Balance=Healthy.

The Dynamic Process of Disease

KETHERIC TEMPLATE BODY.	I believe I am.	Believes he is superior to others.	Tangled or tears in the 7th layer.
CELESTIAL BODY.	I love what I believe.	Loves being superior.	Weak or blocked celestial light.
ETHERIC TEMPLATE. BODY.	I will my beliefs into being.	Tries to be superior.	Distortion in the Etheric Template.
ASTRAL BODY.	I desire according to my beliefs.	Desire to be superior.	Blocks in the Astral. Dark forms or stagnated energy.
MENTAL BODY.	I think according to my beliefs. YES/NO	I think I can be superior. I think I can't be superior. (impasse)	Disturbance of form of the Mental Body. Dissociated thought forms.
EMOTIONAL BODY.	I feel according to my beliefs.	Fear. Anger. Grief.	Dark blocks of energy. Stagnated or depleted.
ETHERIC BODY.	I am according to my beliefs.	Physical pain.	Tangles, breaks or disruptions in the Etheric Layer. (imbalance) of yin/ yang overcharge in the Solar Plexus.
PHYSICAL BODY.	I exist according to my beliefs.	Dis-Ease.	Physical illness, such as ulcers.

Related to distorted belief system.

223

Colour Meaning on Soul Task Level

Colour.	Used for.
Red:	-Passion, strong feelings, love, when mixed with rose.
Clear Red:	-Moving. Anger.
Dark Red:	-Stagnated Anger.
Red/Orange:	-Sexual Passion.
Orange:	-Ambition.
Yellow:	-Intellect.
Green:	-Healing, healer, nurturer.
Blue:	-Teacher, sensivity.
Purple:	-Deeper connection to spirit.
Indigo:	-Moving towards a deeper connection to Spirit.
Lavander:	-Spirit.
White:	-Truth.
Gold:	-Connection to God, in the service of humankind. Godlike love.
Silver:	-Communication.
Black:	-Absence of light, or profound forgetting, thwarted ambition (cancer).
Black Velvet:	-Like black holes in space, doorways to other realities.
Maroon:	-Moving into ones task.

Colour Used in Healing

Colour.	Used for.
Red:	-Charging the field, burning out cancer, warming cold areas.
Orange:	-Charging the field, increasing sexual potency, increasing immunity.
Yellow:	-Charging second chakra, cleaning a foggy head.
Green:	-Charging second chakra, balancing, general healing, charging field.
Blue:	-Cooling, calming, restructuring Etheric level, shielding.
Purple:	-Connecting to spirit.
Indigo:	-Opening third eye, cleaning head.
Lavander:	-Purging field.
White:	-Charging field, bringing peace and comfort, taking away pain.
Gold:	-Restructuring the seventh layer, strengthening field, charging field.
Silver:	-Strong purging field, (Opalescent silver is used to charge sixth level).
Black Velvet:	-Bringing patient into state of grace, silence and peace with God.
Purple Blue	-Taking away pain when doing deep tissue work, and work on bone cells, helping to expand patients field in order to connect to his task.

CHAPTER FIFTEEN

Development

How do you discover you are a medium? Is there some pattern that is common to all of us? Are we born with a gift? The answer is that everyone possesses some psychic faculties and everyone who is in any way receptive to spirit is in fact a medium. Therefore you may assume that everyone or nearly everyone is a medium.

But how near this faculty is to the surface is another matter. With some people it is nearer than with others, but often a great deal of time is needed to bring it to the surface of your consciousness. This is where a good development circle is essential, so one must always look around for one that suits you. Unfortunately there are not enough good private circles around. My advice is to approach the Institute of Spiritualist Mediums, they will know of a good medium near you that may be able to help you.

Each medium generally has their own special quality, so this faculty does not always show itself in the same way, which is why there are a great variety of mediums and phenomena, some of which I have told you about.

You must always remember that all our consciousness and faculties come from God, the Great Spirit, under natural law. We cannot change it. You must understand when you are developing your mediumistic faculties that this is nothing to do with your own personal character. You are not necessarily of a higher stage spiritually because you possess psychic faculties. Your psychic power depends on your development, therefore you can only receive within the limits you are able to tune into, like a radio.

You can obtain success in your development only after a great deal of dedication and effort in a development circle. If it's worth having, it's worth working for and cannot be rushed. I always wanted things done yesterday, and it took me a long time to learn patience, with spirit constantly reminding me of this. In time you will be able to give your best and become a good instrument for spirit to use.

Once you have decided you wish to become a medium and feel the time is right to develop that gift, you need to find a reputable medium to assist you. The medium in charge of the circle will teach you how to relax and meditate. You will then continue this within your own home. You must always open with a prayer asking spirit friends to protect you, to allow only loving and helpful friends to gather around you. If you sit together in the name of God and pray, then no harm will come to you.

There are many different feelings that developing mediums experience during their development, each one progressing in their own way. If you approach your meeting in a loving manner, then the experiences you receive are wonderful.

When you start to see clairvoyantly through meditation it is the etheric world which will reveal itself to you first. If you are dedicated and constantly strive in your spiritual development, putting to one side your thoughts of this dark material world, then you will succeed.

The hardest part of developing one's psychic gifts is having patience. Behind the scenes in the spirit world helpers are working very hard making sure that the condition are right before they are able to work. By constant practice of meditation in your daily life, you will develop a clear vision then spiritual truth is unfolded. The way forward is simple but hard work; there are certain characteristics that are essential. You must possess and aim to develop the qualities of simplicity, humility and perseverance. With these qualities you can receive answers to every question, and you can find a great deal of comfort and peace. You will experience upliftment and healing of the body, mind and spirit, bringing release from anxiety and stress, at the same time gaining in strength.

If you give yourself time to think and to feel, having faith and trust then the door of consciousness and divine spiritual love will be open unto you in humility. The light within will start to flicker like a candle gradually being fanned into a beautiful light, a flame as you unfold. Meditation is the only way to unfold an awareness, which arises from the heart, an awakening, unfolding your spiritual awareness that is in every human being. This light can be seen clairvoyantly – the aura, a coloured radiance that surrounds everyone's physical body and emanates from the emotions of the soul.

When faced with sorrow, bereavement or tragedy, people ask: what is the purpose of all this, what is the point, what can I do and how do I find the key to open the door to all these answers?

The answer to all these questions is simple. The key lies within, a voice in the silence that can be developed.

It is a long, hard road. If you have the qualities then those who feel that life is hopeless can receive and find such comfort as spiritual healing which also comes through meditation. Spiritual understanding is gained through experience and knowledge from the Great Spirit and from those who wish to serve you in the next life. Meditation is the true way to unfold spiritual awareness, which is deep within every human being.

Discipline is a must if you want to follow the spiritual path. Advice for those who sit and feel they cannot meditate: don't give up, persevere, it will come in time. The peace and love from spirit will be felt eventually. Some people may prefer to sit alone for meditation. There is nothing wrong with this but on the whole it is advisable to join others in a circle and concentrate on the spiritual powers within that group. Search for the spark of life within yourself, so that it can shine out in the darkness like a beautiful jewel.

My advice to those who seek to develop on their own at home is to pray for the light of love from spirit to envelope you and protect you on your journey into the realms of the unseen world. Every thought and every action

228

is registered in the spirit world, and every thought is creative. Sit quietly, take a few deep breaths and imagine a beautiful place where you would like to be perhaps a place you have visited in the past. Create your own utopia by thought, enjoy it, relax and know it is for real. Look around and live this place you have created. Take in every detail and eventually with practice the picture will change as spirit ads more and more to your vision. Perhaps you will see relatives who have died and converse with them. You may meet a spirit guide, a teacher who will help you and guide you on the right path towards your spiritual growth and development. By this time you will have realised that spirit is working with you and is trying to communicate with you. Once you have mastered this creative meditation you can go on with other alternative pictures.

I take members of my development circles each week through meditation to various beautiful places, all created from my imagination. After only a few weeks of development my pupils seem to know and can visualise places and objects during meditation before I have chance to describe it to them. This proves that our unseen friends are all working together in harmony, and progress is being made.

I have always created a separate place to meet family and friends from that of meeting with spirit guides. I call it the garden of reunion.

Following meditation you must always close down and seal your psychic centres, your chakras from any possible intrusion by unwanted and undesirable influences or entities from the psychic realms. All you do is mentally close the door, if you do not practice this in the strictest manner then you may as well say to anyone 'come in at any time'. When you go out, or arrive home and retire for the night you lock all the doors, therefore, following meditation you must do the same thing. A prayer before and after meditation should be said thanking God and your helpers for being with you and protecting you.

229

This is only the beginning of the path, leading human beings to the heights of their development.

It is very important to have good mediums, good instruments so that this knowledge can be passed on in love and truth from your friends in the spirit world to those who are ignorant and less fortunate than yourselves. It is the duty of those who have gained knowledge, to share that knowledge with all those who are ready to receive.

Therefore, the object of development is to train you in the practice of meditation, bringing all these chakras, psychic centres under the control and direction of the Great Spirit. Clairvoyants are able to see these round circles of light situated in the etheric body. These points are the windows to the soul. Through these you can receive impressions and messages transmitted from the spirit world. As you develop, your spirit helpers can see these centres growing, developing and changing, becoming more beautiful as one progresses.

It is so important when meditating to be positive thus attracting only the good and to receive love and beauty around you. I believe like attracts like, so if you are a loving considerate person, you can only attract loving spirit people towards you. Entering meditation with the correct motives to unfolding spiritually.

During your development, as you go through different stages and progress, you will find initially that your senses are heightened especially your hearing faculty. The sound of a pin dropping is unbelievably loud. You must always take precautions by taking the phone of the hook and lock your outside doors, so that you will not be disturbed in any way. As you arrive at a stage of deep meditation, you will begin to feel the presence of spirit, either by means of a touch like a gentle stroke of the cheek, a tickling sensation, and a spirit hand placed on your shoulder or spirit overshadowing you. This is a wonderful feeling of love being poured through your body, the power of the spirit. After a while you may see relatives, friends, or spirit helpers.

230

You can be taken spiritually to a level where there is a garden of reunion, to sit and be with those who you have lost physically whom you love.

When your circle leader feels that you have developed your psychic faculty to a degree that your gifts should be used, you should be introduced slowly to the public, with guidance and help from your teacher. After a time you will learn to deliver your messages in a professional and accurate manner. Do not be like some who rush to give demonstrations on the platform in churches, or in private. These people lack the professionalism, accuracy and polish which is essential to the good name of spiritualism.

When you have gone through this process and are confident in your ability to work in the public eye in truth and love, do not feel you that you have completed your learning, it is not the end, but only the beginning. We continue to learn and evolve, gaining more knowledge, more truth and more information from spirit enabling us to prove survival beyond doubt.

It is 35 years since I started working as a professional medium and healer, and it still makes me smile when I look back and remember how I used to work and what I said. My ideas have changed a lot through knowledge gained from spirit, evolving slowly each day.

My advice to all developing mediums is honesty. Never elaborate or fill in even if there is a risk of embarrassment. It never pays; spirit will not use a person they cannot trust. However little information you may receive, it is much better to deliver a good, short and sweet message. If you are not sure of any information you are receiving then say so. I have seen developing mediums start in their early twenties, thirties and even as late as their fifties and have come on in leaps and bounds with dedication and help of a good medium.

I, on the other hand, had to develop by myself. I was very dedicated and spent all my spare time 'tuning' into the spirit realms at the same time each day. On rare

231

occasions when I was late for my meditation, spirit friends were always waiting for me patiently. I always apologised. When all is said and done it is no different than being late for an appointment with someone in this world.

During my early years as a medium and healer I encountered within my area a petty short-sightedness within the spiritualist movement, and should imagine this was widespread throughout the country. I am sure there are many mediums and healers who have come across the same brick wall as I did during their development and afterwards. It isn't easy to establish yourselves and become part of a caring group of so called 'Spiritualists', especially when some are more worried that you may turn out to be a better medium or healer than they are.

There are a number of organisations within the spiritualist movement. Because of my own personal bad experiences with these organisations I thought it a good idea to write about the pitfalls and disappointments.

My first experience when I tried to join a certain healing organisation proved to be less than satisfactory. It was OK to become a probationer member, but forever? Even though I explained that I was turning out good healers from my own development circle, and they went on to become full members within their organisation. I agree with proving oneself. However, I was told I had to train with a full healer member. Good healing results didn't seem to stand for anything. Was I supposed to ask the people whom I had trained, to train me?

Equally I find it hard to believe that some of my circle members who I thought had no potential as a healer and never showed any signs of being able to heal the sick, within a few weeks became registered as healers with this organisation. Perhaps whom you know is more important.

I finally gave up, but continued with my work knowing that results were all that mattered, if I could help the sick that was all that was required of me by my spirit doctors.

Later after a few years of working as a professional

medium, I decided that I would join a church organisation. I had attended my local spiritualist church, two or three times a week for approximately two years when I approached them for the necessary forms to become a member. Yes they would get me the appropriate forms to fill in. Week after week I continually asked about these forms without success. I finally realised that the church did not want good, young mediums working in their church, it was too much of a threat to the older members.

They enjoyed the large donations which I gave from my healing and clairvoyance work, but dare let me trespass onto the platform to give clairvoyance or healing would have been asking too much of them. The excuse they gave me when I wanted to heal was that they had too many healers and not enough patients. I would have brought my own patients along if they had only asked. This sounds very bitter of me, but I am not, it is reality, this is what happens every day in some churches around the country. To all those who recognise what I am saying, please do not give up.

I did finally find an organisation that treated me fairly, who looks at the medium without prejudice and not whether they may be a threat to them. Having said that, it wasn't easy to become a member, they had strict vetting rules, and quite rightly so. But if you are dedicated and true in your determination to become a good reputable medium, then there is nothing to worry about. The organisation I am referring to is the Institute of Spiritualist Mediums, and they will help you all they can to develop and to guide you on the right road to success. I'm afraid I found them only after many years of groping in the dark finding my own way through trial and error and already by then a practising medium.

The human being has an astral body, an etheric body and a spirit body, besides our physical body. They take the same shape as the physical body, but can only be seen by a sensitive or a medium.

Each night we go to sleep, the physical body rests. In our dream state our astral body leaves our physical body with the cord still attached, and visits friends and relatives in the spirit world. The astral body is attached to the physical body with a permanent cord.

Most people can recall having suddenly jumped awake from a deep sleep. Their heart is beating fast as if they have had a shock. This can happen when your astral body has propelled itself back into the physical body with such a force. You often feel disorientated and find you cannot think straight for a while. The best way to overcome this is to go back to sleep and relax.

There is no danger at all. Neither is there any danger connected with astral projection or astral travelling, even if you try to do it consciously or not.

When death comes, slowly the cord dissolves from the physical body and the astral body. Until this is broken, death cannot occur.

I have released my astral body from my physical body (without severing the cord); this is done by will, by conscious manner. There are some people who can recall seeing themselves lying on the bed, looking down on themselves from above, or stood at the bottom of the bed, looking at themselves.

This can cause a little feeling of trauma, a perfectly natural thing and it happens to most people every night as they sleep. It is only the fortunate ones who can remember the following day when they waken.

If you wish to project yourself away from your body consciously, you can do this at any time and is better before you go to sleep when you are relaxed. There is nothing to worry about, the astral body can re-enter the physical body as this is still attached by the cord. Unless the cord is severed, or dissolved, then death cannot take place.

If you leave your body by will you may visit the astral plane and meet those who are physically dead. You can also visit those who are still in the physical body, and communicate with them quite easily. As I said you could achieve this by will, although you may not remember the conversation afterwards or the feeling.

If your astral body remains on the earth plane, the physical environment, then you will find that your astral body can walk through walls. You can travel most places by sheer force of your will, going backwards and forwards in time. The problem is remembering when you return.

You can will yourself, your astral body to rise above the bed. With practice this can be done.

To most people astral travelling often feels as though they have been dreaming. The more experienced person can make it happen whilst they are awake, then returning to the physical body remembering everything they have seen or done.

I have on occasions voluntary travelled. I have rocked my body, my astral body, out of my physical body and gone into the spirit realms and visited people there. Although there is nothing to fear, I personally have never liked this particular experience.

There is much talk on television these days about near death experiences, 'out of body experience's. The most common story is when being operated on, or having been in a coma, the patient has been able to see what has taken place. Many people have been able to describe to doctors and nurses what they have seen, during an out of body experience. The doctors have then confirmed what the patient has told them.

It is more common than we think and happens every day to someone. This of course is only a temporary release from the physical body.

I have on many occasions visited friends and relatives at will, and not just in this country. Distance is not a problem when you are out of your physical body; a thought can take you anywhere. The mind is amazing. It sounds very difficult but it's not. Practice and more practice that's all it takes.

There are people in the spirit world that will protect you from dangers. Although, I do not recommend this until you are aware of spiritual things. Have some knowledge and insight to spiritual phenomena first, and an experienced medium.

It is possible for a person to travel on the astral plane, and get mocked and ridiculed by low spirit entities, this only happens through ignorance. So you must be very careful what you do. If you are not sure, then leave well alone.

The spiritual garden of reunion is a lovely place to visit either in meditation or travelling, although we do not all go to the same place. If, as I have said, everything were created by thought, then our garden would vary from person to person. It would be interesting to talk with other astral travellers and hear their experiences.

I meet my spirit family in a circular garden with wrought iron benches spaced around one side. I sit down to wait for someone to come to visit me. Looking around, I am always aware of the beautiful flowers behind and in front of me. The colours are exquisite, much brighter than on this earth plane. Birds of different colours and sizes are always singing beautifully in the lovely warm sunshine, they perch next to me on the bench. They never show any sign of fear when I reach out to stroke their lovely smooth feathered breasts. I cannot see, but I just know that other animals are playing near by.

My spirit relatives always came from around the bend in front of me. As they approach, they wave, then come and sit next to me on the bench. We talk about all sorts of things, just like we used to do here on earth. When it is time for them to go, I know that I must not go with them, beyond the garden seats. I am not allowed to attempt to follow them around the bend in the garden.

I have never experiencing anything that would upset or offend me. Every journey I take there is always, beauty, love and peace that has surrounded me.

236

What is Meditation?

The difference between meditation and deep relaxation is important. Deep relaxation allows the mind to drift into a pleasant dreamlike state with no direction or focus. Whereas, meditation is a state of relaxed alertness, becoming fully focused on the sensations and the moment. The beneficial effects are similar but meditation has the additional reward of facilitating communication with spirit.

There are many forms of meditation, some of which require an extremely high degree of dedication; others are very simple and yet highly beneficial. 'The method is only the means, not the meditation itself'. It's by practising the method that you reach a state of total presence.

Concentration is the basis of every system, and we learn to quieten the mind and transcend the everyday level of consciousness. The secret of quieting the mind is through using gentle persuasion rather than reprimand.

Lying down is not a good position for meditation, because it is associated with falling asleep, and the aim of meditation is to remain alert. Try sitting comfortably, with your feet flat on the floor.

Try to meditate at the same time and in the same place each day, as the mind is addicted to habit, and once a pattern is established it slips easily into an altered state of consciousness. Once you have found stability in your meditation, noises and other distractions will have less impact, so an experienced meditator can find inner stillness, even in the rush-hour.

Choose a warm place, and avoid harsh lighting. It is advisable to wear loose clothing and comfortable shoes. Never over eat or starve yourself before meditation, the aim is to be as comfortable inwardly as outwardly.

The ability to visualise is one of the most useful skills a medium and healer can develop. Anyone can visualise and it is something we all do naturally, for instance, if I asked you what you would do if you won the lottery, I am pretty sure you have already visualised an answer! We use visualisation in many situations such as pain relief, relaxation, healing, personal growth, insight and intuition and developing spiritual wisdom.

There are many ways we can develop and use are visualisation skills, and the first step we take is to explore our inner senses to enable us to have a clearer picture of how we each imagine. This is because some people are able to see things first, others are able to hear things first, and still others may have a sense or awareness of what is happening. So, there are a few exercises to find out which is your strongest inner sense. It sometimes helps to imagine you are watching a television screen or remembering a similar past experience as a way to begin visualisation. When you are doing this, allow the image to come to you, which means you need to be still and quiet, which has the effect of making room for the image to appear. When you have the first inkling of an image developing, don't chase it, instead, you will discover that as you become ever more still and quiet the image becomes more stable and clear.

Exercise 1

Allow about 30 seconds for each. Imagine you can se the following:

A blue triangle.

A red car.

A yellow hat.

A green teapot.

A pink rose.

Imagine you can hear the following:

A car revving its engine.

Church bells.

Children playing.

A dog barking.

A whistling kettle.

Imagine you can smell the following:

Freshly-made coffee.

Jacket potatoes.

Bread baking.

Freshly-cut grass.

Earth after rain.

Imagine you can taste the following:

Ice cream.

Your favourite fresh fruit.

Chocolate.

Your favourite drink.

Chips with salt and vinegar.

Imagine you can feel the following:

Bubbles.

Flower petals, velvet.

Sandpaper.

Your pets fur.

Silk sheets.

Most people will find they can more easily use more than one of their senses. Whatever you find you are able to sense use this in your visualisations. Therefore create your visualisation first with the senses you have found you can work with.

If for example it is sound, then visualise ball bouncing or children playing etc. If it is smell, then visualise yourself placing flowers in a vase etc.

Exercise 2

Imagine yourself cutting into a lemon. Pick a small piece and suck it as its dribbling. Most people automatically find that their saliva begins to run. This shows that the body responds to what the mind and imagination is telling it.

Continue with similar visual exercises that you think you will be able to do. It can be difficult for someone else to capture your own personal idea of a spiritually uplifting place; so do feel free to alter the examples of meditations I have chosen for you.

Starting your own development circle

If, after reading all that I have had to say, you feel that you want to develop mediumship or healing and you are dedicated, then follow these simple rules:

1) Gather together all those friends who are of like mind.

2) Meet at the same place and time each week.

3) Always make sure that the room you are using is warm and clean, free from cigarette smoke.

4) Play soft relaxing music, and dim the lights or turn them off. You don't need to sit in the dark, but it helps not to have the glare of light in your face, which can cause you to be distracted.

5) Arrange the chairs in a circle. Straight back chairs are preferable, as your spine needs to be erect, yet comfortable.

6) Make sure the telephone is switch off, including mobile phones, and the doors are locked. You don't want to be disturbed.

7) Each member of the circle will need to have a glass of water. The water is to cleanse the inner you. Therefore, you should be clean inside and outside to meet spirit.

8) Do not over-eat or starve you self. Be at ease, this includes clothing and shoes, if necessary loosen your belt etc.

9) Always sit with your feet firmly on the ground, never crossed. Hold your hands, palms facing upwards, or placed one above the other in your lap.

10) Leave all your everyday problems on the doorstep. Be positive.

11) By this time you should have selected one of you to become the circle leader.

12) Start the meeting with a prayer. Each member stands up in turn, when they have finished they sit down, this indicates when the next person should stand up. The prayer should be one continuous, each person starting where the previous person has left off. This is known as a 'round robin'. Remember to ask that only love and light enters the circle, excluding anything that is unloving or unhelpful. Intention is all that matters; your prayers can be simple. In time you will be inspired by spirit. If you are unable, or

don't want to pray, then perhaps you are not the right person for this work. You are sitting for development, to serve God, and without the Great Spirit none of this is possible.

13) The leader of the circle now should lead the circle into a healing meditation, don't forget intention is all that matters so do not worry if you find it hard in the beginning. All the members can then list out loud the names of those whom they know who require healing.

14) Following this the leader once again will lead the circle in another meditation, describing in detail what she can see. You can use any of the meditations I have given, or one of your own. For mediumistic development you should include in any meditation a bridge, stream, gate, or other barrier. Again, it is the intent, and the idea for this, is that when you go through this barrier you are crossing over to the spirit world where you will meet with spirit friends, guides etc.

When you have finished, do not forget to close down. Tea and biscuits and a discussion of what you saw. Spirit usually adds more to your meditations by putting little extras in your picture. Watch for this.

CHAPTER SIXTEEN

Meditations

Relaxation, breathing, centring.

Imagine in front of you a box, any kind of box, and one by one, take your cares and worries and put them into a box. When you have placed them into the boxes, firmly close the lids. Now imagine in front of you all the people in your life who make you feel good, all those kind, caring, generous, beautiful, honest, fun-loving, positive people. Take your time to look at them and to acknowledge their qualities. Recognise that you only notice these qualities if they are within you, so that these people are mirroring your positive qualities back to you. Repeat these qualities to yourself as you see these people.

Bring your focus now to your heart; place your hand there if you wish. Focus on your heart again. Now go into your heart. Imagine you can put the light on, and put it on, and open windows if necessary so that you can explore thoroughly. Do anything that's required to open your heart and to clear it. It may need to be washed or painted.

Now make it warm and welcoming. Do this symbolically by filling it with flowers, music, candles, or anyway you like to improve the heart. When it is warm and welcoming, go to the door, and invite all those positive people in. Let them come and go freely.

Allow yourself to feel loving and warm and open-hearted. Relax more deeply and as you breathe, breathe in a golden light until you consciously feel golden and accepting, open-hearted.

Consciously flow this golden light to the person next to you let it fill the room. Take your time to do this.

When you are ready, return to the room.

Breathing your troubles away.

Imagine yourself standing on a golden road, the road stretches far ahead into the distance. Walk along, holding your favourite crystal. Feel the warm sun, the gentle breeze and the thick springy grass under your feet. You can now see a huge crystal mountain, the same colour and shape as your favourite crystal. Behind the mountain is a beautiful rainbow, look at the colours in turn, red, orange, yellow, green, blue, indigo and violet. The rainbow is reflected through the mountain, which sends out feelings of friendliness and happiness.

You would like to climb up, but your worries are too heavy, so leave them at the bottom. Take them off as if you are removing, a heavy, uncomfortable bag. The climb is now easy, you feel light.

See a magic well in front of you, and the mountain asks you to make a wish. You have a golden coin in your hand. Throw it in into the magic well, and make your wish. Hear the splash, as the golden coin hits the blue, sparkling water.

You have lots of energy and the slopes are very gentle. You find yourself back on the golden, sunny road, coming home.

Breathing, blow out all your worries, fears etc.

For this meditation avoid the use of background music and room scents as they can intrude upon your ability to imagine the sounds and scents I suggest.

Imagine you are walking along a path through a huge green field, it is a warm sunny afternoon, and the gentle breeze carries the scent of hay. The path leads to a weathered door, partially obscured by overhanging ivy. You push the door and it opens slowly. You find yourself standing in a wonderful garden.

In front of you are beautiful rambling roses clambering over the walls, the blooms emanating an exquisite perfume. You breath in a little deeper to enjoy this fragrance, a gentle breeze scatters some petals on the ground.

In a flower bed nearby are tall blue flowers, which rise above floral clouds of pink, purple and white. Aromatic herbs fill the gaps between the stepping stones and ferns grow through cracks in the wall. Everywhere you look,

243

flowers grow in luxuriance.

You meander down to a wooded area of the garden, and find a bronze sculpture of a seated girl; it feels cool and dimpled. You breathe more deeply and enjoy the damp woodland air and earthy smell. The tall grass is full of wild flowers, and looking up you see honeysuckle creeping from tree to tree hanging from branches and making wonderful arches. You hear the fluttering of wings and look up to see a thrush perched on a tree, his song echoing through the wood, impossibly loud.

Walking on through the wood, you see a bank, and in the dappled sunlight are growing clusters of wild strawberries. You pick one and pop it into your mouth, savouring its warmth and sweetness.

You feel the sunshine on your arms and face, as you walk across the soft springy turf towards the hedge. Looking through the hedge, you see a straight path, bordered by flowers, leading to a dancing fountain. When you reach the fountain, you sit on the edge of a stone. A fine spray refreshes your face, and you dip your fingers into the pool, sliding them to and fro enjoying the tingling feeling of energised water moving through your fingers.

A dragonfly lands by the fountain, and its iridescent beauty captures your attention, flashing electric blue as it takes off and disappears over the hedge.

You sit for a while longer, watching the fluffy clouds drifting by, and listening to the tumbling water.

Now it is time to leave the garden, but you know you will soon return.

Magic Garden.

Imagine there is a big gate in the ivy covered garden wall. It is solid oak and has a latch on the left-hand side. You lift the latch and pull the door open and pull it shut behind you as you walk into the garden. There is a flagged pathway weaving its way amongst the raised flower beds. There are roses of all colours and the smell of them is gorgeous. They are all lifting their heads to the sunshine.

244

As you walk following the zig-zag of the pathway, you notice beds of pansies, petunias, Busy Lizzies and fuschias. They all are brightly coloured and are standing up tall and healthy. You go round the corner to the most fragrant herb bed that you have come across in a long while. There is parsley, oregano, mint, basil, thyme and so much more. Bees buzz amongst the herbs and birds are singing amongst the fruit trees.

As you walk along you come across a lovely wooden bench tucked away in a corner. The sun is shining on it and it looks just right to sit on. As you sit and feel the warmth of the sun on your face you close your eyes and listen to the sounds around you. You can hear water running in the distance, the bees humming and the birds singing and you can hear a tractor working in the field across from the magic garden.

As you sit there you feel relaxed and calm allowing your thoughts to wander. You allow your mind to widen and ask that if any friends would like to come and join you they may and, that you would be pleased to see them, or you may just want to sit and enjoy the tranquillity and feeling of calmness around you.

It is time you became aware of the bench that you are sitting on and say goodbye to anyone that has joined you. Telling them that you hope to see them again on another occasion. You slowly rise from the bench and walk back along the path, smelling the herbs once again and noticing that the birds are still singing as sweetly as ever. You walk passed the flower beds, breathing in the perfume from the roses and slowly swing open the big wooden gate in the ivy covered garden wall and walk through, closing it firmly shut.

A Winter's day.

Imagine the day is frosty but bright and sunny and as you put on your coat, scarf and gloves and walk out of the door, the air is fresh and clean. The sky is blue and the trees are various shades of gold and look beautiful as the

245

sun shines on them. The grass is still white where the sun has not yet touched it, and some of the bushes look really spectacular where the frost has touched the branches and leaves.

You look forward to your walk today and have a feeling of anticipation, almost as if you expect something really unusual to happen.

As you turn to walk across the common towards the lake, you notice that there is ice on the water, a few ducks are waddling across the frozen top to an area that has been defrosted by the sun. A few more ducks are scratching the earth around the lake, looking for something to eat and you make a mental note to take some bread for them the next time you go for a walk there.

Your breath is white in the air as you walk around the lake towards the bottom of the hill, but you feel nice and warm, even your face feels warm as the sun shines on you.

As you reach the bottom of the hill, something in the sky attracts your attention and you notice that a number of balloons are floating down to meet you. They are all the colours of the rainbow and as you watch them one colour seems to stand out from the rest.

You reach up to catch hold of a string and suddenly you find yourself floating up and away very gently. You are not scared and feel wonderfully free and light. The ground takes on a totally different look from where you are and you marvel at the way the sunlight catches hold of nature and enhances the colours.

You notice that all the other balloons have disappeared and you are up, up and away, the feeling is wonderful. The balloon seems to know exactly where it is taking you and so you let it float you along, feeling very secure but such a feeling of freedom.

As you float up over the hill you notice...

There I will leave you for a while so that you can go as you wish.

246

You notice that the air is getting a little colder and that the sun has lost some of its warmth, so you catch hold of the balloon's string and ask that you be returned to where you first set off from. You gently and securely float back down the hill and slowly come to rest at the bottom of the hill. You let go of the string and say thank you to your balloon, letting it drift off to join the other ones that are waiting. Away they all float and you know that you can go to the bottom of that hill whenever you wish and your balloon will be waiting for you again.

As you walk past the lake, the ducks huddle next to each other, keeping warm as another frosty night sets in.

You walk quickly across the common and look forward to getting back home. As you reach your door you open it and go in and as you take off your coat, scarf and gloves the warmth of the house seems to greet you. You feel exhilarated and full of life.

A morning run.

Imagine you have woken up after a good night's sleep.

You get up and pull back the curtains to see that the sun is shining and it is warm outside. You can hear the birds singing and playing in the garden below. A wonderful day to go for a run.

You wash and put on your running kit and with a skip in your step, then run downstairs and out of the door.

As you stand outside doing your stretching exercises in preparation for your run, you think how good it is to have the freedom to go for a run on a day like today.

As you walk to the gate, the sun is warm on your back and everything smells fresh and clean. When you reach the gate you go through it and turn to your left and slowly start to jog along the road outside your house.

Gradually getting into your rhythm, you are aware of the sound of water gurgling on the other side of the hedge on your right. There is a gap in the hedge halfway along the road and you turn through it and run along the little path that is beside the stream.

The sun is shining through the leaves on the trees, making lovely patterns on the ground, the smell of wild garlic is in the air and the bluebells make a wonderful carpet of colour all around you. You feel content and that everything in your life is as it should be.

As you travel along, the pathway becomes slightly more uneven, there are several small rocks and stones sticking up and the occasional branch is lying across your path. But you are feeling good and fit so you simply jump over these obstacles and continue on your way. Some of the bushes are overgrown and stick out across the path, pushing them to one side you keep going.

You feel content. Nothing is insurmountable. You feel fit and alive and the feeling is good.

As you come out of the wood, there is a slight incline up a lovely grassy track that leads home. As you run up the track you think 'how good this is, and how fit and well you are'. You briefly stop at the top of the track, turn and look at the view below. You can see where you have run.

You turn away and continue on your journey back along the stream and then through the gap in the hedge and out onto the road. You reach your gate, stop and take a few deep breaths and stretch your body. Walk through the gate, up the path and back into your home.

You feel refreshed, happy and content.

Along the mountainside.

Imagine it is a cold morning as you set off down the road. You turn left at the bottom of the hedge and start to walk up the mountainside. Your breath is visible as you walk up and up the long path to the top. As you walk you feel the temperature drop, but because of the exertion of climbing you feel warm inside.

You soon start walking in the snow as you get nearer the top. When you reach the summit of the mountain, the sun peeks out of the clouds and all around you are bathed in a beautiful orange light and the view from the top is breathtaking. You notice the river down below is sparkling as it makes its way down the valley and the wood to your left is such a picture of oranges and copper colours as Autumn starts to go into an early winter. An aeroplane is going through the navy blue sky, leaving a white trail behind it. You can't help wondering where it is going and you wish that you were on it too.

You decide to stop walking along the summit to eat your lunch. You notice that the little ledge that is just big enough for you to sit on and shelter from the cold wind. You eat your food and as you sit there watching the view you feel that life is not so bad after all. You close your eyes and absorb the peace around you...

You become aware that it is getting dusk and that it is time to make your way down the mountainside. You take a last look at the river and wood and notice that the colours of the leaves are less intense as the sun drops down behind the mountain top. You turn and make your way carefully down the mountainside; you climb through the gap in the hedge and head home.

A Spring day.

Imagine that you are walking along the road on a misty spring day and you can hear the birds singing in the bushes next to a path. As you walk along you notice that the grass is a beautiful green and that the hedgerows are starting to burst into flower. Then as you turn round the corner in the road you cannot believe your eyes, there in front of you is the most beautiful carpet of pink carnations as far as the eye could see. The smell of them is just wonderful. They sway gently in the breeze and form patterns up the hillside. You decide to go and have a closer look.

As you make your way carefully along the pathway that weaves through the carnations, you notice a tree in the distance and decide to walk to it and sit among the branches. It is a lovely strong tree with beautiful green foliage and one branch sticking out at an angle: just the right shape and size to sit on. As you get closer you notice that at the base there is a lovely blue pool. The grass is very long and wafts against the tree, making a restful sound.

Taking off your shoes you wade into the pool, it's cool and clear as you make your way across to reach the tree. You then climb onto the branch of the tree and find it is a wonderful fit as you rest your back against the trunk. As you gaze at the view of pink carnations and the blue pool you appreciate the breathtaking scene before you.

As you sit admiring all that is before you the sun starts to break through and the mist disappears. In the distance a small wood surrounded by lush green fields is canopied by the beautiful blue sky. The longer you sit the more you are able to captivate.

The birds are flying high in the sky and you can hear the bees busy collecting pollen from the carnations. As you relax, your thoughts drift away...

You are disturbed by the breeze rustling the leaves on the tree and realise that it is time to move and return home. Gathering your thoughts you reluctantly climb down off the branch and walk around the edge of the pool still enjoying the freedom of the cool water on your feet. Stepping out of the water you put your shoes back on and make your way through the carpet of pink carnations.

Reaching the road you turn back and take a final look at the view. The colour of the carnation's complement the colour of the sun as it starts to dip behind the hillside making the hill look as if it is on fire. Reluctantly you return along the road to home.

Jewelled Cave.

Imagine you are walking along a path through a wood. You are aware of the sound of water. As you walk, it

becomes louder and louder. Suddenly you find yourself in a clearing and there is the most wonderful waterfall you have ever seen. It's falling into a deep clear pool and looks so inviting. There is a beautiful rainbow arching up from the pool, caused by the water vapour of the waterfall.

Ferns grow out of the rocks that surround the waterfall and as you look down you notice the edge of the pool is

250

quite sandy. Around the pool there are different trees and lush growth like an oasis in the middle of a wood. You can hear wood pigeons cooing in the background and a blackbird singing high in the tree- tops. On the left hand side your attention is drawn to a rustling sound made by a squirrel rushing through the bushes.

As you approach the pool you notice that the pathway is quite rocky and full of tree roots. You have to pick your way through very carefully, concentrating where you place each foot. All around are beautiful wild flowers. You know that the blue ones are forget-me-knots and that the yellow ones are celandines. You also notice that there are some pretty pink flowers, with dainty petals, slim stalks and big green leaves. Looking closer you see a ladybird struggling through the undergrowth and smile to yourself. It is such a beautiful and peaceful place you can't help wishing that you had known about it before.

As you sit on a log, you can see the ripples on the water caused by the waterfall and where the sunlight hits it the colour is completely different, almost green. In the more shaded areas you can see the bottom of the pool and marvel at the clearness of it all. You can see a few branches lying there with tiny little fishes swimming in and out amongst the rocks and wonder how deep the water is.

You can't help thinking how nice it would be to have a refreshing dip in the coolness of the water and so you take off your shoes and walk to the water edge to have a closer look before you take off your clothes. You become aware that the wood seems to have become very still, all you can hear is the water falling and splashing into the pool and how crystal clear it is. You take in the beauty of the nature all around you as you step into the wonderful pool. While enjoying the soft silk water you notice a path behind the waterfall and decide to step up behind it. In front of you is a cave hidden behind the rushing water. Fascinated, you decide to investigate further.

At first it seems to be very dark, but as your eyes become

accustomed to the light you notice that something is gleaming on the other side of the cave. Approaching you notice it is another cave. You cannot believe your eyes as you walk in and see every colour you can imagine. Pinks, blues, greens, purples, oranges, violets, the colours seem to go on and on. You're dazzled at first as you sit on the floor and absorb the energy from the healing colours. After a while you notice that the roof of the cave is covered with many different crystals and gems sending the wonderful rays down to you.

You sit for quite a while until you become aware that the energy is beginning to fade and you start to feel cold. It is time to trace your steps knowing you would return at a later time to enjoy and revitalise yourself.

You walk down and out of the first cave and step down from behind the waterfall and walk around the pool picking up your clothes and shoes where you left them, thinking how good it is to be alive and well. You trace your steps along the rocky path and through the wood where you began your journey.

A healing journey.

This journey takes us to a place that allows for total and complete healing of body, mind and spirit. If you are not ill you can gain from the input of energy, relaxing, knowing you are protected.

Breathing in deep and slow. Begin to look out from within your 'third eye'. This allows you to see what is real.

As you look, imagine yourself on a path at the bottom of a hill, which slopes gently upwards in front of you. Around the path you can see thick growth, of tangled choking weeds. Pause and examine this closely.

You can see thorns and sharp spikes among the weeds and you have to tread very carefully as you begin to move along the path. Allow the image of this place to unfold naturally in your mind. Look around and accept what you see. The path is faint and winding, you look around you as you progress. You are aware that you are climbing all the

252

while and have climbed further that you realised. You spot a stream running beside the path and when you look closely, you see that the water is hardly flowing at all, and that it is dirty and polluted. You continue regardless, still seeing weeds and different plants that look dull and listless.

To one side, you now notice a smaller path that leads off at an angle and climbs more steeply. Take this fork and follow the path, putting a little more effort into your climb now.

Soon you arrive on the top of a hill; this juts out higher than anything else around you does. The atmosphere is different here, and the air seems charged. You find a place to sit or lie down, perhaps against a tree trunk. Look around and find the right place for you.

Now relax, and feel the rain as it starts to fall, it is warm, and soon you feel wet through. When you look round you find that this is no ordinary rain, but it is filled with shimmering, rainbow drops of liquid. It feels pleasant and refreshing, and you can feel it seeping into your being. Stay where you are and enjoy this pleasant, healing rain as it washes over you, through you and heal you.

Let the rain stop of its own accord, then stand up once more, and begin to walk back down the path. Walk slowly and carefully down the steep path to where the fork is, down the side of the hill. Now the going is much easier and the path straighter. Pause and take a look around. You will see that the weeds have gone, and in their place are lovely, vibrant growth of flowers of dazzling colours. Even the grass looks glowing and healthy. The stream is clear now, and flowing freely. Everything is in a state of radiance and bliss. Your step is light as you return and soon you are back where you began.

Let the image fade, knowing you can return any time you wish. Take a few deep breaths and wriggle your fingers and toes. Open your eyes and return to the room.

Imagine yourself in a lovely place, maybe a green open meadow with a small brook, or on white sand by the sea.

Picture all the beautiful details and see yourself really appreciating and enjoying it.

Now begin to walk, and soon you will find yourself in totally different surroundings- perhaps in a field of golden grain or swimming in a tranquil lake. Wander around and explore, finding more and more beautiful environments of different variety, mountains, forests, and deserts, whatever you like. Appreciate each one.

Now, imagine yourself taking a boat to a lush tropical paradise. Picture yourself arriving at a huge castle where you are made very welcome with an enormous feast, music and dancing. Then you are taken to a vast treasure room where you are presented with incredible jewels, precious metals, and gorgeous clothes, more than you could ever use. Use your imagination; see yourself wandering around the world being given everything you could ever want, in huge quantities.

Imagine the world as a magnificent paradise in which everyone you meet is experiencing the same fullness and abundance as you are. Enjoy it thoroughly. Wherever you go you are given miraculous things. Infinite possibilities.

Eventually you come home, happy and contented, and think about the fact that the Universe is truly a place of incredible wonder and abundance.

You can contact Barbara Bridgford at:

38, Nunthorpe Road
Rodley
West Yorkshire
LS13 1JS

or

Chapel House
Chapel Lane
Scropton
Derbyshire
DE65 5PS